The Life and Death of
Secondary Education for All

Is there life after death for secondary education for all?

This book focuses upon the quality of learning. Educational 'reform' too often begins with qualifications, examinations, institutional provision, paths of progression. Whilst these are important, their value lies in the support they give to learning in its different forms. This book starts with the aims of education and progresses on to what it means to learn (practically, theoretically, morally), taking into account the very many different needs of the learners.

In so doing, the book will be both philosophical in analysis and empirical in example. So much is happening 'from down below' that goes unrecognised by policy makers. But innovations too often get hampered by government interventions, by a bureaucratic mentality and by failure to spread good practice. The general argument of the book, therefore, will be illustrated throughout with detailed references to practical developments in schools, colleges, the third sector, youth work, independent training providers and professional bodies, all expressed from an international angle. It is split into three parts:

- aims, values and culture
- putting aims into practice
- provision of education.

Building on *Education for All* (2009), which was based on 14–19 research into secondary education, this book transcends the particularities of England and Wales and digs more deeply into those issues which are at the heart of educational issues, policy and practices and which survive the transience of political change and controversy. The issues (the aims of education, standards of performance, the consequent vision of learning, the role of teachers, progression from school to higher or further education and into employment, the provision of such education and training and the control of education) are by no means confined to the UK, or to this day and age. Pring identifies similar problems in other countries, especially the USA – and, indeed, as in the Greece of Plato and Aristotle – and offers solutions with a comparative perspective.

In addressing 'learning' and the 'learners' first and foremost, the book will argue for a wider vision of learning and a more varied pattern of provision. Old structures must give way to new.

Richard Pring was Professor and Director of Educational Studies, University of Oxford, UK.

The Life and Death
of Secondary
Education for All

Richard Pring

Routledge
Taylor & Francis Group

LONDON AND NEW YORK

First published 2013
by Routledge
2 Park Square, Milton Park, Abingdon, Oxon OX14 4RN

Simultaneously published in the USA and Canada
by Routledge
711 Third Avenue, New York, NY 10017

Routledge is an imprint of the Taylor & Francis Group, an informa business

© 2013 Richard Pring

British Library Cataloguing in Publication Data
A catalogue record for this book is available from the British Library

Library of Congress Cataloging in Publication Data
Pring, Richard.
    The life and death of secondary education for all / Richard Pring.
        p. cm.
    1. Education, Secondary. 2. Educational change. I. Title.
    LB1607.P68 2012
    373–dc23   2012012974

ISBN: 978–0–415–53635–6 (hbk)
ISBN: 978–0–415–53636–3 (pbk)
ISBN: 978–0–203–09515–7 (ebk)

Typeset in Galliard
by Swales & Willis Ltd, Exeter, Devon

MIX
Paper from
responsible sources
FSC
www.fsc.org   FSC® C004839

Printed and bound in Great Britain by
TJ International Ltd, Padstow, Cornwall

To Isaac, Eleanor, Dominic, Isobel, Lucy and Mary

Contents

Introduction

It is a critical time.

Old patterns of education and its provision are less and less suitable for facing the twenty-first century. Modes of communication, which affect access to knowledge, have changed radically in just a few years and those changes are quickening in pace. The economic context has been transformed, affecting the skills and knowledge needed for employment. The social world of young people raises fresh demands, hopes and fears. A global recession has affected young people disproportionately, making quality of life and self-fulfilment ever more difficult to attain.

It is not surprising, therefore, that many countries are dissatisfied with the educational provision for young people, especially at the secondary stage. Reforms are called for. The comprehensive high school in the United States, which pioneered secondary education for all within the same educational institution, is increasingly criticised (see Franklin and McCulloch, 2007). The government paper in England, *The Importance of Teaching* set out a range of radical reforms. *Curriculum Excellence* in Scotland heralds changes which provide a better education for all as young people meet the challenges of a changing society. *Learning Pathways* in Wales similarly addresses perceived problems in preparing all young people for the difficult way ahead.

However, 'reform', so-called, too often begins with qualifications, examinations, institutional provision, paths of progression. All those are very important, but their value lies in the support they give to learners and to their sense of fulfilment. We need to start with what it means to learn (practically, theoretically, morally). We need to question critically the value of that learning. We need also to respond to the many different needs of the learners and of a democratic society into which they are entering. That is what this book aims to do. In addressing 'learning' and the 'learners' first and foremost, the book argues for a wider vision of learning and a more collaborative pattern of provision. Old structures must give way to new.

Once there was hope that secondary education would embrace all young people whatever their ability or background. Changes were needed, certainly, because of evolving social and economic environments. And there was, also, a degree of scepticism about the claim that all young people were capable of being educated. But hope prevailed. Now, however, those sceptical voices are being heard again.

Perhaps, so they say, we should be satisfied with a well-trained rather than a well-educated workforce – education being the privilege of a minority.

The matter is urgent.

In the pursuit of 'reform', we have been witnessing the most radical changes to the educational system in England since the Second World War. But unlike the reforms of 1944, the present ones are being pushed through with the minimum of parliamentary or public debate. I have in mind the draconian increase in central ministerial power, the destruction of local responsibility for education and training provision, the impoverishing system of accountability through testing and league tables, the narrowness of learning experiences, the undermining of teachers' professionalism, the privatisation of education in place of a public service.

This book relates closely to what is happening in England but, as shall be shown, the issues which are covered extend much more widely than England. Britain is but one side of an 'Atlantic bridge'. At the other end, we are seeing, too, the very same narrow conception of 'standards', the testing to those standards, the undermining of public service, the opening up of the public system to for-profit and market forces, and the dominance of a regime of performance management.

The flow of the argument, therefore, is as follows.

Part I gets back to basics by questioning the values which do, and should, govern and guide secondary education for all.

Chapter 1 provides an introduction to the aspiration for 'secondary education for all'. But was it but a dream? Deep in the bowels of society are firmly held views that only a few can be really educated – Plato remains alive and well in the minds of many. Others see that 'education of all' simply substitutes mediocracy for meritocracy. Yet others reluctantly concede that education cannot compensate for the overwhelming cultural and social conditions which, for many, militate against education.

Chapter 2 examines one aspect of this search for, and yet ultimate doubts over, secondary education for all, namely, the identification of and pursuit of higher standards. In the global comparisons of educational success, 'standards' (as identified in international surveys) become politically important. But the concept of standard is rarely examined, or seen to be logically related to answers to more fundamental questions about the aims of education.

Chapter 3, therefore, turns to this question: *What counts as an educated young person in this day and age?* Perhaps those doubts about 'education for all' arise from the failure to ask this question. Therefore, close attention is given to what it means to be educated, and to what qualities and capabilities all young people should be enabled to acquire if they are to live fulfilled lives and if they are to manage their lives intelligently. But to do that – to question what is worthwhile – requires a rejection of the Orwellian language of targets, audits, performance indicators and efficiency gains which now shapes educational policy.

Chapter 4 takes a crucial aspect of this exploration of what is worth learning. 'Culture' is rarely examined now, as once it was, in our understanding of education, whether that be culture in the sense of 'the best that has been thought and said' (upon which the curriculum should draw) or culture in the sense of the values and understandings of social groups, which dominate young people's understanding of the world.

Chapter 5 is a sort of interlude – a reflection upon the essentially philosophical issues which underpin the controversies about 'education for all' and which characterise the arguments of this book. The philosopher Wittgenstein (1958: 1.464) said that his main task was 'to teach you to pass from a piece of disguised nonsense to something that is patent nonsense'. There is a lot of disguised nonsense in educational policy and practice.

Part II translates these questions about the aims of education into practice.

Chapter 6, harking back to the difficulties raised in Chapter 1 concerning the failure of education to compensate for social disadvantage, looks more carefully at the evidence and the arguments.

Chapters 7 and 8, accordingly, see the solution to many of the difficulties to lie in a much wider vision of worthwhile learning. We are mesmerised by an indefensible notion of 'academic learning' which excludes so many young people and even handicaps those who apparently succeed. The dualism of academic and vocational is but one example of the disguised nonsense. That wider vision embraces the equally demanding practical learning, the moral sense of respon- sibility, the wider social commitment to community and its well-being. It takes seriously, too, the experiences which the learners bring with them into the school or college.

Chapter 9 extends this wider vision of learning to the community basis of learn- ing – to the significant interactions within the group, to the community of learners, and to the possibilities of technology for enhancing interpersonal enrichment.

Chapter 10, however, recognises that such learning needs formal organisation in a curriculum. But, in keeping with the constant criticism of the book of the top- down management of learning, so too is there need to reject the commonly held idea of a curriculum as 'something to be delivered'. Rather, it is 'a proposal' which needs constantly to be refined by the teacher as he or she initiates the diverse group of learners into worthwhile knowledge and practices.

Chapter 11 follows directly from this – a plea to 'bring back teaching', to respect the teacher as a curriculum thinker not a curriculum deliverer, and (if the aims of education are to be open to all) to ensure the possibility of continuing professional development. There is no curriculum development without teacher development.

Chapter 12, however, issues a warning. Learning is narrowed and impoverished by the all-pervasive system of testing. Teachers are deprofessionalised. If there is to be 'secondary education for all', then a much more positive system of assessment and accountability must be recognised. Assessment is killing education.

Chapter 13 argues for one important component of the curriculum, given prominence in the book because it is usually neglected. Information, advice and guidance (IAG) is crucial for students in navigating their way through the different pathways, in making the right choices of subject, and in knowing about the different training and employment possibilities. But it needs to be independent and pro- fessional.

Chapter 14 completes Part II by examining more closely the different routes through secondary education and then into employment, further training and higher education. Is there not a great deal of deception here?

Part III, finally, addresses how such an education for all might be provided.

Chapter 15 points to the dramatic changes which are taking place, without public or parliamentary debate, in the very provision, funding and accountability of education. This is a global revolution indeed, and one which undermines the tradition of public service in the interest of all. A mixture of central power and control, combined with openness to market competition, fragments further an already segregated system. Perhaps secondary education for all was but a dream after all.

Chapter 16, however, shows where salvation lies. Let us not give up just yet. There is a need (which surely all must soon recognise) that no one school can go it alone. Partnership and cooperation are essential if the learning needs of all young people are to be provided for. The challenge is to restore some form of local accountability and responsibility for the range of opportunities which will do justice to all young people.

Chapter 17 examines one key aspect of that provision. An essential element in local authority provision has been the faith schools. But can we, in the much more ethnically and religiously diverse society, sustain these any longer? Do we not need 'the common school'? The arguments are explored.

The concluding chapter sets out what must be done, in the light of the previous chapters, if there is to be secondary education *for all*, not just for a privileged minority in a country which is increasingly divided economically, socially and educationally. We must remember that an educational system should serve the general as well as the personal good – serving to enrich the sense of community as well as the betterment of individuals. To that end we must constantly ask the question: what counts as an educated person in this, the twenty-first century? And, in our answers to that question, we should ask further about the kind and quality of learning to be developed and the institutions and resources in which that learning can best be nurtured. Unless we pursue those questions, then the hope for an education of all young people irrespective of background will not be realised. It will remain but a dream.

Part I
Aims, values and culture

1 Secondary education for all
Dream or reality?

Secondary education

In a purely descriptive sense, all developed countries claim to have secondary education *for all* – namely, the provision of compulsory schooling to the age of about 16, with its continuation beyond that for many who choose to benefit further from formal education.

However, one might question whether there is secondary *education* for all. In England, the Newsom Report (1964) showed that the aspirations of the 1944 Education Act had not been achieved by *half our future*, even though they remained in secondary schools until the age of 15. Subsequently there have been many attempts to reform the system in order to embrace the other half of our future. But critics remain – many of them. Is education *for all* possible? If so, what changes are needed?

In most countries there is a break in the provision for young people somewhere between the ages of 11 and 13. That break takes place between primary (including elementary and preparatory) school, on the one hand, and, on the other, secondary (including high and senior) school.

Precision here is not important. It is assumed that changes take place about then which demand a different kind of curriculum and a different context for learning. The Hadow Report (1926) for England and Wales, aptly entitled *The Education of the Adolescent*, set the tone in claiming that 'there is a tide which begins to rise in the veins of youth at the age of 11 or 12. It is called by the name of adolescence.' The adolescent, so it is argued, needs a different environment – one that is more 'grown up', more oriented to the adult world for which he or she is being prepared.

However, it is increasingly felt that in this period from 11 to 18, when the young person changes from dependent child to adult (entitled to get married, to earn a living and to fight for their country), changes are so great that they cannot adequately be responded to for all young people in a totally uniform secondary system. Different opportunities and environments should be available at 14, and also (or alternatively) at 16. At least there should be collaboration between different kinds of institution (for example, between schools and colleges of further education) which offer different pathways from 14 onwards.

Indeed, recently in England there have been calls for a 'transfer' at 14. Some have argued that 14 is when young people are able and need to make choices about the most appropriate educational pathway – influenced by their aspirations for the future, their preferred modes of learning, the range of possible courses available, or the need for a more 'grown-up' environment. Kenneth Baker, once Secretary of State, is promoting University Technical Colleges (UTCs) for those who, at the age of 14, see their future in the more practical and technical, but equally demanding, world of engineering. Several have already opened. In the USA, transfer at 14 is the norm as young people progress from junior high to the high school.

All such claims emerge from the recognition of the need for a wider range of learning opportunities and for different environments to meet the needs of growing young people. Educational provision should be based on the learning needs of young people, not on the needs of inflexible institutional provision.

Therefore, the definition of 'secondary education' is fluid in terms of institutional provision, learning opportunities, appropriate environments, and progression routes into further training and higher education.

Some areas of concern

How such secondary education is shaped depends on answers to several issues of concern.

First, the change at the age of 11 from one environment to another is smooth for most, but somewhat disconcerting for others. Croll *et al*. point out from their extensive research:

> Children had very mixed views on the transition from primary to secondary. Some of them had been happier in primary school and found secondary school to be too big and impersonal. Others, however, had welcomed the transition as a move from a claustrophobic environment into a more varied and grown-up world offering them much wider academic and social possibilities.
>
> (Croll *et al*., 2010: 101)

That shift from a small, cosy environment to a larger, more impersonal one with a variety of teachers and a complex timetable can be difficult to cope with. Therefore, secondary education *for all* needs to attend to this transition and to the larger and less personal nature of the school. At the same time, importance is attached to a 'more grown-up world' which is seen to characterise the secondary phase. Perhaps the US division between elementary, junior high and high school is the best after all.

Second, development is gradual. It occurs at different paces, depending on the individual, on their environments and on the opportunities offered. Part of what one might expect from a secondary phase is the recognition of different levels of attainment, of pacing and of motivation within the same age group – and thus a great deal of flexibility in the ways in which the educational aims might be realised for different young people. Individual progress should not be tightly constrained by 'standards' defined for age groups.

Third, as the journey through the secondary phase progresses, so educational development needs to acknowledge a more adult environment. There is surely a connection between educational development and recognition by young people themselves (and by others) of their growing adult status. Such an environment and such recognition can, of course, be reflected in many different ways – relationships within the school between teacher and learner, opportunities for learning in the workplace, or transfer to the more adult world of the further education college.

Fourth, by their second decade young people have accumulated a lot of experience which shapes their sense of relevance, their aspirations and their very perceptions of schooling. There is a need to acknowledge the informal learning through which their minds and their values have already been provisionally formed.

Fifth, modern communication technology has opened up in revolutionary ways social networks, conversations beyond immediate acquaintances, ready access to information and opinions – even to the extent that some argue for future classrooms without teachers. Florida State, for example, is using virtual classrooms called e-learning labs with on-line teachers. And many, if not the majority of, young people in the secondary phase have developed independently an expertise in the use of technology. Perhaps the normal institutional framework for providing education for all, with its carefully controlled curriculum, should be questioned.

Sixth, the time approaches, during the secondary phase, when decisions have to be made about further or higher education or about training for employment. Opportunities to anticipate the future, in terms of both personal aspirations and realistic employment possibilities, should be part of the educational experience for all.

Hence, a lot depends on the characterisation of a secondary phase. It is when young people move into a different and potentially less personal environment, when they are soon to see themselves as young adults, when there emerges a wide range of abilities, achievements and aspirations, when their prior and contemporary experiences sieve the formal curriculum through different perspectives, when a command of communication technology opens up a much greater social and academic freedom, and when crucial decisions are made about their respective pathways to the future.

All these characteristics of the secondary phase demand flexibility of provision, respect for the learner's voice, and collaboration between educational providers (schools, colleges, Youth Service, voluntary bodies, employers and training providers). Are the institutional arrangements we have inherited appropriate for secondary education for *all* in the twenty-first century?

The dream

In the USA, the 'common school' was an ideal promoted by, amongst others, the philosopher John Dewey (1916). A principal aim of education was to help nurture a sense of community. This sense of community should be characterised by mutual respect and by learning through the interactions between learners of different backgrounds and experiences. 'Education', 'preparation for democracy' and 'community school' went together.

In England and Wales, secondary education for all was established by the 1944 Education Act. This was to be achieved (following the recommendations of the Norwood Report, 1943) through recognition of three broad areas of innate ability, each to be nurtured through a separate kind of school. There were those who were good at abstract thinking for whom the traditional grammar school was appropriate; there were those who were motivated by technical interests and were good at applying ideas, for whom technical schools and colleges were appropriate; and there were the rest who were motivated by practical activities and the more immediate environment, for whom secondary modern schools were relevant, followed by an early departure into the world of unskilled work. A very different 'dream' from that of the American High School!

This is not the place to rehearse all the criticisms of such an arrangement, in particular, the inequality of opportunity, of respect and of funding amongst those so categorised. But four criticisms stand out.

Equal opportunity to acquire intelligence

In England and Wales certainly, prevailing assumptions (spelt out in the Norwood Report, 1943) about 'different kinds of children', characterised by an objectively measured level of intelligence, came to be questioned. Far from being fixed and unchangeable, intelligence can, where the opportunities are provided, be 'acquired', as the Conservative Minister of Education, Sir Edward Boyle, declared in the Foreword to the Newsom Report (1964). The essential point is

> that all children should have an equal opportunity of acquiring intelligence, and of developing their talents and abilities to the full.

There was much evidence for this – for example, that of Vernon (1957) whose research demonstrated that coaching for the 11-plus examinations (by which children were selected for grammar school) could boost the intelligence scores by as much as 15 points.

A wider vision of achievement

The Newsom Report was scathing about the treatment of the 'half our future' which was denied the educational opportunities enjoyed by the other half. They deserved better. The curriculum needed to be broadened and enriched, and their achievements, too, should be recognised in public examinations. Indeed, until the implementation of the Beloe Report (1960) in the establishment of the Certificate of Secondary Education (first sat in 1965), there were no publicly funded examinations for anyone beyond the (roughly) 20 per cent selected for the GCE 'O' Level examinations.

More to education than academic success

There is much more to education than academic success. The rarely examined word 'academic' usually excludes the practical and demanding studies leading to engineering and design, and to the creative arts. Schools and colleges should be enabling young people to live more fulfilled lives and to live and work together as fellow citizens.

Economic needs

There was the economic argument. A more sophisticated economy needed a more sophisticated workforce – a higher level of literacy and numeracy, and a broader basis on which to build the skills and knowledge for the world of work.

All in all, there should be meaningful secondary education *for all*.

That, of course, was the rationale for the development of the comprehensive school – the kind of school which would bring young people across the socio-economic spectrum of society and across the ability range in order to mitigate social differences, provide greater equality of opportunity and create a less socially divided society. Those who welcomed the birth of comprehensive schools as the attempt to provide 'education for all', not for just an elite in the independent sector or in the grammar schools, saw the creation of a 'common culture', through the provision of a 'common curriculum' (and preferably in a 'common school') to be central to that vision.

Yet, despite the evidence to the contrary, the tripartite mentality lives on. One pioneering comprehensive school in south London was reopened in May 2011, divided into three 'houses' or 'mini-schools' – one for the gifted and talented, one for the middle ability and one for the lowest ability. Membership of each 'house' warrants a different coloured tie – purple for the gifted and talented, red for middle ability, and blue for the lowest ability. They are taught in separate buildings, play in different fenced off playgrounds and eat at different times. This is seen by the head teacher as the 'only way to survive in the brave new world of market-driven education', where the school is competing for children with the nearby grammar schools in Bexley. According to the head teacher, mixed ability teaching has failed and hence back to the tripartite system within the school – with a vengeance (*Education Guardian*, 26 July 2011).

The end of a dream?

The 'dream', which helped to shape the American High School as the twentieth century progressed, came under critical scrutiny. Such education for all was seen not to be possible without compromising educational aims – 'a fragmented curriculum that lacks a unified purpose and focus', and a compromise of academic rigour and demanding standards.

> As a result, it is often suggested, the effort of the high school to provide for everyone has created an institution that serves no one particularly well.
>
> (Franklin and McCulloch, 2007: 7)

Further problems emerged where the common school reflects only what is common within economically and racially segregated communities, or where 'choice' enables some learners to take flight from their community schools. As Ravitch points out in relation to New York City:

> As it elevated the concept of school choice, the Department of Education destroyed the concept of neighbourhood high schools. . . . Neighbourhoods were once knitted together by a familiar local high school that served all the children of the community, a school with distinctive traditions and teams and history.
>
> (Ravitch, 2010: 83)

In Britain, despite massive investment in schools, a large proportion of young people is regarded as uneducated, school failures, disengaged from the formal learning, ill-prepared for the world of employment, untouched by the prospect of social upward mobility. Employers complain about the lack of employability skills. Critics point to the lack of 'social mobility' amongst those from the most disadvantaged sections of society. Universities speak of the lack of preparation of 18 year olds for the demands of university work (Wilde and Wright, 2007). Politicians blame the schools for their lowly places in the league tables based on test scores and examination results (Ed Balls, when Secretary of State, had a list of over 600 'failing schools'). And the OECD PISA (Programme for International Student Assessment) comparisons of 65 countries indicated not only were the United Kingdom countries no more than average in educational attainment in the core subjects of reading, mathematics and science, but also there was a greater proportion of young people in the very low categories (OECD, 2009).

This suggests that there is not secondary *education* for all.

Reasons for doubts

Why, after universal provision of secondary *schooling* for all, should there be doubts about secondary *education* for all?

This is not an easy question to answer because there are different ideas about *educational* success. What some think to be educational progress, others reject. Why, for example, should the 'educated young person' be assessed solely on academic achievement, howsoever practically incompetent he or she might be? And why should the young person who displays a great deal of practical intelligence (in outdoor pursuits, in design and construction, or in a range of technical matters) but who fails in the textbook-based so-called academic core of the curriculum, be regarded as an educational failure? Qualities and capabilities obtained through different forms of learning and experience are frequently omitted from the prevailing list of 'performance indicators'.

Nonetheless, though a difficult question to answer, it is answered and the answers seem to be of three different kinds.

Reason 1. Plato lives

There was until recently, especially in England, a rather Platonic idea of the sort of education in which, 'in a place set apart', the guardian class would receive a special sort of education partly through what was taught but partly through the initiation into a particular tradition, social ethos and network. This was accessible to a relatively few (what the philosopher and poet, Coleridge, 1830, referred to as the 'clerisy') brought up, if not on gymnastics and mathematics, then at least on the classics and games. Prep school, public school and Oxbridge would provide the right kind of educational background. Indeed, this was argued to the Bryce Commission in 1895 by Herbert Warren, President of Magdalen College when discussion was conducted on whether the University of Oxford should be concerned with the training of teachers. The student who has read Plato's *The Republic* and Aristotle's *Politics* and *Ethics* has whatever theory is necessary for the practice of teaching. But in addition it would be helpful

> that a young man who has passed through an English public school, more particularly if he has been . . . a prefect . . . has had experience in keeping order and maintaining discipline . . . Thus the average Oxford man, more especially the classical student, ought not to require so long an additional training, either in theory or practice, as is sometimes necessary for students elsewhere.
>
> (Bryce Report, 1895: v.257)

Such a secondary education is certainly not for all. But is this set of assumptions now not just a matter of history? Hardly, when so many ministers in the present government come from the narrow world of public school and PPE at Oxford. Herbert Warren vindicated!

But this went further than the privileged world of the 'guardian class'. Geoffrey Bantock in his 1971 essay, 'Towards a theory of popular culture', was concerned with the many young people whom secondary education for all seems to have failed, namely, those 'of low achievement, probably though not invariably of low I.Q., come from culturally deprived homes, wish to leave school as soon as possible, and find themselves employed on leaving in unskilled or semi-skilled jobs' (Bantock, 1971).

His anxiety arose from the intention to raise the school-leaving age to 16. With due references to D. H. Lawrence's analysis of twentieth-century working-class consciousness and Basil Bernstein's 'Social class, language and socialisation', Bantock points to the disadvantages of those who inhabit a more oral tradition, a practical way of working, a set of cultural expectations which fit ill with a school culture which is book-based and demands disciplined entry to the various modes of more abstract thinking. There are two cultures and, in providing secondary education for all, we either water down the literary and more academic education or we preserve it at the expense of alienating a large number of young people.

Hence, such learning should be, according to the philosopher Michael Oakeshott, 'in a place set apart', far from the rumblings and business of everyday life. 'What is special about such a place or circumstance is its seclusion, its detachment from what Hegel called the '*hic et nunc*', the here and now, of current living' (Oakeshott, 1975: 24).

This is hardly the picture of the American High School or the British comprehensive school, open to all, connected with the community and economic context, far from secluded.

Reason 2. Incompatibility of inclusiveness and standards of excellence

A similar basis for the difficulties in providing secondary education for all lies not in the notion of exclusiveness to a limited social group, but in the *de facto* reduction of standards in the attempt to be all-inclusive. This is a most important point for when we come to consider '*general education* for all'.

The USA's National Commission on Excellence in Education published in 1983 *A Nation at Risk: the Imperative for Educational Reform*. It declared:

> The educational foundations of our society are gradually being eroded by a rising tide of mediocrity that threatens our very future as a nation and a people. What was unimaginable a generation ago has begun to occur – others are matching and surpassing our educational attainments. [The nation has] been committing an act of unthinking, unilateral educational disarmament. [Beset by conflicting demands, our educational institutions] seem to have lost sight of the basic purposes of schooling, and of the high expectations and disciplined effort needed to attain them.
>
> (from Ravitch, 2010: 24)

Those basic purposes of education, which were being eroded, lay in an initiation into the broad cultural traditions which we have inherited and which demand disciplined effort to enter into. The danger in extending initiation into these cultural traditions to everyone is that those traditions themselves become a superficial reflection of the real thing – what Allan Bloom (1987) referred to as 'the closing of the American mind'.

In the late 1960s in Britain, the Black Papers provided a hostile critique of the comprehensive trends in Britain – secondary education for all, identified with an ideology of egalitarianism and a 'progressive' approach to education, inimical to high standards and excellence: 'No longer can it be accepted that progressivism and comprehensive schemes are necessarily right, or that the future inevitably lies with them' (Cox and Dyson, 1969). One contribution to Black Paper 1, from H. J. Eysenck, was entitled 'The rise of the mediocracy'.

Another major contributor to the Black Papers, Rhodes Boyson, associated comprehensive schools with a slow decline in general culture since the First World War. He stated much later in a radio programme: 'If a balanced system of grammar schools, technical schools and apprenticeships had been created in the post-war years, I don't think we would ever have moved to comprehensive schools and the *lumpenproletariat* we have created' (BBC Radio 4, 23 October 1993, see Franklin and McCulloch, 2007).

Many agreed with the claim made by Eric James over 60 years ago that comprehensive schools would precipitate 'grave social, educational and cultural evils which may well be a national disaster' (quoted in Rubinstein and Simon, 1969: 37).

We see, therefore, an intensive debate in the USA, as well as in Britain, about the fall and rise of standards. Such a debate, with profound impact upon the content and structure of education, has a number of ingredients – an implicit elitism in that only a few are capable of benefiting from what powerful people recognised as 'education', the suspicion of making education relevant to a much broader group of learners (especially the *lumpenproletariat*), concern about seeing education in terms of its relevance to economic performance, the close or distant relation of school to the wider community, the perennial battle between so-called 'academic standards' and a wider vision of learning, which often is rejected as 'having lost sight of the basic purposes of schooling'.

Some are deemed, through lack of intelligence or through lack of cultural background, not capable of accessing such cultural forms and values. They should be in different schools or apprenticeships, preparing more practically for their future.

Reason 3. Education cannot compensate

A third kind of reason given for the failure of secondary education for all (that is, for there being so many failing or disengaged learners), is not so much cultural discontinuity or lack of intelligence, but social conditions which education cannot compensate for. 'Education cannot compensate for society' was the title of Basil Bernstein's influential paper published in 1970.

Chapter 6 will look at this in greater detail, but here let it suffice to say that education does not occur in a vacuum. It is *influenced* by social and economic contexts in which policies are developed. The sceptics argue that such influences are too great to be affected by educational interventions – except at the margin. Indeed, such scepticism has a long and pervasive history. The Jenks (1972) and the Coleman (1967) reports in the USA concluded that schools made no difference. And it was the case that many young people were dismissed in terms of educational achievement because of 'their background'. That is why the Rutter Report (1979), which demonstrated that schools do make a difference, was such an important piece of published research. But the work of the American prophet of doom, Christopher Jenks and his colleagues, in their 1972 book *Inequality*, argued that 'the egalitarian trend in education has not made the distribution of income appreciably more equal over the last 25 years'. When I was training to be a teacher, Jenks' book was on the reading list. There was no doubting the influence which this conclusion had upon schools – many young people could be contained but not really educated as that term was conventionally understood.

Conclusion

It is a critical time: a changing economic and employment context, different social networking, access to information at the press of a button, more vocal and demanding youth. Does not the provision of education in the twenty-first century need to change in response?

The last 50 years in England, since the Crowther Report (1959), *15 to 18*, and the Newsom Report (1964), *Half Our Future*, have witnessed many policy interventions aimed at transforming the educational provision for those in secondary education in order to meet the needs of the twentieth and now the twenty-first century. And these interventions are by no means confined to Britain.

But have they worked? Are we not still left with 'half our future' – underqualified, disillusioned, disengaged, ill-equipped for life after school? And if that is the case, do we finally accept defeat, or do we try even harder to transmit the knowledge which those in authority think that all young people should have? Or do we think more radically about what, in this day and age, counts as an educated person, and re-examine, in the light of the answer to that question, the standards by which young people, their teachers and their schools are judged?

There are many different responses to these questions, set against constant and often hostile criticism of the ways in which different national systems have developed secondary education for all. Is there any hope?

This book will say there is room for hope. In doing so, it argues for a wider vision of learning, respect for the informal learning and the voice of the learner, and in consequence a collaborative pattern of provision. Old structures must give way to new.

But in doing so the book questions many of the assumptions which have underpinned 50 years or more of disputation. Above all, it asks:

> *What counts as education – or, more accurately, an educated person – in this day and age?*

Those who question the hopes and aspirations for *secondary education for all* rarely pursue this question. They invoke, in their defence, the cultural basis of education without close analysis of what is meant by a culture which excludes so many.

Hence, in Part I, these wider questions will be explored – educational aims, standards, and culture. Part II brings out the implications for learning in its different modes, for curriculum, for teaching and pedagogy, and for the relation of schools to the wider community. Part III then indicates the consequences for the provision of education – the kind of system which will ensure secondary education for all.

2   The rise and fall of standards

The central worry: 'standards'

The main difficulties over secondary education for all arise from a concern about 'standards', namely,

- the apparent dilution of standards (as 'the best that has been thought and said' is extended to an unappreciative majority), or
- sheer lack of ability (Norwood Report's (1943) third category of adolescents), or
- the inability to attain those standards because of social background and culture ('education cannot compensate for society – Bernstein, 1970), or
- poor quality of teaching (not 'teaching to the standards').

The solution is to try harder, or to recruit more highly qualified people into teaching, or to provide those who can't be educated with good vocational training, or to change the institutional structure so as to benefit from the 'effective methods' employed by the business world.

This chapter seeks to look beneath the surface of these controversies. 'Standard' would seem to be a relatively straightforward concept. We all know what it means to say that the students display a low standard of behaviour, or that there is a high standard of teaching in that school, or that only students who show good standards of academic work will be able to proceed to university.

Or at least we think we do. But in effect it is not as clear or as simple as that. One must understand a word within its usage, and 'standards' have been adopted by the discourse of performance management which shapes its meaning and thereby affects what is meant by 'improving standards'. This extremely important matter will be developed later in this chapter, especially in the context of the USA and the UK.

International comparison of standards

Problems are exacerbated by the now regular comparison of standards between countries which are economic competitors. Such comparisons are based on surveys of performance in core subjects at different ages. Much hangs politically on the result of such surveys. As a government White Paper in England says in its Foreword: 'What really matters is how we're doing with our international competitors. That is what will define our economic growth and our country's future' (DfE, 2010). And recent international comparisons were taken as evidence of a 'decline in standards' over the last decade or so. Secondary education for all would seem to be failing.

There is, therefore, the need to look at the recent international comparisons of standards as a backcloth to the concern about education for all.

The OECD has, since 2000, provided detailed and comparative data on the performance of 15 year olds every three years. In the 2009 survey of performance in reading, mathematics and science, 65 countries took part, 34 from the OECD. These surveys are referred to as PISA. The detailed reports give important insight into how 'standards' are perceived and measured, but also into factors which affect performance. The PISA survey (OECD, 2009) indicates that both the UK and USA are falling behind many countries which they once felt superior to in their core achievements. Thus, on reading competency, the UK came 27th and the USA 24th in the league table of 65 countries; in mathematics, their positions were 28th and 31st, respectively; in science they were 21st and 30th, respectively. They were close to the mean in reading competency – not statistically significantly different from the OECD average. But, for example, more than 20 per cent in Britain are failing to achieve a baseline proficiency in maths. The US fares a little worse, fuelling the already fierce debate about falling standards and the need for school reform – as is described below.

To grasp the discrepancies between countries, one should compare the mathematics scores of Shanghai, China with those of the OECD countries. More than 25 per cent of 15 year olds could 'conceptualise, generalise and creatively use information based on their own investigations and modelling of complex problem situations'. In the OECD area, just 3 per cent reached that level of performance.

Four points of caution arise for the purposes of this book.

The first concerns the limited range of areas on which the measures are based. Is there not much more to education than reading, mathematics and science? No doubt there would be different league tables if other considerations were taken into account (for example, the ability to engage in open discussion, preparation for democratic communities, enjoyment of the arts, or the desire to carry on learning). But the OECD would no doubt reply that not everything can be measured and these three 'competencies' are central to functioning effectively in present-day society.

The second point concerns the identification of competencies within each of these three core areas. Obviously there will be disagreements about what should and should not be included. But the ones identified are thought to be necessary in meeting the challenges ahead if young people are to function effectively in modern societies, to contribute to economic well-being and to live fulfilled lives. There is, of course, a constant need to analyse what those challenges are. What, for example, do young people need to get a job, to be self-sufficient, to cope with the problems which inevitably arise? These questions were thoroughly examined in literacy and numeracy by the Moser Report (1999). Yet, another international survey, that of TIMSS (2007), arrives at different conclusions from those of the OECD as far as mathematics competency is concerned, putting Britain much higher in the league table.

Third, as the demands of society change, so do the standards against which one assesses competency. For example, the reading measures in the 2009 survey, but not in previous ones, include understanding and navigating around electronic texts. Quite possibly many who scored high in the 2006 survey would have done badly on the 2009 one – including the author of this book. Standards change as education tries to keep up with changing social and economic challenges. Nonetheless, the pointers to poor standards in literacy remain, confirming the problems which the Moser Report (1999) identified some time ago.

Fourth, league table ordering can be deceptive – where, for example, there is clustering of countries with only a marginal difference between them, and that possibly due to the imprecision of the testing. To drop several places might not be as serious as it sounds.

Therefore, international comparisons of standards are important, but only if they are properly used. They do not include areas which many would think are central to the aims of education. They do require a constant questioning of what it means to function competently and confidently in meeting future challenges. And they change over time. Longitudinal comparison is difficult. The social and economic demands have changed and will continue to do so. And it is no doubt partly due to these factors that other international standard measurements produce different rankings. England performs much better in *Trends in International Mathematics and Science Study* (TIMSS, 2007) than it does in the PISA rankings.

Context counts

The PISA surveys provide a lot of background context, country by country, for the results: information on the learners' home background, different approaches to learning, and school learning environments. They show, for example, wide variation within particular countries as well as between those countries. There is significant performance variability in the UK – larger than in other countries, much of this explicable by socio-economic background.

The argument is that there need not be such a gap, as there is in Britain, between the advantaged and disadvantaged young people. Policy and practice could do something to narrow the gap. In schools with mixed socio-economic intakes, the least advantaged students do better, but in England certainly there is an increasing polarisation between schools that serve the most disadvantaged and those that do not.

What then is the advice to governments?

First, many of the world's best performing educational systems have moved from bureaucratic 'command and control' environments towards school systems in which the people at the front line have much more control of the way resources are used, people are deployed, the work is organised and the way in which the work gets done.

(OECD, 2009: 4)

Second, where there is success, there is greater discretion over the content and curriculum, and teachers work together to frame what they believe to be good practices including conducting field-based research. There is less standardisation.

Third, it is not so much a matter of spending more money overall (only seven OECD countries spent more money per student than the UK), but more a matter of directing the money where it can make a difference. The UK is one of only 13 OECD countries where schools, dominated by socially disadvantaged learners, have similar staff/student ratios to schools which serve more advantaged neighbourhoods. There is little discrimination in funding according to need.

In sum, the evidence seems to show that, if national performance is to improve, there should be less top-down control, greater opportunity for teachers to work together in planning the curriculum and their own professional development, a redirection of resources to those most in need, and much more balanced entry to the secondary schools than is the case in the socially polarised English system.

Standards debate in the USA

If anything reflects the ebb and flow of educational debate and policy over standards, it is the continuing controversy in the USA, wherein 'traditionalists' berate 'progressives', and vice versa. The American philosopher, John Dewey, was seen as the most significant proponent of 'progressive education', a child-centred approach in which 'the child becomes the sun about which the appliances of education revolve; he is the centre about which they are organised' (Dewey, 1910: 103).

The 'project method', developed by W. H. Kilpatrick, a colleague of Dewey at Columbia University, translated Dewey's ideas into a curriculum in which the practical and interdisciplinary project provided the relevant interest to motivate the learner (Kilpatrick, 1918). Start with the interests of the learner, not with 'the standards' embedded in the traditional subjects.

This shift in 'the centre of gravity' away from education as a 'transmission of knowledge', wherein *standards* of truth, argument, and evidence are embodied, came to be a classic war over the fall and rise of standards. So much was this the case that Dewey was

hailed as the saviour of the American education by those who welcome greater involvement of students in their own planning and activity [but also] has been called worse than Hitler by some who felt that he infected schools with epistemological and moral relativism and substituted socialisation for true education.

(Noddings, 2005)

And such has been the apparent influence of Dewey in the UK that he was believed to be the cause of problems in British schools. Anthony O'Hear (1991: 28) argued: 'it is highly plausible to see the egalitarianism which stems from the writings of John Dewey as the proximate cause of our educational decline'.

Hence, the economic difficulties faced by the USA in the 1970s against increased economic challenges from Japan and other overseas competitors were placed firmly at the door of the 'progressive' educational approaches. They had abandoned the standards which were the hallmark of traditional education and the transmission of knowledge.

It is, of course, this very dualism between progressive and traditional which Dewey (1938a) so vigorously attacked. The broader aims of education, and the concept of 'standards' built in to such aims, do not fit into such a simplistic distinction. But it continues to shape the very public arguments about schools and education both in the USA and in Britain, especially where concerns arise about economic failure and international comparisons.

The continuing economic difficulties (blamed in part on 'poor standards' in schools, particularly in numeracy and literacy) and then the apparently lower scores in the Scholastic Aptitude Tests, which are used as measures of quality for entry to higher education, resulted in President George Bush's *No Child Left Behind* (NCLB) programme which entered federal legislation in 1972. Standards became identified with national test scores, and the raising of standards became linked, not with curriculum development or improved pedagogy, but with 'total quality management' (TQM).

Such TQM required precise definition of standards in terms of targets and the conditions which would spur on teachers and their schools to reach those targets – greater accountability with lots of high-status testing, parental choice, deregulation of schools so that they might pursue those targets in a competitive market, and merit pay for the successful teachers. As in business, schools would improve through 'the invisible hand of the market', in which failing schools would disappear, unable to attract customers.

A popular book at that time, made much of in Britain, was Chubb and Moe's *Politics, Markets and America's Schools*, arguing for school choice (helped by a voucher system) since this was the only way of breaking the power of the vested interests of the educational establishment (the so-called experts in educational aims and methods). Choice 'has the capacity all by itself to bring about the kind of transformation that, for years, reformers have been seeking to engineer in myriad other ways' (Chubb and Moe, 1990: 217).

Diane Ravitch sums it up well:

> NCLB introduced a new definition of school reform . . . In this new era, school reform was characterised as accountability, high-stakes testing, data-driven decision-making, choice, charter schools, privatisation, deregulation, merit pay, and competition between schools, Whatever could not be measured did not count.
>
> (Ravitch, 2010: 217)

This then was the recipe for raising standards all round. The doubters and the progressives would be defeated.

What was lacking in this reduction of standards to the language of TQM was any sense of vision of what education is for, of the relation of education to the public good (as opposed to private gain), of the content and quality of learning, of the relation of standards to professional judgement, or of progress made (slowly perhaps) within difficult social circumstances. This is an issue which will be at the heart of the discussion of educational aims and values in Chapter 3, but also of the provision of education in Chapters 15 and 16.

Standards in Britain: up, down and sideways

As in the USA, so in Britain, there has been a concern about declining standards. Take, for example, the 1977 consultative document *Education in Schools*, in commenting on the speech made by the then Prime Minister at Ruskin College, Oxford:

> [it] was made against a background of strongly critical comment in the press and elsewhere on education and educational standards. Children's standards of performance in their school work was said to have declined. The curriculum, it was argued, paid too little attention to basic skills of reading, writing and arithmetic, and was overloaded with fringe subjects.
>
> (DES, 1977)

It is important to note the two areas where standards were a matter of concern – first, in the 'basic skills' and, second, in the neglect of more traditional subjects usurped by 'fringe' ones (possibly the document had in mind such subjects as media or peace studies). There is an assumption (as in the PISA survey) that standards overall required meeting standards in 'basic skills' – part of the essential equipment of the educated person. But it is also assumed, first, that certain subject expertise is intrinsic to the aims of education, and, second, that detailed analysis and discussion of matters of deep human concern are not. Without success in basic skills and in traditional subjects, you are an educational failure – you do not 'come up to standard'.

Sir Keith Joseph, when Secretary of State, continued this theme. He expressed his deep concern with the poor standards of many young people and affirmed the aim of bringing 80–90 per cent of all pupils at least to the level achieved by pupils of average ability. Hence, poor standards there might be, but this signalled the need, not to abandon hope for secondary education for all, but, with a renewed and radical effort, to raise those standards. And his successor, Kenneth Baker, to that end, introduced the 1988 Education Act in which a detailed National Curriculum was introduced, with detailed targets expressing the expected standards to be reached by specific ages.

There was a need for establishing targets, performance indicators, methods for reaching those targets, and assessment of whether the targets had been hit.

Standards and management-speak

It is here that the arguments in the UK became not dissimilar from those in the USA. That is not surprising since the language of TQM spans the Atlantic Ocean. But also one of its chief advocates in England, and education policy adviser to Prime Minister Tony Blair, was exported to the USA, and in particular New York, to apply the formula believed to have been so successful in England. An interview with Joel Klein, then Chancellor for the New York School System, revealed that he [Klein]

> is a fan of Blair's education reforms and 'learnt a lot' from talking to Sir Michael Barber, the former No. 10 education adviser. 'The UK is performing better on international tests and moving in the right direction', he says. 'They have a lot of the challenges we have'. He is surprised when I mention the sense of failure, especially in London. 'The work just hasn't finished', he says blithely.
> (Ravitch, 2008)

Quite clearly Klein had not read the PISA reports.

The consequence is that standards are identified with the targets which are increasingly narrowed so that they can be more easily measured. To improve standards, one needs to spell these out in detailed specifications of 'can do's', teach more effectively to these targets, measure the outcomes, evaluate the programme in the light of the results, and possibly change the targets or means in the light of the evaluation. That is – TQM.

'Greater effectiveness' is created by the extension of 'customer choice', increased competition between schools for their 'customers', rewards (or bonuses) for teacher performance, and punishment through naming and shaming of the schools which do not 'come up to standard'.

Standards are said to be 'driven up' by such measures – and data are produced to show it. For example, schools in inner city neighbourhoods, particularly London, showed dramatic progress in the time of the Labour Government. In Hackney, Lambeth and Islington, the proportion of pupils with five good GCSEs, including maths and English, rose between 1998 and 2009 by 35, 34 and 29 per cent, respectively. This partly reflects the extra investment; funding almost doubled – from £2,900 per pupil to £5,310 (*Guardian*, 14 January 2010). But such 'dramatic progress' often reflected politically astute substitutions by head teachers of so-called 'vocational qualifications' for the GCSEs, which were officially deemed 'equivalent' to GCSEs, albeit of a very different kind – and regarded as 'easier' by the Wolf Report (2011). The significance of this is developed in Chapter 12. Where standards 'go down', on the other hand, or remain low, then the school (in this more publicly accountable and competitive system) will be declared a failed school and possibly closed through lack of 'customers'.

All this might suggest that precise definition of standards, the publication of school-by-school attainment of standards, the spur all this gives 'to teach to standards', the institutional framework in which parents might migrate their children to schools with higher standards are a good thing. That might be the solution to the failing school, to the decline in national profile of standards, to the final salvation (as believed in school reforms in the USA) of secondary education for all.

Focus on standards: warning voices

Teaching to standards

The most regularly articulated concern lies in the tendency for the officially defined 'standards' to become the targets of the teaching. Teachers feel obliged to teach to the targets and, indeed, to focus upon that group of learners that would help the school move up the league table – in England, the group just below the threshold of five GCSEs graded A to C (or their officially sanctioned equivalent).

The consequences of this are several, well articulated by a sixth former in his evidence to the Nuffield Review (2009: 67):

> Far too often in education the emphasis is on achieving targets and regurgitating what the exam board wants, as opposed to actually teaching children something. As a sixth form student myself, this frustrates me on a daily basis, especially in history, when we must learn to write to the specifications of the exam board, instead of actually learning about the past.

There is overwhelming anecdotal evidence from teachers on the frustration of having to teach to targets, which define the standards with precision, militate against a deeper sense of understanding, leave no room for the struggle to understand, focus on inappropriate content for these learners in this context, and give undue attention to specific groups of learners (see Chapter 12).

The evidence, however, is by no means just anecdotal. The Smith Report (2004) on mathematics points to the

> serious concerns about the frequency of assessment of material in GCE AS and A Level Mathematics. This is felt by many respondents to hinder the development of learning and understanding of mathematics at this level. It is the consensus view that far too much time is devoted to examinations and preparing for examinations – 'teaching to the test' – and that this is at the expense of the understanding of the subject itself.

The Chief Inspector in England expressed her concern about teaching to the test in her submission of evidence from national inspections to the government's Select Committee on Testing and Assessment (HoC, 2008). Learning experience is narrowed.

Wilde and Wright (2007) conducted discussions with some 250 admissions tutors in 21 higher education institutions and these revealed perceptions of the mismatch between the forms of teaching and learning in the 14–19 phase and those in higher education. The key comment was a variation on the theme of 'over assessment' and 'teaching to the test', prior to entry to higher education. This criticism was shared by universities which were able to recruit exclusively from candidates with excellent grades.

So, what is happening? Schools want to raise standards (who would possibly say they were trying to lower them?). They therefore identify the standards precisely. They teach to those standards. But that, it is then claimed, leads to lower standards.

Moveable standards

The government in Britain does not dispute that schools have improved according to the officially defined standards (the proportion who obtain GCSE Grades A*–C including maths and English). However, it does now dispute that these standards are 'good standards' (that is, meet the standards by which standards themselves are to be judged). It has introduced, therefore, an English Baccalaureat (EBac) which requires obtaining GCSE A*–C grades at GCSE in mathematics, English, two sciences, a modern language, and history or geography. Thereby, at a stroke by the new Secretary of State for Education, schools which previously had been judged to be successful (came up to standard) were now seen to be failing schools. According to evidence to the Select Committee, when the EBac was applied retrospectively in 2011 to the previous year's results only 15 per cent of pupils met the requirements for the EBac, and less than one-fifth of the pupils in the English grammar schools qualified for the EBac on the basis of GCSE 2010 results (*TES*, 18 March 2011; HoC, 2011a: ATL evidence).

This is of no little political importance. A key government policy for school improvement has been the creation of free standing schools, called 'academies' and 'free schools', which are claimed to improve standards (namely, achieve better GCSE results than local authority schools). However, 'at a stroke of the pen' this would no longer appear to be so. In only three-sixteenths of such schools did as many as 6 per cent of pupils qualify for the EBac (HoC, 2011a: ATL evidence). Two explanations might be given. One is that the academies are not as good as the political rhetoric would have us believe. The second is that the academies are doing well but only against standards which have now been rejected, without, according to the Select Committee, consultation 'with key stakeholders and the wider public'. The new standards, according to the Select Committee, 'focus on a narrow range of subjects' and they 'are not part of a balanced score card', especially for the many children on free school meals.

Might there not be yet more changes in standards when new Secretaries of State feel it necessary to re-define them? None lasts very long – there have been 17 since 1974. Perhaps a new EBac would include technology or the arts. All this underlines the need for a much more thorough examination of the aims of education, for only in the light of such an examination might there be sensible, though tentative, statements about standards.

'Performance indicators' are not standards

To deal with these dilemmas, therefore, it is necessary to think critically about what we mean by standards, their assumed identification with performance indicators, and their absorption into the language of TQM with all its consequences and implications.

Imagine that a major educational aim was to make all the learners happy, and indeed that the top place in the educational league table was reserved for the school which caused the greatest amount of happiness of the greatest number. And why not? Was not Jeremy Bentham correct? States of happiness would be graded on the performance criterion of smiling (total quantity of smiles and measurable size of each smile). And that would not be a foolish criterion. Happy people generally smile, just as happy dogs usually wag their tails. In comes the inspector of 'happiness education', quantifies the number of smiling faces at regular intervals, measures a randomised sample of smiles and gives a starred A Grade for prolonged laughter so as to help top universities discriminate more finely. He congratulates the school on the quantity and quality of smiling, and recommends a distinction. The standards in that school are very high.

This has been very important for the school. Its place in the league table of smiling schools will attract, at a time of unregulated choice, future customers and the added income which comes with them. Hence, the teachers have prepared the students well. They have learnt to smile at appropriate occasions, to respond smilingly to appropriate prompts. They have been well trained by a teacher who is expert in delivering this part of the happiness curriculum.

The only problem is that the learners are as miserable as sin. They have simply been well trained to meet the performance indicators. Indicators are not the same as the states of mind (happiness, understanding, willingness to learn, kindness, etc.) which they are supposed to be indicators of. Furthermore, those states of mind can be revealed in different ways. There are many possible indicators – such as humming a tune from *The Marriage of Figaro*. But they are not what one *means* by happiness.

Sometimes one thinks that someone has learnt how to approach a particular mathematical problem, only later to withdraw that judgement on the basis of some further behaviour in a different context. He or she has only partly understood. And the standard reached – the standard of understanding – will be revealed in a number of contexts. Moreover, the judgement is always open to revision in the light of further judgement.

If one attends to the experts in any one area – those whose work has been judged to have reached high standards – the standards they adhere to are not logically reducible to simple performance indicators. They exercise judgement. They argue about the worth of a piece of work. They have come (as a result of study, argument and criticism) to recognise the standards which are to be appealed to in the arts, humanities and sciences. And, as teachers, they initiate the next generation into those standards which become part of their understanding, often implicit, of the activity they are engaged in.

Elliott Eisner, drawing particularly on the arts, sees this judgement to be a kind of connoisseurship – a coming to appreciate the quality of a proof, of an artefact, of an argument. This is done even where there are few, if any, explicit criteria with which to measure its value. And yet people are able to argue about the judgements concerning standards, and even about the standards themselves, through critical engagement and argument. Such judgements (as in connoisseurship) and such criticism, without reference to 'performance indicators', should not seem surprising to those who are familiar with art appreciation and criticism, or indeed with the controversies amongst historians, geographers or writers of literature. But, as Eisner points out, that might be one reason why, under systems dominated by TQM, less importance is attached to the arts and humanities (Eisner, 1976).

What, then, are standards?

Standards are benchmarks against which we judge what is good or bad, true or false, correct or incorrect, elegant or inelegant, aesthetically pleasing or not pleasing. They are implicit within any activity, and they relate logically to the purpose of the activity. And educational standards, therefore, *a fortiori*, relate logically to the aims of education.

Different activities have different purposes and therefore refer to different standards as to what counts as performing that activity well. Standards of success in riding a bicycle relate to the purpose of the activity. And these standards change as those purposes change to meet different contexts. The standards appealed to are different for those who wish to win races from those required for leisurely exercise. And yet those standards, though not measurable, remain objective in the sense that they are open to critical enquiry, articulation and debate.

Such an understanding of standards makes nonsense of the vast qualification structure which is supposed to show equivalence in standards between very different activities and disciplines. Standards relate to the nature and purpose of the activity. In what sense can Level 3 in hairdressing be seen as equivalent to Level 3 in engineering?

It might be argued that two different activities might be equivalent in difficulty, but that could depend as much on the specific abilities of the learner. Level 3 hairdressers might find Level 3 electronics too difficult. But equally Level 3 electronics engineers might lack the aesthetic sensibility and the dexterity ever to become Level 3 hairdressers. It makes no sense to say that, due to certain equivalences, they are both achieved at Level 3.

Equivalences do, of course, need to be made between competing qualifications concerned with similar activities. Does a BTEC in engineering provide similar foundations for university courses in engineering as the more traditional A Level route? To answer such a question, it is necessary to look at the content of each and to the different modes of learning. The Smith Report (2004) devotes some space to the claimed equivalences between different mathematics qualifications (or units within them).

Conclusion

Standards do not go up or down or decline, despite the many claims that they are doing so. Rather, performance improves or gets worse in relation to those standards. If standards were to rise or fall, that rise or fall could only be judged to be so against a different type of standard – namely, those standards whereby one assesses the standards of standards, and thus one is into an infinite regress.

But what are those educational standards against which we want to assess performance? Standards are the benchmarks which are distinctive of those activities which we believe are worth pursuing. Educational standards depend on what we believe education to be about – what counts as an educated person.

Very often those standards are implicit only, embedded in the very nature of the activity. To learn a craft or a subject is to be initiated into those standards – learning how to think appropriately, to move elegantly, to behave politely, to create beautifully – but to do so without necessarily being able to articulate those standards explicitly. But how does all this affect the deep concerns which we have detected in relation to secondary education for all?

Educational standards relate to the aims of education. What counts as an educated 19 year old? Only in answering that question might one begin to see the standards which should shape the aims and content of secondary education for all. Possibly those who focus almost completely on academic achievements have failed to ask that question, and have too narrow a view of what it means to be educated.

On the other hand, in the failure to ask this question, both Britain and the USA have adopted a seductive but superficial model for 'improving standards' – one which confuses standards with performance indicators. The so-called 'school reforms' have transformed the language of education into one of effective management of performance, whereby standards are identified with measurable outcomes.

The answer must be in asking: What is the purpose of education? What are the values, the qualities and the understandings which, at different levels and in different ways, we believe ought to be the possession of all young persons? Only in that way might we be able to articulate the standards whereby schools, the school system and the young people themselves are to be evaluated. Perhaps secondary education for all, far from being impossible, depends on a wider vision of education in terms of its aims and a wider range of worthwhile achievements (and thereby standards) than is generally recognised.

Personal development is central. But first we must ask what it means to be and to develop as a person.

3   The aims of education
Watch your language

Old rhetoric is out of date

What, in terms of political rhetoric, has been the message for selling 'education' to young people and their parents? For several decades, it has been that more education will maximise opportunity, ensure better jobs, create greater social mobility and raise living standards.

What, then, if this is no longer the case – or even if it never was the case for many young people as they struggled to get qualifications which had no, or only marginal, financial returns? In the UK wages have not risen in real terms since 2005. Upward social mobility for some has meant downward social mobility for others. There can be no universal opportunity for betterment in such social and economic terms.

There is, of course, the belief that, as manual work is exported to centres of cheap labour overseas, there will be an inexorable increase in 'knowledge work' in the more 'developed world', absorbing the increasingly better educated young people. The latter will more than compensate for the former if only we have better educated workforces.

However, that 'knowledge work' is now being exported, too. Alan Blunder, former Vice-Chair of the US Federal Reserve, estimated that one-quarter of all American service sector jobs could go overseas. A skilled chip designer in India costs ten times less than one in the USA (Wilby, *Guardian*, 3 July 2011).

One might expect, however, that this does not apply to the top 30 per cent or so – those who, as a result of their education, achieve high-level and satisfying jobs. Surely, it is a justifiable aim of education for more young people to go to university and to acquire the knowledge and skills for gaining and enjoying more responsible and satisfying employment. But, again, this is challenged. There is predicted a 'digital Taylorism' (i.e. a routinisation of once mentally and personally demanding jobs in the same way that had happened to manual jobs decades ago), leading even university graduates into less satisfying careers.

Those young people, who, for whatever reasons, may not aspire to university education, are 'sold education' and the pursuit of vocational qualifications on the grounds that they will better find employment or apprenticeships leading to employment. But can such claims for more education be any longer justified? Youth unemployment (16–24 year olds) in Britain is reaching one million – 20 per cent of that age group. And that is caused, not so much by lack of education as by lack of opportunities. Graduates, unable to get graduate-level jobs, fill the posts once taken by less qualified young people and requiring no graduate-level qualification.

Surely, then, the justification for (that is, the aims of or the values embodied in) 'education for all' must lie elsewhere. Why believe in education even when it will not bring greater opportunities, social mobility, more money, or a satisfying career?

The key question

Educational 'reforms' which are continually being pursued in many countries, often as a knee-jerk reaction to the latest PISA survey, should be accompanied by a thorough examination of the aims of education. That, however, rarely happens.

> *But what should count as an educated 19 year old at the beginning of the twenty-first century?*

Perhaps, as a result of the answers to that question, many more educational successes might be discovered than are recognised in PISA surveys.

However, it is not easy to arrive at statements of educational aims which avoid empty rhetoric – that is, statements which are so general that nothing specific follows from them or would be excluded by them. Statements of aims should be sufficiently clear that we know what we want from education and where the system which is to be reformed went wrong. Furthermore, they should be sufficiently well-grounded in a defensible understanding of human well-being as to make the changes genuine 'reforms' – that is, transformation of the system and its practices for the better.

One might claim that that is precisely what has happened in the USA and Britain, where long lists of standards and targets have been enumerated. However, as we have seen in the last chapter, standards, and the targets associated with them, are not educational aims. Therefore, in failing to recognise the distinction, the language of education changes and the key philosophical issues get ignored.

Watch your language – was Orwell right after all?

In January 2011, Sir Michael Barber (founder of the U.S. Education Delivery Unit, head of 'global education practice' for the world-renowned management consultancy McKinsey, chief education adviser to Pearson 'the world's leading learning company' with interests in 70 countries, and former chief education adviser to the British Prime Minister, Tony Blair) met with Kentucky Department of Education staff to share insights on 'deliverology' (http://www.kypost.com/dpp/news/state/institute-to-help-ramp-up-educational-improvement).

'Deliverology' is the systematic process for 'driving progress' and 'delivering results' in education. It has the 'tools' with which teachers might *deliver* more effectively at the student level what is intended at the system level. These 'tools' enable the school reformers to set precise and measurable targets, plan strategies for attaining those targets, gather the data on learner-by-learner performance, monitor that data and then, in the light of the monitoring, solve any problems which are related to the implementation of the reforms as these are reflected in the targets.

In what George Orwell would have described as the 'newspeak' of education, a new 'deliverology language' has developed in Britain and the USA, borrowed from the business world where *outputs* are related to *inputs* and where *effectiveness* in meeting the *performance indicators* is the key criterion of success. Schools are now subject to *audits* of their performance in relation to the *targets*, set 'at the system level'. Teachers are seen as the *deliverers* of what, at a system level, has been prescribed. And they have to comply because, otherwise, the *customers* might take their custom elsewhere.

The problem is reflected in *A Survival Guide for College Managers and Leaders* by David Collins, the newly appointed Chief Executive (*sic*) of the Learning and Skills Improvement Service. Not one of the ten chapters is devoted to teaching or learning, and there is no mention of the distinctive educational purposes of further education, but much on efficiency gains, value for money, marketing products, income targets for each subject, examining performance, quality control. All the experts referred to come from management and business. It is assumed that the main purpose of further education is improved economic performance and that private firms offer the model for the public sector (see Coffield, *TES*, 24 July 2009).

The contrast between 'oldspeak' and 'newspeak' is poignantly illustrated by Larry Cuban in his book *The Blackboard and the Bottom Line: Why Schools Can't be Businesses*. Cuban meticulously shows through many examples, and through reference to pertinent documents, the many ways in which the world of business has shaped the aims and values, the governance and (above all) the language of education. The reaction in the past to the perceived failure of schools has been to run them more like businesses, and in doing so, to shift the moral language of education to that of the management theory which pervades the business world.

But can schools be run like businesses?

Perhaps the most succinct and effective response to this is given through Cuban's story which might be abbreviated as follows. A successful businessman, dedicated to improving public schools, told an audience of teachers: 'If I ran my business the way you people operate your schools, I wouldn't be in business very long.' Cross-examined by a teacher, he declared that the success of his blueberry ice cream lay in the meticulous way in which he selected his blueberries, sending back those which did not meet the high quality he insisted upon. To this the teacher replied:

> That's right . . . and we can never send back our blueberries. We take them rich, poor, gifted, exceptional, abused, frightened . . . we take them all. Every one. And that . . . is why it is not a business. It's a school.
>
> (Cuban, 2005: 3)

But what is the significance of 'we take them all – every one – that is why it is not a business'?

The poverty of 'newspeak'

Whatever their personal background, personal problems and characteristics, the learners are persons – distinctive moral individuals, capable of yet further development in their capacities for thinking, feeling, appreciating, aspiring, acting responsibly. As Oakeshott (1975: 17) said, 'man [*sic*] is what he learns to become: this is the human condition'. That learning to become human, in its many dimensions, is the focus of education. It cannot be captured in a few measurable behaviours, nor in the business language of 'performance management'. It cannot be treated as but the 'means' to some non-person-centred 'end' such as that of a successful economy – though of course there may very well be economic benefits from such personal development.

The problem, as Cuban perceives it, lies in what he refers to as the 'logic of action'.

This 'logic of action' has the following characteristics. First, there is an identification of precise and measurable objectives – these are the educational aims. Second, there is the identification of those 'means' which can be shown empirically to achieve those objectives. Third, therefore, the 'means' are logically different from the 'ends' – they are what can be shown, *as a matter of fact*, to be the way in which the technically competent deliverer (the teacher) can hit those targets.

The teacher need not think about the ends or aims – they are decided elsewhere, away from 'the action'. Teaching becomes a technical science of delivery. And now worksheets can be downloaded for teachers, who may know little about the subject matter, to enable the learners to hit the targets. There is little or nothing (nor can there be) in the science of deliverology about the aims of education or the means through which those aims might be decided upon.

A different voice – that of 'liberal learning'

Change the language and you change the way in which you conceive the educational enterprise and its very aims. How do we conceive learning? Is it always choosing a 'means' to arrive at some 'end', preconceived by 'the system'?

That surely does not fit the *informal* learning whereby children adapt to new circumstances, internalise what is experienced, come to see things differently through interactions with others, seek to understand what is puzzling, re-conceptualise the world tentatively in the light of experience. They are learning what they become – 'that is the human condition'.

Formal education, then, is the way in which that *informal* learning is consciously helped by others who are able to put the young learners in touch with the wisdom we have inherited as they attempt to make sense of the physical, social and moral worlds they inhabit. Education is an 'engagement' between the learner and what others have said and done. Such an engagement, rightly conducted, illuminates their experiences, enriches their understandings of the world, and makes possible what Dewey referred to as 'the intelligent management of life'.

In this 'engagement', Oakeshott likens education to a 'conversation – an endless unrehearsed intellectual adventure in which, in imagination, we enter into a variety of modes of understanding the world and ourselves' (Oakeshott, 1975: 39).

Liberal learning, therefore, is 'an initiation into the art of this conversation' in which we learn to recognise the voices of science, of history, of poetry, of religion, of philosophy, and 'to distinguish their different modes of utterance, [and] to acquire the intellectual and moral habits appropriate to this conversational relationship, and thus to make one's *debut dans la vie humaine*' (ibid.).

In a nutshell, there are, on the one hand, the learners with their own and limited way of understanding the world, and, on the other hand, the knowledge and wisdom of previous generations which should illuminate those understandings. Education requires the interaction between the understandings we have inherited and the limited modes of understanding of the learners. The teacher is the one who facilitates this interaction – acquainted with the 'best that has been thought and said', on the one hand, and the limited understandings of the learners, on the other.

But a broader conversation is needed

There may appear to be two aspects of Oakeshott's conversation missing: the first, the broadening of the conversation to the wider community of which the learners are part; the second, the kind of 'conversation' which takes place within practical traditions of making and creating which are not articulated within written language and which thereby are too often neglected in formal education.

Involving the wider community

With regard to the first aspect, Oakeshott felt that the engagement with the ideas, which we have inherited and through which we are enabled to make sense of the human condition, is best achieved in a 'place set apart', secluded from and undisturbed by the noise and business of everyday life. It is interesting to note how many of Britain's famous 'public schools' and newer universities were in 'places set apart' free from the distractions of the non-educational world.

That would hardly be a rallying call for education through work experience, endorsed by the Confederation for British Industry. Indeed, it has the overtones of that Platonic ideal, referred to in Chapter 1, in which the relatively few who are deemed to be capable of engaging in this conversation might be educated apart from those who are seen to be less able and less motivated to enjoy this cultural inheritance. The few become the new 'guardian class'. Oakeshott would not appear to his critics to be an advocate of 'secondary education for all'.

The similarities and differences between two very different philosophers help us to understand the issue. John Dewey refers to the fundamental factors in the educative process as

> an immature, undeveloped being and certain social aims, meanings, values incarnate in the matured experience of the adult. The educative process is the due interaction of these forces. Such a conception of each in relation to the other as facilitates completest and freest interaction is the essence of educational theory.
>
> (Dewey, 1902: 123)

As with Oakeshott, so with Dewey, education lies in that 'reconstruction or reorganisation of experience which adds to the meaning of experience' (Dewey, 1916: 76), arising from, on the one hand, the teacher's expert acquaintance with those 'social aims, meanings and values' which we have inherited and the relating of these to the more limited understandings of the learner.

However, that 'reconstruction of experience' occurs not simply from the interaction with the selected culture we have inherited (what Dewey refers to as 'the wisdom of the race') but also through the interactions with others in the community who bring to the learner a wider range of experiences. This very range of experiences often challenges preconceptions and prejudices. Moreover, some of those 'others' are the young people whose own 'popular culture', gleaned from the media and developed through their powerful social networks, shapes how they perceive and evaluate the social and moral worlds to which they are being formally introduced.

It is important to remember in this connection that Dewey was writing at a time when thousands of immigrants from very different ethnic, religious and social backgrounds were entering the United States, often poor and illiterate. How might people of such different backgrounds become a mutually supportive community rather than remain divided and divisive, to the detriment of all? The common school was where people of different backgrounds and experiences would learn from the different experiences of the others, would learn to deal with the challenges which such differences created, would question their own assumptions in the light of these challenges and would, above all, learn to respect these differences – to see and benefit from 'the dignity of difference', the title of Chief Rabbi Jonathan Sacks' book (Sacks, 2002).

As Dewey succinctly put it:

> Men live in a community in virtue of the things which they have in common. What they must have in common in order to form a community or society are aims, beliefs, aspirations, knowledge – a common understanding – likemindedness as the sociologists say.
>
> (Dewey, 1916: 4)

It must be emphasised that learning to live in community is not just added on to the more fundamental aims of education (knowledge and understanding, say) but is seen as central to the development of a person. 'Seclusion in a place apart' or the barriers dividing different classes of citizenry impoverish the lives of those so separated – they are cut off from important occasions of growth and under-standing.

Can we still have *secondary education for all*, including the privileged and wealthy, without the common school and the educational advantages of more socially and economically mixed communities?

Recognising traditions of practical excellence

The second limitation in the 'conversation between the generations', which traditional schooling has drawn upon and which cuts out so many young people, is reflected in Richard Sennett's *The Craftsman*:

> History has drawn fault lines dividing practice and theory, technique and expression, craftsman and artist, maker and user; modern society suffers from this historical inheritance. But the past life of craft and craftsmen also suggests ways of using tools, organising bodily movements, thinking about materials that remain alternative, viable proposals about how to conduct life with skill.

> (Sennett, 2008: 11)

Part of the 'conversation' we have inherited lies in the practical accomplishments which have demanded intelligence in the most demanding way – the building of cathedrals and churches by the medieval stone masons (who had no degrees in engineering or architecture), the great engineering creations of Brunel or Morris (later Lord Nuffield, who, leaving school at 15, never passed an examination), the inventiveness of Thomas Edison (who had but three months of formal education in school), the awesome constructions of Brunelleschi (who had been an apprenticed clock maker). In the nineteenth century, the Victoria and Albert Museum in South Kensington, London, was built as a monument to the achievement, artistic imagination, and practical capability, indeed genius, of woodworkers, weavers and skilled craftsmen. Unfortunately, those great achievements of practical making, doing and creating have so often been divorced from what might be called the 'higher pursuits' of learning.

Such traditions are acquired through doing rather than theorising (although there is theory embodied in the practice), through experimenting and learning from mistakes, through being apprenticed to master craftsmen who show how something is made, through engagement with difficult tasks. Such doers and makers are part of a continuing tradition in which one generation learns from another – for example, the architect thinking through the tentative sketches with pencil in the light of previous constructions, or the horticultural worker envisaging new creations albeit within an inherited and learnt tradition.

These traditions of practical capability are not a matter of just knowing the right technique to achieve a preconceived goal – mastery of the 'means' which will inexorably deliver the 'end'. The ends of the activity often emerge from the deliberation which takes place in the very engagement. In arguing this, one has in mind the achievements not only of great inventors and discoverers, such as those just mentioned, but also of the many people who master the arts of cooking, gardening or decorating from practice, from reflection on practice and from following the example and criticism of others.

The American philosopher turned motor mechanic, Matthew Crawford, shows the problems arising from the separation of thinking from doing. 'The disappearance of tools from our common education is the first step towards a wider ignorance of the world of artifacts we inhabit' (Crawford, 2009: 3).

Formal education has a key role in ensuring the continuation of such practical capabilities (the intelligent arts and skills of living) just as much as it has of initiating young people into the different modes of understanding and appreciating the world.

On becoming human

This 'learning to be human', therefore, involves: first, the acquisition of knowledge and understanding to help one manage life intelligently; practical capabilities; and a developed sense of community with which our own well-being is connected.

There is, however, still something missing from this analysis, namely, the moral dimension in which young persons are enabled to foresee life as a whole, to think seriously about the life worth living, to recognise excellence and to want to pursue it in the activities they are engaged in. Life is shaped at every level by the values one adheres to, even if these be but implicit. Let us call the caring about those values (for example, the readiness to examine them in the light of criticism, attending to alternative viewpoints, respecting the examples of others, or cherishing demanding ideals) 'moral seriousness'.

That moral seriousness is not something separate from the other dimensions we have referred to. The humanities and the arts are the very voices through which the human condition – its ideals and possibilities as well as its failures and weaknesses – is portrayed and made available to the new generation of learners. Nor is this moral dimension separable from the pursuit of practical capabilities or the more vocational pursuits, because these themselves have inbuilt values as to what are the appropriate standards to be embodied in practice. The good bricklayer is rightly proud of the elegantly constructed wall that he has built.

However, that moral dimension – the essential characteristic of becoming and being a person – is more than a matter of obeying the right rules of behaviour. Rather, it is a matter of acquiring and developing the appropriate dispositions, both intellectual and moral. For example, the intellectual dispositions or virtues are essential to the serious pursuit of knowledge. 'Understanding', of whatever kind and at whatever level, requires a concern for the truth – *honesty* in presentation of what one claims to know, *modesty* in terms of what one might achieve, *open mindedness* in the face of well-meant criticism of others, *patience* in the search for answers, *perseverance* in the often difficult task of solving problems.

Similarly with the engagement in the distinctive practices of the craftsman. As Sennett argues: 'The carpenter, lab technician, and conductor are all craftsmen because they are dedicated to good work for its own sake. Theirs is practical activity but their labour is not simply a means to another end' (Sennett, 2008: 20).

That 'dedication to good work for its own sake', not for the sake of a higher reward or wider recognition (although no doubt such would not go amiss), has no room on the one hand for sloppiness, nor on the other for excessive zeal which would get things out of proportion. And the disposition to seek excellence welcomes criticism, is ready to correct what does not come up to standard, and delights in doing something well. Virtue is its own reward.

What might be referred to as the moral virtues are precisely these dispositions which enable one to live the distinctively human life, ensuring a proper balance between destructive extremes. 'Courage' disposes one to pursue what is worthwhile despite setbacks and pain, and yet it shuns the foolhardiness that fails to recognise danger or faces dangers unnecessarily. The disposition to respect other persons reflects the perception of them as ends in themselves, not as objects in one's personal game and drama, whilst at the same time not blinding one to their faults.

Formal education, in its concern for the development of persons and helping each to acquire those qualities which make them distinctively human, cannot ignore this development of moral seriousness, that is, the development of the virtuous human being, reflecting on what is a life worth living, and disposed not only to take the question seriously but also to act accordingly. Chapter 7 (concerned with a 'wider vision of learning') shows how such an aim is not only deeply held by many teachers but also the inspiration for much excellent practice – but, alas, too often neglected in the impoverished world of 'deliverology', with its own rewards and punishments.

Personal or public good

This moral seriousness might be tackled from a different angle. It is true of much schooling that formal education is, and should be, concerned with the achievements of individuals within the school or college. There they gain, one hopes, the experience, skills and understanding to live more fulfilled lives and the qualifications to enable them to proceed to university or to employment. Success of the system is, in fact, partly assessed by the degree of social mobility it creates.

Such an emphasis on personal enhancement has not been universally held. The guardian class of Plato's *The Republic* were educated to serve the republic justly under the guidance of their philosopher king. The nineteenth-century 'public schools' in England saw themselves very much in that mould, as reflected in Coleridge's idea of a 'clerisy'. Societies institute systems of schooling as much for the general good of society as for the personal good of individuals. After all, the two are intrinsically linked. We are all members of the wider community and benefit from the health and moral ethos of that society. The 'public value' of education, as a recent report on life-long learning demonstrated, lies in the reduction of discrimination, crime, poverty and ill-health (Schuller and Watson, 2009).

This contrasts with a view of education as essentially a personal and 'positional' good, reflected in the predominant emphasis on parental choice. The respect and enhancement of each person, howsoever modest his or her position, requires a fair society – for example, one which eliminates discrimination on the basis of gender, ethnicity, religion, sexual orientation and social class. Fairness and the social cohesion are more urgent today in the light of increased diversity, lower social mobility, and the widening gap and segregation between rich and poor.

But more than that. To be educated is not only to recognise oneself as a person (capable of understanding the world in which one lives, of being practically capable within it, of being an integral member of a community, and of being morally responsible for the kind of life one lives) but also to recognise others as persons – thereby worthy of respect whatsoever their capabilities or background. A system which militates against such recognition and respect is to that extent less educational; it fails to generate that learning and understanding which is at the heart of social justice. It makes the very same error as the 'deliverologists', namely, that of treating others as means to some further end rather than as ends in themselves. As Michael Sandel (2009) argued in his Reith Lecture, there is a need to think afresh about 'the common good' – whether we need to foster deeper moral and spiritual values in our public life. In that education has a crucial part to play.

The aim of the educational system, therefore, should be, first, that of bringing the best that has been inherited in our culture to the self-understanding of all, irrespective of capability or background, and, second, that of enabling each to respect the contribution of everyone else to that understanding. That requires the generation, as far as possible, of a common culture as a basis of mutual respect – a point to be developed in the following chapter.

There is a need, therefore, as Sandel argued, for democratic debate about fundamental values. 'The better kind of politics we need is a politics oriented less to the pursuit of individual self interest and more to the pursuit of the common good', especially:

- a more demanding idea of what it means to be a citizen;
- a more robust public discourse – engaging more directly with moral and spiritual questions;
- a focus on big questions that matter – in particular the role of markets in public life and their moral limits.

Conclusion

There are two related senses of 'education'. There is the descriptive sense as when, for example, we talk of the 'educational system' or ask where someone 'received their education'. Both examples are compatible with critical and negative answers. The educational system might be thought of as 'mis-educational'. Similarly with the so-called education received. Indeed, in both examples, one might question the claims that 'education' so-called had anything to do with education!

That would be because the primary use of 'education' is evaluative. It claims that something of value has taken place, that the educated person is thereby a better person. Its descriptive use is parasitic upon the evaluative. Richard Peters (1965: 27) likened it, in that respect, to the word 'reform'. To talk of 'reforms' (the 1832 Reform Act, the reform of the Senate, a reformed person) entails that those who introduce that term believe that there was a transformation for the better.

Similarly, to be educated implies that something of value is happening. It is not an 'end' separate from the 'means' of arriving – a qualification bestowed or a lump of knowledge transmitted. Rather, it is giving its *imprimatur* to the kind of knowledge and understanding being entered into, the practical capabilities acquired, the sense of community recognised, the moral seriousness developed and the self-worth or dignity achieved.

Such understanding, capability, community mindedness, moral seriousness and sense of dignity are the essence of what it means to be human, and education lies in the further development of these distinctively human traits and qualities – enabling young people to acquire yet further understanding of the world they experience, to work practically and capably within it, to promote active contribution to the communities of which they are part, to take seriously responsibilities for life's decisions and to acquire a sense of self-worth and human dignity.

Hence, an educational transaction is more than mere training – the preparation for a specific end. One is trained as a plumber; one is educated as a human being – although, as Sennett and Crawford show, one might be educated through training which is pursued in an educative way!

In my first teaching post, I was given Form 1x, the bottom form of a five-form-entry comprehensive school. The head teacher addressed the class and said that they must work hard for otherwise they would end up as street cleaners and dustbin workers.

This was puzzling. Most of the class were the sons and daughters of street cleaners and dustbin workers or occupations equally lowly. Is to be educated to have a disdain for the worthy and important occupations of one's parents? Is it to be ever upwardly mobile – particularly difficult in an economy where there are limited opportunities for such mobility? Many of those parents, despite their lack of formal educational opportunities, were serious and thoughtful human beings, taking pride in work well done, deeply concerned about the quality of their children's lives, maintaining a sense of dignity in circumstances militating against it, contributing voluntarily to the wider community.

People are *more or less* educated, and formal education is a matter of enhancing the knowledge and qualities which people, young and old, have in order to enable them to manage their lives intelligently and responsibly.

The contrast between education in the descriptive sense (without reference to the underlying aims and values) and education in the evaluative sense (with reference to human development) was put most emphatically and clearly by the principal of an American High School I visited in Cambridge, Massachusetts. The school had several thousand students, and so a relatively large turnover of teachers each year. This is the letter which she sent to the new cohort of teachers, quoted in Strom (1981: 4):

Dear Teacher

I am the survivor of a concentration camp. My eyes saw what no man should witness:

Gas chambers built by learned engineers.

Children poisoned by educated physicians.

Infants killed by trained nurses.

Women and children shot and burned by high school and college graduates.

So, I am suspicious of education.

My request is: Help your students become human.

Your efforts must never produce learned monsters, skilled psychopaths, educated Eichmans.

Reading, writing, arithmetic are important but only if they serve to make our children more human.

If our main purpose were 'to make children more human', in the different dimensions outlined in this chapter, would we have such a narrow view of 'education for all' – one which leaves so many young people with a sense of failure, which assesses so narrow a range of attainments, which ignores the experiences which they bring to school?

The purpose of this book is to advocate a secondary education for all which, in the light of these aims, embraces a wider vision of learning, a distinctive role for the teacher in providing the cultural basis for that vision, and a provision of opportunities through which all young people (howsoever modest their circumstances) might have a sense of pride and fulfilment.

4 Transmission of culture
But whose?

A dilemma

On the one hand, seeking 'secondary education for all' is seen to undermine educational values (for example, 'the rise of the mediocracy', or 'the closing of the American mind', as pointed out in Chapter 1). The reasons for such a view are that the basic purpose of education is the initiation into the cultural traditions, which we have inherited, and that, through lack of ability or social disadvantages or countervailing cultures, many, if not most, young people are unable to access them. Hence, 'traditional learning' is diluted or abandoned in the pursuit of 'relevance' either to the learners' interests or to the economic needs of society. There can be *real* secondary education only for the few.

On the other hand, Chapter 3 closed with the aspiration of bringing the best that has been inherited in our culture to the self-understanding of all, irrespective of capability or background. And that requires the generation, as far as possible, of a common culture as a basis of mutual respect.

How might we reconcile these two positions?

Many think they are not to be reconciled. The exponents of 'traditional learning' will, more often than not, see culture to be embodied in the subjects from which most curricula are constructed. There is a content to be transmitted, and literary and artistic achievements to be appreciated which the educated person should be familiar with. That is an argument well put by O'Hear (1987) in his paper, 'The importance of traditional learning'.

However, those who wish to widen learning may see such cultural inheritance to be only marginally relevant to the concerns of most young people, especially those whom Bantock (1971) referred to as inhabiting 'a more oral tradition, a practical way of working, a set of cultural expectations which fit ill with a school culture which is book-based and demands disciplined entry to the various modes of more abstract thinking'.

This division, indeed conflict, is nothing new. 'Progressive education', so-called, has taken on several forms, but many of its exponents argue that learning should arise, not from the exposure to the culture we have inherited (embodied in subjects and ultimately determined by the academic structures of the university), but from the interests and experiences of the learner. Indeed, it was with a concern for the pupils' interests that developments took place in school organisation, teaching methods and curriculum content in America during the 1920s and 1930s. Thus Kilpatrick (1918) spoke of the children's interests *determining* curriculum content and structure, and of common learning resulting from common interests. In introducing the account of 'An experiment with a project curriculum', he denied that the aims of the school were the 'conventional knowledge or skills'. The starting point was 'the actual present life of the boys and girls themselves, with all their interests and desires, good and bad'; the first step was 'to help guide these children to choose the most interesting and fruitful parts of this life as the content of their school activity'; and the consequent aims were

> first to help the boys and girls do better than they otherwise would the precise things they had chosen, and second, by means of the experience of choosing and through the experience of the more effectual activity, gradually to broaden the outlook of the boys and girls as to what they might further choose and then help them better effect these new choices.
>
> (Kilpatrick, 1923)

Thus the child's interests rather than 'history' or 'geography' constitute the subject matter of the curriculum.

But do we have to accept this dualism between 'traditional' and 'progressive' learning? Is there not a way in which the two can be brought together and so make possible a 'secondary education for all'? Dewey argued so, and, though blamed for the so-called ills of the progressive movement in the USA, he condemned equally both progressive education as it was then depicted and traditional learning as it was reflected in the 'transmission of knowledge' (Dewey, 1938a).

We need to think more carefully about the concept of culture, and what could be meant by 'a common culture'.

A common culture?

'Culture' is a neglected concept in current thinking about education in general and the curriculum in particular. It would seem that fear of elitism sidelines its pursuit, as education is made 'relevant' to the needs of all young people or as it is to be seen much more in business terms.

It was not always thus. Those who welcomed the birth of comprehensive schools as the attempt to provide 'education for all', not for just an elite in the independent sector or in the grammar schools, saw the creation of a 'common culture', through the provision of a 'common curriculum' (and preferably in a 'common school'), to be central to that vision. Lawton in 1975 argued for the common school which will 'transmit a common culture and provide an adequate means for individual development within the general framework of that culture' (Lawton, 1975).

In saying thus, Lawton was speaking within the tradition of R. H. Tawney who believed (as indeed this book seeks to argue) that

[s]ocial well-being depends upon cohesion and solidarity. It implies the existence, not merely of opportunities to ascend, but of a high level of general culture, or a strong sense of common interests, and a diffusion throughout society of a conviction that civilisation is not the business of an elite alone, but a common enterprise which is the concern of all. And individual happiness does not only require that men should be free to rise to new positions of comfort and distinction; it also requires that they should be able to lead a life of dignity and culture, whether they rise or not.

(Tawney, 1938)

Hence, that 'common culture' would mean, not uniformity or lack of flexibility, but a framework of common understandings – the product of generations of thinking, enquiry, criticism and creativity – within which society, and individuals within society, might function coherently and attain fulfilment.

However, there was the problem already referred to. There was the scepticism, shared by many, that 'culture' and its pursuit were essentially 'elitist' – that is, something judged to be worthwhile by but a few. It contained an air of superiority in the kind of knowledge and especially the artistic and literary tastes of those privileged to have been initiated into them through their upbringing and education. Could 'education for all', that participation in a 'common culture', mean that all young people from whatever social background should be initiated into the knowledge, tastes and understandings which were generally the prerogative of an educated minority?

Moreover, culture so described was seen, even in some universities, whose *raison d'être* lay in preserving and promoting it, to be irrelevant to the big issues which engaged young students. Allan Bloom, writing of the disturbances at Cornell University in the 1960s, condemned the betrayal of its educational purpose because

hardly any element in the university believed seriously that its distinction was based on something true and necessary, the self-confident possession of the kinds of standpoint outside of public opinion that made it easy for Socrates to resist the pious fanaticism of the Athenian people.

(Bloom, 1987: 314)

That 'standpoint outside of public opinion' is based on traditions of thought, enquiry and criticism, difficult to attain and hence in need of a systematic initiation.

Here, however, distinctions have to be made, lest the concept of culture, which once was seen to be the key to an *education for all*, is so narrowed as to justify an education for the few.

Meaning of culture

An authority, to which the advocates of a 'common curriculum' based on a 'common culture' referred, was Raymond Williams, whose book, *The Long Revolution* (1961), analysed the changing, though intertwining, meanings of the word 'culture' as it evolved in response to changing social conditions and attitudes.

In so doing, he made three important distinctions.

Culture as 'an ideal': high culture

First, culture refers to 'the ideal' – to the ways of life, reflected in literature, the arts, the sciences, philosophy – the value of which 'can be seen to compose a timeless order, or to have permanent reference to the universal human condition' (Williams, 1961: 2).

That culture emerges from what Oakeshott (1975) referred to as 'the conversation which takes place between the generations of mankind' in which the voices of history, of philosophy, of the sciences, of the arts have evolved through criticism and through refinement in the light of further evidence and arguments. It is that 'conversation' which constitutes the culture we have inherited, which enlightens our understanding of the human condition, and which therefore is relevant to everyone and the basis for common learning experience. Clearly, it should not be frozen in time, because past understandings are challenged by new insights.

Culture in this sense is much more than the transmission of past knowledge. It is not a collection of inert ideas. It contains the very attitudes, dispositions and processes for an active participation in those 'conversations' – a challenging of these ideas in the light of experience and critical appraisal. It embodies the resources, generated over time through scholarship, creativity and critical enquiry, upon which people draw, at different levels and in different ways, to make sense of their lives and to act intelligently within them. It is embodied in what people have written (poetry, drama, stories), in the arts (music, painting, sculpture), in technical achievements (architecture, engineering), in the sciences and mathematics, in practical skills and crafts (carpentry, cookery, horticulture). These ways of thinking and of practising have evolved over the generations through personal creativity and public criticism – different elements in 'the conversation between the generations of mankind'. The internalisation of such cultural attainment frees us from the 'here and now', enables us to see things and our various predicaments in perspective, challenges the superficial analysis, frees us from mental slavery to passing fashion or mistaken authority.

Such 'high culture' has frequently been seen as the privilege of the few who alone are able to access it – an educated class, referred to by the philosopher and poet Coleridge as 'the clerisy, whereby a true education . . . was seen as the monopoly of an elite' (see Simon, 1985: 144). As such, the idea of culture would not be seen as something for the many, for then it would lead to 'the plebification of knowledge'.

Culture as a particular form of life

The second, though historically related, meaning of culture outlined by Williams was that in which it described a particular form of life – one which might seem quite distant from that depicted above. We do talk about the distinctive culture of a nation or of a group of people, even of a gang. We talk of 'youth culture'. Such cultures might reflect economic contexts in which people work and live, as in the 'working class culture' described by Richard Hoggart, which, in his case study of Leeds poor, even included a distinctive cuisine reflecting the economic necessity of poverty yet the skills acquired through coping with poverty (Hoggart, 1957: 37). This second meaning of culture is what Williams refers to as 'the social definition of culture, in which culture is a description of a particular way of life, which expresses certain meanings and values not only in art and learning but also in institutions and ordinary behaviour' (Williams, 1961).

It is important to recognise the coherence given to this more specific idea of culture in two related ways.

The first way in which coherence is given is by the values which bind people together and which support shared understandings. However, such values and understandings might clash with culture understood in the first sense. The 'gang culture' might see the values inherent in 'the best that has been thought and said' to be antithetical to its own. There arises a clash of cultures. On the other hand, less dramatically, but nonetheless significantly, one might talk, as E. P. Thompson (1957) did, in *The Making of the English Working Class*, of the evolution of a distinctive and self-conscious culture, which gradually enters into our wider understanding of society and the human condition – that is, into the inherited culture in the first and wider sense.

The second way in which this sense of culture gives coherence to experience is expressed by Dewey. The material world is experienced and evaluated through the connections already established through social activity. Those connections constitute the cultural environment. Indeed, such are the interconnections between the physical and the cultural that Dewey argues:

> Of distinctively human behaviour it may be said that the strictly physical environment is so incorporated in a cultural environment that our interactions with the former, the problems that arise with reference to it, and our way of dealing with these problems are profoundly affected by incorporation of the physical environment in the cultural.
>
> (Dewey, 1938b: 46)

Educationally, of course, this is significant. The learners might enter the school from very different cultures (in this second sense) from that which is embodied in what the school thinks to be worth transmitting (culture in the first sense). The physical world itself, the modes of working, the artefacts used have different significances. The learners see no point in, or even feel hostile to, values which undermine their own values and ways of seeing things.

Hence, a major problem in education lies in bridging the gap between the two cultures – that which is seen as the best (changing and provisional though that might be) that has been said through literature, the arts, sciences, etc., about the human condition (and therefore relevant to everyone) and the cultural understandings which are brought into the school from diverse economic and social backgrounds. For Dewey, bridging the gap lay in the transformation of experience of the learners through their confrontation with the experiences of others, enshrined in what he referred to as the 'wisdom of the race' in poetry, arts, humanities, theology and sciences.

Culture as criticism

The third sense of culture, which Williams refers to, is really the offspring of the first, namely,

> the body of intellectual and imaginative work, in which, in a detailed way, human thought and experience are variously recorded . . . the activity of criticism, by which the nature of the thought and experience, the details of the language, form and convention in which these are active are described and valued.
>
> (Williams, 1961)

This, it would seem, refers to the particular exemplifications of culture picked out, let us say, in the National Curriculum, examined, criticised, transmitted. It will include the list of 'good books' and the traditional criticisms of them. The problem is that such can be frozen in time, become ends in themselves, or indicators of being an educated or cultured person, whilst at the same time disconnected from that illumination of the human condition as that is endured by the learners.

Therefore, there have evolved these different yet interrelated senses of culture. The emphasis given to one or to the other affects the idea of an educated person and the extent to which being so educated can be reconciled with the values and ways of life of young people from very different backgrounds.

Conclusion: relevance to *education for all*

Education avoids the two sides of the dilemma when the knowledge and wisdom captured in the so-called 'high culture' are connected with and illuminate the thinking, aspirations, interests and concerns of the learners. Those connections are what the good teacher makes. The ability to do that is at the heart of pedagogy. The classroom thus becomes a place where this dialogue occurs between the learner trying to make sense of experience, the other learners similarly engaged, and the teachers facilitating that growth of understanding through providing access to what others have achieved in knowledge both theoretical and practical. Formal education then becomes a 'selection from that culture' (see Lawton, 1989) based, on the one hand, on what is seen to be relevant to the young learners, and, on the other, on what is part of that corpus of knowledge and understanding which has withstood critical appraisal – whether that be in the arts, humanities, sciences or crafts.

History, for example, enables young people to understand themselves and their society in terms of what has happened before. Their worlds are shaped by past achievements and failures, by technological developments and discoveries, by the heroism and duplicity of individuals, by the power struggles between ambitious people, by a steady progress to the achievement of democracy, by political and philosophical exponents of freedom and equality. Furthermore, our understanding of all these depends on systematic study, exposure to critical discussion, analysis of evidence, interpretation of recorded events, creative imagination as the past is re-invented in the light of data available. History is much more than a set of facts, and history teaching is much more than a transmission of those facts. It is an inter-pretation of the past through disciplined enquiry which is embodied in our culture.

All this might, at this stage in the argument, seem a little abstract, and yet it is at the heart of the struggle to provide *education for all*, not betraying 'half our future' by denying them access to what can and should illuminate their lives and enable them to be more insightful into their human condition. Abstract though it might be, it has massive implications for practice, as will be shown in Chapter 7, 'Learning: a wider vision', and in Chapter 10, 'Bring back curriculum thinking'.

5 A pause

The need for a little philosophy

Thinking philosophically

Policy answers, which are given to perceived problems, are often muddled because they have not addressed questions that philosophers from time immemorial have been asking. It is the job of philosophy to scratch beneath the surface of 'agreed meanings' – the 'self-evidently true' pronouncements – and to show that life is much more complicated than is assumed. Indeed, as the philosopher Wittgenstein explained, 'My aim is: to teach you to pass from a piece of disguised nonsense to something that is patent nonsense' (Wittgenstein, 1958: 1.464).

There is a lot of disguised nonsense in what policy makers say and write. Therefore, one task of philosophy is to make people – especially those who think they have the right answer – uncomfortable.

A good example of what I mean is provided by Plato in *The Republic*. The rather arrogant Thrasymachus defines (cynically, maybe) 'justice or right' as 'what is in the interest of the stronger party' (Plato, Part I.338). Socrates sees a problem in that definition (one which would have been common amongst the sophists of the time). What is meant by 'in the interest of'? Socrates enlarges on his puzzlement.

> For instance, Polydamas the athlete is *stronger* than us, and it's in his *interest* to eat beef to keep fit; we are *weaker* than him, but you can't mean that the same diet is in our *interest* and so *right* for us?

Thrasymachus now gets irritated as he refines his original definition to embrace the state or government as the stronger party. In other words, those in power are the ones who define what is right and just – which, in fact, would often seem to be the case. Socrates presses on with counter-examples to this definition. Eventually Thrasymachus exits in a fit of temper. What seemed straightforward had been proved not to have been so.

Therefore, philosophy requires close attention to the meaning of often contestable concepts as these are revealed in different usages of key words. Through systematic examination of language, through asking for examples of what one means and through giving counter-examples, one might contribute to the solution of problems which often arise from the 'bewitchment of intelligence' by the unreflective use of language. The analytic tradition within the philosophy of education took seriously the advice of Wittgenstein.

Words and concepts

The words we use embody concepts – that is, the way in which we mentally organise experience and describe the world. Our experiences reflect not only what happens independently of us (the material world we live in and the social world we interact with), but also the ways that material world and those social interactions are organised in the language we have inherited. Imagine an isolated society which had no schools – the word would be entirely missing from its language. When confronted with schools in a visit to another society the visitors would not recognise a school as such in coming upon it; all they would see is a building, say, and perhaps a few funny looking tables which we call desks. To learn a language is to learn a particular way of viewing and understanding the world and of experiencing it.

Furthermore, concepts do not exist in isolation, but are part of a system of concepts through which we understand the world. It is often important to make clear the relations – the logical entailments – within such a system. For example, 'indoctrination' is logically related to 'teaching' and to 'education'. 'Training' is related to, but not the same as, 'educating'. In learning physical sciences, one needs to grasp not specific concepts in isolation (e.g. atom) but the logical interrelation of such a concept with others such as 'particle', 'electron', 'neutron', 'proton', 'element'. To understand a concept is not only to know when to apply it but also to see how it is placed in a broader conceptual map.

Hence, a frequently asked question is 'What do you mean?' Of course, such a question would be tedious in most everyday conversations, but it should not be considered tedious where key words are 'contested' – that is, where the words have a history which reflects conflicting understandings and where these conflicting understandings often go unrecognised.

The following are examples of what I mean, relevant to the developing argument of this book.

Education

An obvious example of the disagreements which beset educational policy would be the contested concept of 'education' itself, and that is why Chapter 3 looked long and hard at what we mean by 'an educated person'. People may well disagree with that analysis. They might have a different understanding of the word, from which therefore different conclusions are drawn.

For example, new kinds of school are established to reflect these differences. Steiner schools are very different from the normal community school, reflecting a different view about the *aims* of education. A. S. Neil's Summerhill was famous or infamous depending on what you thought *education was for*. Dewey (1938a: ch. 2) was highly critical of the educational systems of the United States because he believed the prevailing transmission of knowledge, disconnected from the experience of the young learners, to be *mis-educational*.

It is important, therefore, constantly to ask policy makers and teachers to spell out what they mean by education. Often the grammar of our language makes it look as though people are talking about the same thing in relation to education, when all the time they have in mind something significantly different in terms of the kind of knowledge worth pursuing, the underlying idea of personal fulfilment, and the link between individual autonomy and social well-being.

Of course, given the use of the word within our language, not *anything* could be referred to as an education. In its general usage it refers to the promotion of learning. But in its evaluative sense, not any kind of learning would be counted as educational, only that kind of learning which somehow changes the person for the better. Education in this evaluative usage is concerned with learning what is considered worthwhile. And there is the rub. Pursuing educational issues is necessarily to move into the area of value judgements and to the sort of discourse (ethics) in which problems of value judgements are argued about.

We have seen in the previous chapter how the importation of a language from performance management creates a different way of thinking about persons, their education and its formal provision. There is a need to challenge that language, and all that it entails, in the light of the insights which are embedded in our normal usage of 'education'. Change the metaphor (from that of 'performance management' to that of 'conversation') and you change what you mean by educating young people.

Language matters.

Learning

Central to educating all young people must, by definition, be the effort to bring about or to enhance learning. And, given that success in life requires constant learning, it is now a truism that the educational system should enable young people 'to learn how to learn' – to acquire 'learning skills'. Learning is measured and those measurements become the criteria by which young people and their schools and colleges are judged to be educational successes or failures.

But rarely is it asked: 'What does it *mean* to learn or to have been a successful learner?' Can one just learn, or does one not learn *something*? And does not the nature of that 'something' affect the analysis of learning? Thus, to learn how to ride a bicycle is very different from learning algebra. One learns to be practical as well as one learns facts, concepts, principles and theories. What we mean by learning depends on the logical nature of that which is to be learnt. The significance of this will become apparent in Chapters 7 and 10, when we consider the nature of the subject matter which is thought to be worth learning and of the distinctive mode of thinking which defines the different subject matters. 'Learning how to learn' is one example of the 'disguised nonsense'.

Recently, a well-regarded teacher was declared failing by the visiting inspector because, in the 20 minutes of observed teaching, 'no learning was observed' by the inspector. But what does it mean to observe a piece of learning? How, from a brief observation of 30 young people, can an inspector with an observation schedule know that there has not been a shift in understanding, newly conceived solutions to old problems, resolution of a struggle to understand, doubts arising about previously held beliefs, patience acquired in the pursuit of a solution? All these are aspects of learning. And a lot is learnt in silences as well as in conversations.

Skills

Emphasis in policy is placed on 'skills' (the importance of basic skills, thinking skills, social skills, emotional skills) as though the same word means the same in each of these uses. There are, of course, overlapping usages, and that often leads to confusion as though one can transfer the meaning from one context to another (as in 'skill training'). But a careful analysis of these different usages would reveal differences of meaning, which, if not recognised, lead to misguided policy and practice. For example, although one might well isolate the training of a manual skill in woodwork from a particular work context, one cannot equally (as is often supposed) isolate the training of 'thinking skills' from the wider conceptual contexts of, for example, historical or scientific thinking.

One talks of a 'skilled craftsman', and one might take the paradigm case of a knife grinder. The skill lies in the hand–mind coordination in the use of tools to do a particular kind of job. That ability or skill is achieved through constant practice, usually under the correction of someone else who is skilled, until the activity meets certain standards and is carried out without conscious reflection on what he is doing. The ability to handle the tool has been internalised. Hence, one talks of being trained in a skill, and also of a well-trained workforce. But such skills do not add up to an *educated* workforce. Education suggests a wider understanding, a cognitive perspective on the nature, purposes and use of the skills (see Winch, 2010: ch. 6, for an extended account).

On the other hand, to be educated would more often than not require being trained in certain skills and being trained in these skills might be the context in which young people become more educated. That is why, traditionally, apprenticeships required an integration of skill training in the workplace and a broader theoretical understanding through education in a college of further education.

Academic versus vocational

Unexamined use of language bewitches policy and practice in many ways: for example, in the questionable distinction between 'academic' and 'vocational' – especially where the 'practical' is confused with 'vocational'. Upon analysis this dichotomy not only does not make sense but also is extremely dangerous for practice. It excludes important activities, especially in the arts, which were, under a previous government in England, disapplied from the National Curriculum post-14. Are these academic or vocational? They can become academic (theorising about drama or studying the history of art) but then they lose their distinctively practical and aesthetic character.

Again the meaning of 'vocational', as indeed that of 'skill', is so elastic as to stretch from the very narrow skills training relating to a particular occupation such as window cleaning to intellectually demanding apprenticeships in engineering, through which young people can move into higher education.

One danger in such a dualism between academic and vocational, as we shall see in Chapter 7, is that practical learning, such as that pursued in woodwork, metalwork, horticulture and cooking, not being seen as academic, are referred to as vocational with all that that implies for status. There is no 'parity of esteem'. And yet, properly taught, such practical pursuits are the ways in which young people engage intelligently with the material world, coming to understand and appreciate its properties, able under the teacher's guidance to get a deeper grasp of the social cultures in which they play a part. The material world is experienced through the connections established through physical and social activity. Those connections constitute the cultural environment.

Educationally, of course, this is significant. In pursuit of a better education for all, the practical learning (often mistakenly referred to as vocational) has given way to what is referred to as academic, thereby not only disengaging many young people who are bored with the academic but also depriving the so-called academic student of a rounded education.

Free school

As we shall see in Chapter 15, the future of secondary education is seen to lie partly in the creation of 'free schools'. But one is never just *free*. One is 'free from' something or 'free to' do something. What are 'free schools' free from? They are free from local accountability, but thereby they lose their freedom from central control through the contract signed with a now all-powerful Secretary of State. Free but enslaved.

Interim conclusion

These are but a few examples of the way in which apparently straightforward words or concepts, which play important roles in educational discourse, when more closely examined, often cover up confusion in thought and action. Could the inspector really have said he observed no learning in 20 minutes if he had really thought about what that means? Could authors of reports on vocational qualifications have divided all qualifications into academic and vocational if they had attended seriously to the meanings of these words? Would the success or failure of an educational system be measured in terms of a few targets had there been deeper consideration of what it means to be an educated person in this day and age?

The following chapters will constantly point to the need for more careful philosophical reflection on what is meant by those words that shape the deliberations about policy and practice.

Areas of philosophical thinking

What, however, makes these and many other words contestable is that their meaning involves deeper and disputed questions which philosophy has traditionally been concerned with in the theory of knowledge, ethics, philosophy of mind, political philosophy, and philosophical understanding of the major disciplines of thinking such as history or religious studies. The teaching of history, for example, presupposes a particular view of what it means to understand society historically, and that particular view is contested by historians. Acton's understanding of history was different from that of Collingwood.

Ethics

We have already seen this in Chapter 3 in relation to what it means to talk of an 'educated person'. That meaning implies an evaluation of the kind of learning and its value which has been acquired by young persons – what, in the words of the head teacher (p. 39), makes them 'more human'. If one emphasises one aspect of being a person, namely, the capacity to think systematically and deeply about the arts and the sciences, then one will associate 'educated' with the sort of academic elite and the inhabitants of a distinctive culture, and exclude the rest as uneducated and even ineducable. But if one recognises the achievements of practical learning, the rigorous standards whereby practical people engage with the physical and social environments, then one widens the notion of an educated person – and indeed questions the education standards by which academic success is so elevated.

The ethical issues are frequently dodged by the claim that education is a matter of enabling all young people to realise their potential (DCSF, 2004) – and many a wise head nods when politicians pronounce this. But think. Some years ago a visiting five year old pinched my handkerchief from my pocket, unknown to me, and then stuffed it down the lavatory. A potential artful dodger, if ever there was one. But do I want him to realise his potential? One glance at the newspaper makes one realise that we have as much potential for evil as we do for goodness. Some potential we want realised and others not so. Which are which is a matter for ethical debate.

Theory of knowledge

It is impossible to go far in the study and the practice of education without struggling with the nature of knowledge in general and its different forms in particular. Knowledge is 'transmitted', and the amount of knowledge acquired is assessed through constant testing. But what is this 'knowledge' which is transmitted? Can it be acquired without 'understanding', as would seem to be the case according to several critical reports? The Smith Report (2004: 93) *Making Mathematics Count* spoke of the acquisition of knowledge suitable for the tests but without the underlying understanding. But can one be said to have knowledge without understanding? One might be trained to make the correct answer to a certain sort of question – to state the right facts. But does one *know* the answer or at least know what it means?

A traditional analysis of knowledge is that it is (a) a belief, (b) which is true, and (c) whose claim to truth can be justified. One might have true beliefs, for example, without any good grounds for believing that they are true. But here lies the problem, for different sorts of belief have different sorts of justification. A true belief in science is thereby logically different from a true belief in history. And many people would question whether it makes sense to speak of 'true beliefs' in morals, politics and religion.

If that is the case, can we be justified in teaching these beliefs as if they were true – as if they counted as knowledge? Furthermore, in teaching scientific or historical knowledge as such, one would need to teach the underlying justification as to why this is knowledge – the basis of the knowledge claims. To teach science is more than a transmission; it is an enabling of young people to think and to practise scientifically, to have a grasp of scientific method, and to realise that scientific conclusions are always tentative and open to refinement in the light of further discoveries. One learns through criticism and correction. In teaching, there needs to be room as much for doubt as for certainty, as much for questioning as for seeking secure foundations.

Moreover, this applies equally to the development of educational policy. Governments talk of evidence-based policy. But too often evidence is confused with proof, and proof is too often seen as leading to certainty. But there can be no certainty, and evidence can range from the strong to the weak. So many decisions have to be made in life after the careful weighing of evidence, knowing that there might well be further evidence to show that one got it wrong. Conclusions have to be tentative, drawing on the best evidence that is available at the time. That has profound effects upon how the educational system should be run and reformed. Too often big changes are made without taking into account what the evidence suggests and without being open to possible contradiction by further discoveries. That is certainly true in the introduction of academies and free schools.

Philosophy of mind

Philosophy has traditionally pursued the difficulties which arise in relating the physical world of human beings to the mental world. Is a person two substances – that of the mind and that of the body – or one? If two (mind and body), how does the one relate to or affect the other? When, for example, the pupil behaves naughtily, was there a preceding mental event (an intention) which caused the physical behaviour? And if there was, how can we know, since it is impossible to peer into a person's head to see a thing called an intention? And if there was not, has anyone the right to punish for the naughtiness? One way of solving this problem is to eliminate the mind as a separate substance – as an unnecessary 'ghost in the machine'. In fact, so it has been argued by such influential psychologists as B. F. Skinner (1968). We are but machines, and behaviour can be (or will be one day) entirely explicable by the laws of behavioural science. However, if that is the case, then we need to revise our understanding of young people (to develop the science of behaviour modification, for example) and our attribution of responsibility for actions performed. Bad behaviour is a form of physical malfunction – the miscreant needs medical treatment rather than punishment.

Let us take a further example of the way in which a philosophical position is implicit, but rarely recognised, in the kind of educational discourse which shapes radically the educational fate of young people. Chapter 1 introduced the reader to the policy debates on school organisation in England following the 1944 Education Act. So much depended on the idea of intelligence – whether this 'thing' referred to by the noun 'intelligence' was innate or could be acquired. But let us shift from using nouns to using adverbs. Can a person be enabled to think and to act more intelligently? When you examine this question more closely, you might want to know in what context one is asking about intelligent thinking and actions. The philosopher might be unable to act intelligently when mending his or her bathroom leak, whereas the plumber (demonstrating the capacity to act intelligently in the bathroom) is not able to engage very intelligently in an ethical dispute with his philosopher employer. One can see why, in recognising the diverse ways and contexts in which one might be considered to be acting intelligently, the notion of an innate 'intelligence', basically unaffected by nurture and learning, becomes increasingly unintelligible as a reason for segregating learners.

Social and political philosophy

Is society simply an aggregate of potentially autonomous individuals? Schools would be places created by ambitious parents to assist their offspring to realise their potential – the pursuit of personal benefit. And one reflection of such a realisation of private gain would be the development of 'free schools', released from the chains of a bureaucracy which otherwise would decide what should be taught, how it should be taught and by whom it should be taught.

One could think of the other extreme in which the society comes first, and the personal good is entirely subordinate to the wider good of society as that is conceived by those with the wisdom to detect 'the general will'.

Many of the debates about policy making and control of educational practice make assumptions about where one should stand between these extremes. On the one hand, how far can we conceive of individuals as autonomous beings, whose identities owe little to the social and cultural framework in which they learn and live? On the other hand, on what grounds might central government take to itself powers over what schools teach and what the young people should learn? What are the limits of government power in such matters?

Chapter 1 referred to the shift in Britain from a 'hands off' approach to educational content and methods (that is none of government's business) to one of detailed intervention. Such a shift makes assumptions, not only about the ability of government to know what is best and 'what works', but also about the rights of government. These issues of autonomy versus central control, democracy versus autocracy are developed further in Part III when we consider who should run the system.

Conclusion and relevance to the book

The narrative of this book is to move, first, from the consideration of the aims of education (and what those aims signify for all learners, not just for a selected few), second, to the kind of learning and its assessment which should be pursued in order to embody these aims and to address the educational needs of all young learners, and then, third, to the organisation which enables this to happen. Does the traditional provision of learning which we have inherited (in the words of the head teacher) 'serve to make our children more human'?

In following that narrative, we need to pay particular attention to *what is meant*, first, by educating everyone irrespective of background and aspiration; second, by the different kinds of learning which such education might and should embody; third, by the kinds of knowledge (theoretical and practical) which such learning should draw upon; fourth, by the professional role of the teacher in that transaction between the learners and the cultural resources at their disposal; fifth, by the connection between such formal education and the wider society and economy; and, finally, by the control of such provision. What, as Dewey asked, is the connection between education and democracy?

All these issues are fraught with puzzling questions about 'what do you mean?', and the answers, insofar as they can be reached, are rooted in the perennial problems of philosophy.

Part II
Putting aims into practice

6 Can education compensate for society?

Must education *for some* be but a dream?

Frequent reference was made in previous chapters to doubts concerning the aim of secondary education *for all* – at least, if that means the sort of education which leads to significant social mobility and to the kind of learning traditionally associated with being an 'educated person'. Indeed, as pointed out in Chapter 1, the US National Commission on Excellence in Education, *A Nation at Risk: the Imperative for Educational Reform*, declared, 'the educational foundations of our society are gradually being eroded by a rising tide of mediocrity that threatens our very future as a nation and a people' (quoted in Ravitch, 2010: 24). And, in England, Rhodes Boyson did not mince his words in arguing that we should never 'have moved to comprehensive schools and the *lumpenproletariat* we have created'.

One reason for those doubts was the belief that education cannot compensate for society. Schools are struggling against social, cultural and economic forces for which they are not responsible, and against which not even the most strenuous efforts and ever-increasing investment can prevail.

How true is this? Were those who fought for *secondary education for all* (those, for example, who fought for the 'common school' where educational success would no longer depend on social and economic background) living in cloud cuckoo land? The evidence would seem to point to such a conclusion.

Therefore, 'Education cannot compensate for society' was the title of Basil Bernstein's influential paper in 1970 – which put weight behind the growing belief that more was needed than the reform of schools if there was to be genuine education for all.

To that end, Educational Priority Areas were established in England and Wales for the allocation by government of extra resources for school building in low-income areas and for supplementing the salaries of teachers working in those areas. Indeed, Donnison (1974) referred to the 'boom in priority area policy', namely, the compensations for the economic and social disadvantages which held back the hoped-for educational achievements of so many young people.

Yet there remained criticisms of low standards, disengagement of many from formal learning, disenchantment with the system and its achievements, connections between poverty, social class and underachievement, and lack of social mobility.

The same initial hopes and later dismay characterised the ambitions for educational reforms in the USA. The growth of the American comprehensive high school, especially in the post-war period, arose from the belief that all young Americans, irrespective of race or social background, would be enabled to have secondary education, leading to graduation, to successful careers, and to active participation in a democratic society. The expansion of the comprehensive ideal, as assessed through enrolments, was highly successful (Rury, 2007).

But again elation was followed by disillusion. As Rury concludes from his extensive analysis of high school expansion in the post-war years, 'the negative association of poverty and teenage enrolments suggests that a significant portion of the population remained alienated from the institutions that were supposed to represent the comprehensive ideal' (ibid.: 64).

He points to the fact that the 'American secondary school ultimately failed to reach a critical segment of the nation's youth'. Social and economic factors such as poverty, race and class seriously affected participation and achievement in the high school.

The facts seem to bear this out in Britain. Children from the poorest families are half as likely to get 'good' GCSEs (namely, five A to C including maths and English); white children from low-income families perform worst at GCSEs; black Caribbean children are three times more likely to be excluded and their boys perform well below the average (Equality and Human Rights Commission, 2010).

To give a deeper understanding of the issues, let us consider the rival positions and how they enter into the political arena.

Thesis: education can compensate for society

There had been the belief in the USA and Britain that a reformed educational system (for example, the creation of a fully comprehensive one) would provide the conditions for secondary education *for all*, in particular (in England and Wales) for Newsom's 'half our future', the educational neglect of which was the focus of that report. That was equally true of the USA, as shown, for example, by the Commission on the Reorganisation of Secondary Education in 1918, and by the Progressive Education Association's Eight Year Study in 1932.

Hence, post-war settlements did in fact create the provision of secondary education for all. That surely was a step in the right direction. Everyone, not just the privileged and the academic few, could benefit from continuing with their education.

However, in England and Wales that was but a small step because that settlement, resting on the recommendations of the Norwood Report of 1943, advocated a tripartite system – grammar schools for the few who were capable of abstract thought and interested in learning for its own sake, technical schools for a few who were capable of applying ideas and more interested in technology, and 'modern schools' for the majority who would be motivated by practical activities and an interest in the immediate environment. There was a strong correlation between the type of school and the social class from which the students came. And, although the examination for grammar schools selection was supposed in theory to transcend such class differences, few from the so-called working class made the transition, and of those that did many subsequently performed badly in their O Level examinations.

Inequalities of educational achievement there will always be in society, but those who believed that 'education can compensate for society' strove to overcome the grossest of those inequalities and to make sure that they were not caused by such non-educational factors as social class or wealth. The creation of the comprehensive system was a major reform to ensure greater equality not only of opportunity but also of outcome. It would create the 'common school' with a 'common curriculum' reflecting a 'common culture'. Holt (1978), in his aptly entitled book *The Common Curriculum*, drew upon Tawney's (1943) advocacy of 'the common culture which at present we lack', for 'to serve the educational needs, without the vulgar realities of class and income, is part of the teacher's honour'.

Along similar lines, Pedley (1963), in his pioneering book *The Comprehensive School*, referred with approval to the 'common school' in the USA. Indeed, it was that common and community school which Dewey believed to be at the centre of a more egalitarian society where everyone would be enriched by the communication with others of different faiths, different ethnicities, and different social and economic backgrounds. Such common understandings, and indeed such growth through the interaction with other young people from different backgrounds, would mitigate the social and economic disparities within it.

The Rutter Report (1979) in Britain gave firm evidence that schools do make a considerable difference. Of 12 comprehensive schools, matched carefully in terms of socio-economic context, some out-performed others against a range of significant criteria. The only variable which could account for such differences was the quality of teaching in the schools. From that report emerged project after project on school improvement and school effectiveness.

'London Challenge', through which funding was directed to supporting schools in the inner city, transformed many of the schools in some of the most disadvantaged areas (Ofsted, 2010a). London is the only major world capital where pupil achievement is above the national average. Dylan Wiliam attributes this to government investment in the schools and their communities through London Challenge (interview, *Guardian*, 24 September 2011).

Schools really do make a difference.

Antithesis: education cannot compensate for society

However, the dream that 'education can compensate for society' – that is, help overcome the gross inequalities of social class, poverty and lack of social mobility – seemed to fade following so many criticisms of under-performance, especially in centres of disadvantage. Perhaps these inequalities are too deeply rooted in our society for education to have the required impact.

Therefore, Beverley Shaw's book, *Comprehensive Schooling: the Impossible Dream?*, expressed the doubts, which many felt, that changes to the educational system could not achieve what they set out to achieve: 'In short, comprehensive schools have failed to fulfil the aims so confidently set for them by their advocates' (Shaw, 1983: 151).

Again, Nick Davies' *The School Report: Why Britain's Schools Are Failing*, questioned not only the politicians' and the Chief Inspector's blaming of teachers for poor performance, but also the statistical evidence upon which such blaming might be based. The scene for the battle over explaining educational failure is set nicely in these contradictory passages:

> I emerged [from his investigations] with the clear view that school failure was primarily caused by bad teachers, and in particular by bad teachers who had been led astray by 'trendy teaching methods' from the 1960s.

Then, however, Davies started to go into schools!

> I realised that my working theory was complete garbage, that the truth was simpler, nastier and very plain to see . . . You cannot make sense of why some schools fail and some succeed without taking account of the corrosive impact of child poverty, which has soared in this country in the last 20 years.
>
> (Davies, 2000)

The impact of poverty and other social disadvantages occurs again and again as 'the cause' of educational failure. The Nuffield Review (2009) pointed to the fact that, despite considerable public investment in education, the more disadvantaged a child, the lower the level of educational attainment. Such disadvantages included: 16 per cent of young people growing up in workless homes; 25 per cent growing up in households with one parent (with a strong correlation between one parent households and poverty); 10 per cent of young people suffering from psychiatric disorders; 64,000 who are in care; 40,000 who are teenage mothers. According to Marmot (2011), 60 per cent of five year olds in Britain's poorest areas do not reach a 'good level' of behaviour and understanding (compared with 30 per cent found in wealthier suburbs).

Furthermore, those with such disadvantages tend to be concentrated in specific geographical areas, increasingly segregated from those who are well-off, as Dorling's (2010) studies show. Post-code is a good predictor of future achievement.

Therefore, increased economic prosperity is counterbalanced by increased poverty for many and growing segregation of the well-off from the disadvantaged. That inequality is spreading across the UK. The consequences are reflected in the differences in attainment between children at an early age. Children from the poorest families are a year behind the children from average income families when they start school at age five (Waldfogel and Washbrook, 2010). Such differences accumulate throughout formal education and affect individuals in later life. Indeed, according to the report from the Equality and Human Rights Commission, 2010, by the age of three, a baby's brain is 80 per cent formed, and his or her experiences before then shape the way the brain has grown and developed. That is not to say, of course, it is all over by then, but ability profiles at that age are highly predictive of profiles at school entry. There is little sign that schools close these attainment gaps, with children who arrive in the bottom range of ability tending to stay there.

Therefore, the damning conclusion of Joseph Rowntree research is that

> all the evidence over many decades and from many countries seems to show that family background continues to be a major determinant of educational outcomes . . . far from offering a route out of poverty, education seems simply to confirm existing social hierarchies.
>
> (Raffo *et al.*, 2003)

Unlike the conclusions of the Rutter Report in Britain, reports in the USA (Coleman *et al.*, 1967; Jenks *et al.*, 1972) concluded that schools made no difference.

Can thesis and antithesis be reconciled?

Who is right? Can education (the curriculum, different provision, quality of teaching) make much impact on the aspirations and achievements of those who live in communities characterised by economic and social disadvantage, and by a social class culture which seems inimical to the educational ideals and measures of success which characterise the system? Can, in other words, education compensate for society?

Education does not occur in a vacuum. Commenting on the poor attainment of the white working class in particular areas, the Schools Commissioner for England argued that

> the white working class can be the most challenging [culture] . . . In a monoculture, in particular seaside areas . . . they haven't come from a culture where they've got work, they think there's a more limited range of things they can aspire to. You have to open their minds that they can go to the city, they can go abroad. You can't turn around a school without turning around a community.

Education success or failure, therefore, is affected by social and economic contexts in which policies are developed. But so much depends on the strength of that word 'affected' and thereby on the possibilities of countering disadvantage through educational intervention either alone or along with others not directly educational.

There are three prevailing ways in which education might be seen to compensate – each having profound implications for what we mean by *education for all*.

Applying 'what works'

It is in the interest of policy makers to hold schools and colleges responsible for the effects of wider social problems for two reasons. First, it passes the blame to others than themselves. Second, it makes the solutions look much simpler – for example, getting rid of the 15 per cent of poorly performing teachers supposedly identified by a former Chief Inspector, or detailing a National Curriculum for all young people, or providing pedagogical instruction for the teaching of literacy. If education can compensate for the ills of society, one needs to know 'what works', and then to ensure that schools and their teachers 'deliver what works'.

That, in turn, requires close specification of what it means for the educational system to work, and this is duly done in the setting of targets and the measurement of these. A system of testing, publication of results, league tables, financial incentives and 'customer choice' becomes the machinery for making educational provision effective and thereby overcoming the disadvantages which previously had been seen to be insuperable. Education *can* compensate for society if we know and apply what works. Teaching should become much more of a science.

However, Diane Ravitch, writing about such policy solutions in the USA, gives a different story as she speaks of how testing and choice, targets and performance indicators, measurement and incentives – the instruments politically chosen for ensuring that 'education' has an impact even amongst the least advantaged – are impoverishing what it *means* to educate. Following such approaches borrowed from the business world, schools might be seen to succeed (raising standards as measured, achieving higher scores) but what they are succeeding in has little to do with education. (The importance of such a critique demands further development and therefore Chapter 12 will be devoted to it.)

Furthermore, it alienates yet further those whose disadvantages are most prominent. The Barnardo's Report (Evans, 2010) points to the number of suspensions from secondary schools, as such a policy is pursued – one out of every 20 pupils sent home, two-thirds of these suspended more than once and 40 per cent repeatedly. Those on free school meals were three times more likely to be suspended. Those with special needs, seven times more likely. Education for all must include these. They are not equally distributed around the schools, and so some schools, often seen as failing, have the gigantic task of compensating for the society from which they come (*Guardian*, 25 November 2010).

It is essential, in reflecting on the application of 'what works', to pause a little and to think more philosophically about how to explain personal and social behaviour. Educational hopefuls recoil at any suggestion of 'determinism' (namely, that despite educational intervention, young people from disadvantaged backgrounds are pre-determined to low educational achievement). On the other hand, those very hopefuls believe that the correct formulae, discovered through empirical investigation, will ensure educational success – leaving only the teachers to blame through their failure to deliver what has proved to work.

What does it mean to explain human behaviour? There is a view that education policy and practice need to research empirically 'what works', to communicate this to the teachers and to ensure that the successful recipe is vigorously applied (or 'delivered'). There is, in other words, a 'science of teaching'. Once one knows what the causes of human behaviours are (and we are seeing increasingly the application of Randomised Control Trials to solve empirically 'what works'), then one can 'cause' those behaviours to change.

There are, indeed, ways in which causation in human affairs does resemble causation in those of the physical world (for example, drowsiness in the classroom might be 'caused' by overheating and lack of fresh air). Nonetheless, there are logical differences between causal explanations of physical phenomena and causal explanations of human behaviour. It is difficult to guarantee that a policy will work because instructions, which are clear to the politician, get re-interpreted and evaluated by those who are being instructed. Further down the 'causal chain', along which such instructions travel, the greater the chance of further re-interpretation.

Those 'delivering what works' (the teachers) and those 'in receipt of the delivery' (the young people) dwell in a world of ideas through which they interpret the social worlds they inhabit. The students bring to the school understandings that are rooted in the cultural lives of their families and social groups, through which are percolated instructions from above. It is not surprising that the targets set for many of them seem totally irrelevant – indeed inimical to their conception of what is worthwhile. Similarly with the teachers. They, too, come to school with understandings of what is educationally worthwhile, rooted in a professional culture. Political formulae of what works are necessarily filtered through such preconceptions.

Therefore, a straightforward account of causality (where a particular intervention can be predicted to have a desired effect) is hardly applicable in human affairs and *a fortiori* to educational engagements. In that sense, 'education cannot compensate for society' – and so much educational policy and intervention, based on that assumption, is grossly mistaken.

Broader vision of education

Causality does enter human, as well as physical, explanations, though not in the same way. How young people engage with formal education (e.g. with meeting the targets set for them) depends on the preconceptions, the values, and the cultural understandings which they have inherited from their respective families and social groups. Where educational provision takes these seriously and gets to grip with the social understandings and concerns of those to be educated, then it can have an impact and 'education can compensate for society'.

But that requires different views of curriculum from that of a collection of targets, and of teaching from that of delivering those targets. It requires a different view of the relation between school and the community from that of autonomous and competing institutions.

Therefore, reconciling thesis and antithesis, as described above, needs to question the narrow aims and impoverished values of those who think they know what works. Brian Simon, in answering the question 'Can education change society?' argued that in one sense it cannot, but, in another more educationally defensible sense, it can.

> We will not, I think, find our answer from the techniques of contemporary social science since these studies . . . necessarily leave out of account, or lose sight of, the crucial human factor – subjective experience; and it is this which determines outcomes – not whether it can be shown statistically that schooling and/or a particular innovation, has a marginally positive or negative effect on the distribution of income, or life opportunities, however measured, or on social mobility. . . . Contemporary theorising and empirical studies on this issue – that is, on the relation between education and social change – are both seriously misleading and, in many ways, short-sighted. They ignore human subjective experience – people's capacity for movement, for acting on the environment, transforming it and so for self-change. It is this process which is educative, and profoundly so.
>
> (Simon, 1985: 30)

Such transformative experience of education, as teachers engage with the different concerns of the young learners, is nothing fanciful. It is what so many teachers aspire to and what, despite the pressure of targets, many continue to attain. But in so doing they take seriously the ways in which the learners see and understand the world, the subjective experiences through which they perceive the relevance of learning, the cultural values which they bring from their own communities. Teaching is an engagement with the minds and hearts of the learners, not an imposition of targets.

What can 'compensate for society' too often gets marginalised in a system which, working from very different premises, employing the deceptive language of performance management, and seeking very different targets, inevitably fails so to compensate. What is required is a wider vision of learning

Partnership in learning

It is difficult for individual schools to provide the wider vision of learning or to give the extra attention to those who are disengaged, have special needs or are in danger of repeated suspensions and final exclusions. Disadvantages created by poverty, cultural deprivation, or domestic circumstance require broader social support. The wider vision of learning requires a wider range of resources and expertise. Lack of aspiration or the lack of known opportunities requires highly knowledgeable and professional advice and guidance. No one school can go it alone. Partnerships between schools and voluntary bodies, Youth Service, social services, further education colleges, employers and careers counselling are crucial – a matter to be developed further in Chapter 16.

Let us take two examples.

Example 1

'Restorative justice', introduced to a partnership between schools and police in Oxfordshire, showed how the contribution of the community policeman attached to a school or a group of schools could have a positive impact upon those young people most likely to fall foul of the law, saving them from court appearance, exclusion and the downward spiral of crime. This manner of dealing with social problems outside the school had measurable impact upon what was possible within the school (Pring and Hudson, 2003).

Example 2

The head of a London comprehensive school, recognising that each year seven or eight children are in hostel accommodation and another 20 homeless, living with the most vulnerable elements of society, is finding a family house for homeless sixth-form students. He spoke of Vincent,

> who achieved three As and A*s at GCSE and had been sleeping on a bench in Hyde Park for four-and-a-half months. He would wake up cold and tired and make his way to school, where he would shower. It wasn't until he told us that we became aware of the situation. At first he wanted to keep it to himself, but he thought we were his only hope of hanging onto a normal lifestyle.
>
> (*TES Magazine*, 18 March 2011)

The head teacher sees the 'family house' as an extension of the ethos of the school, from supporting families and young people to physically replacing those families. The saving of Vincent might not shift the statistics on social mobility or promote the school in the league table, but it might have saved him, and given him the opportunity to live a fulfilling life. But the school needs the wider community and social support in order to provide that service.

Social mobility: an insuperable problem?

Perhaps the issues come out most starkly in debates over social mobility. Despite so-called *education for all*, the evidence would seem to show that there is now less rather than more social mobility than used to be the case or than was hoped for. The Institute for Social and Economic Research at Essex University looked at the test scores of 15,000 children born in England in 1989/1990 and compared these to previous cohorts born in 1958 and 1970. Fifty-six per cent of children from degree-educated parents were in the top 25 per cent of test scores at age 14, whereas only 9 per cent of children of parents who left school without O Levels were in the top 25 per cent. This is much greater than the gap in Australia, Germany and the USA. The Sutton Trust's analysis of people at the summit of the social and political ladders showed that over 35 per cent of MPs elected for the 2010 Parliament attended fee-paying schools which educated only 7 per cent of the school population. Just under two-thirds of the Cabinet went to independent fee-paying schools and 70 per cent to Oxford University (Sutton Trust, 2010).

However, a major obstacle to education's role in creating social mobility was found to be, not poor teaching or disadvantage as such, but high levels of social segregation in English secondary schools. This is not just a factor of the private/public divide, but also of the growing social segregation between schools within the public sector. The PISA report, referred to in Chapter 2, shows how such segregation of rich and poor into separate schools is a significant factor in overall educational performance. The Sutton Trust found that the country's top 164 comprehensive schools took only 9.2 per cent of children from income-deprived homes although they drew pupils from areas where about 20 per cent were income deprived (Sutton Trust, 2011). In other words, social mobility is hampered at least in part by admissions arrangements within neighbourhoods, on top of the increasing social segregation across neighbourhoods. The discrimination in admissions could be addressed if politicians had the courage and will to do so.

Conclusion: a way forward?

The considerable increase in social disadvantage and the increasing segregation of the affluent from the poor, both across neighbourhoods and in schools, affect educational performance and social mobility. They militate against education for all. Schools can make a difference, but only if, at the same time, wider social issues are tackled. Individual schools cannot go it alone.

What then needs to be done?

First, invest in pre-school years. Difficulties at secondary level arise partly because disadvantage has not been addressed as early as that. According to Sir Michael Marmot (2011),

> by the age of 10 a child from a poorer background will have lost any advantage of intelligence indicated at 22 months, whereas a child from an affluent family will have improved his or her cognitive scores purely because of his/her advantaged background.

Second, widen the vision of learning. That is argued in the next chapter. The present narrow and target-driven curriculum leads to the disengagement of many learners from education.

Third, widen the vision of schooling to embrace partnerships with those who have the resources and expertise for this wider vision of learning and for the personal and community support needed – from Youth Service, further education, employers and voluntary sector. That will be argued in Chapter 16. Sir Aynsley Green, former Children's Commissioner, deplores the decimation of the youth programmes and centres, and

> the destruction of many of the building bricks of support for children and young people to achieve their potential in life. It is desperately worrying. I see

little in their place to inspire confidence that this generation will be looked after by Government. It could spell the end of hope and expectation of many of them.

(quoted by Benn, 2012)

Fourth, involve parents in the educational enterprise and help develop, where necessary, parenting skills, such that they will appreciate and reinforce what the teachers are trying to achieve. (See page 94 on Family Links.)

Fifth, provide stable accommodation and intensive support for young people released from custody or 'in care'. According to Barnardo's (2011) thousands of young people leave custody each year without a proper home to go to. The youth re-offending rate is 74 per cent. The cost of a young offender caught in a cycle of homelessness and re-offending can cost the government £116,000 over three years.

Sixth, ensure that a much greater proportion of students from low-income groups go to university, including (in Britain) the Russell Group universities. Only 45 on free school meals got to Oxbridge in 2010 and only 1 per cent to Russell Group universities (*TES*, 2 September 2010). The fact that they have not had the opportunities to get the highest grades does not mean that they do not have the same potential as those that did have these opportunities (see Chapter 17).

Seventh, maintain a highly professional information, advice and guidance (IAG) service for those who have low aspirations, so that they may see further education, training and employment opportunities (see Chapter 13).

Eighth, put more resources into those who are most vulnerable and disadvantaged – it would be a good financial investment (for example, a restored Personal Education Allowance for the education of children in care and Education Maintenance Allowance for those who otherwise struggle to remain in education post-16).

Postscript

At the time of writing this book, riots were breaking out in several areas of London as well as in other urban centres. Several of the rioting hotspots were amongst the ten areas of the country where the largest number of claimants are chasing each job vacancy. Riots came as no surprise to young people in London who live either with or alongside the deprivation and social exclusion that many adults and politicians were so shocked to have seen erupt into lawlessness.

Many explanations were quickly given – dysfunctional families, general breakdown of morality, 'broken society', greed, gangs, etc. But, as Martin Luther King said, 'a riot is the language of the unheard'.

Listen, then, to the voice of one, who was out that night. Gary (not his real name), aged 16, would not go any further up Hoxton Street.

> I don't associate with Hoxton, or London Fields. I'm in the Pembury Boys Gang so I would get shot or stabbed if I went up there. You have to be in a gang because when the other estates come round they can be a lot older than

you, you're not just fighting people your own size. Poles, baseball bats, guns, knives, whatever, anything. It's a fight to the death. I ain't scared of death or nothing.

Excluded from school at 13, he never returned and was too young for benefits. His sweat pants are holed, he is thin and hungry. 'I do what I have to do', he says of his lack of money.

Gary's re-engagement with education requires much more than 'the discovery of what works'. It requires a deeper rethinking about educational aims and the nature of learning. And it requires cooperation between the educational and other services.

7 Learning – a wider vision
'Learning how' as well as 'learning that'

The problems we are facing

Doubts about *secondary education for all* are, as we have seen, of different kinds:

- so many disengaged from formal education;
- the impoverishment of culture in its accommodation to all;
- the 'counter-culture' of the social worlds that young people inhabit;
- the debilitating effects of social and economic disadvantage.

A report by Demos (2011), entitled *The Forgotten Half* (50 years after Newsom's *Half Our Future*), claims that half the teenagers in England and Wales are being failed by secondary schools which focus on brighter children.

To counter consequent doubts about the possibility of secondary education for all, many point to the narrow aims of education that dominate policy and practice. They are narrow not only in the dominant focus on economic returns and qualifications, but also in the way knowledge and its transmission are perceived. In questioning those aims, in returning to the idea of education as the development of the whole person, in connecting (apropos that development) our inherited culture with the cultural worlds of young people, and (in the words of the school principal – see Chapter 3) in helping young people 'to become more human', so we need to have a wider vision of learning than presently prevails.

In so arguing, this book says little that is new. There have been, and are, many attempts by teachers to provide that wider vision, though too often frustrated by assessment regimes, inspection criteria, policy initiatives, league tables, and lack of progression routes to higher education and employment. As Learning Futures (2010), which successfully supported a wider vision of learning in schools, observed, 'it is particularly important that school leadership teams provide a "buffer zone" between the Learning Futures innovative pedagogies and the fear which can be engendered by a performance-dominated external agenda'.

In many respects, this book articulates what is already understood and felt by many. However, to re-iterate what was concluded in Chapter 3:

> understanding, capability, community mindedness, moral seriousness and sense of dignity are the essence of what it means to be human, and education

lies in the further development of these distinctively human traits and qualities – enabling young people to acquire yet further understanding of the world they experience, to work practically and capably within it, to promote active contribution to the communities of which they are part, to take seriously responsibilities for life's decisions and to acquire a sense of self-worth and human dignity.

To meet such aims, a wider vision of learning is needed.

'Learning how' and practical knowledge

One does not simply *learn*. One learns *something*. And the nature of that something affects how we characterise learning. That makes any single theory of learning impossible and a nonsense of such aims as 'learning how to learn'. Learning how to ride a bike is very different from learning that something is the case.

We need to distinguish between 'knowing that' (propositional knowledge such as 'I know that it is raining') and 'knowing how' (practical knowledge such as 'I know how to ride a bicycle'). Such practical knowledge cannot be reduced to propositional knowledge, at least in the sense that the knowers (the cyclists) might know how to ride a bicycle without being able to explain that knowledge 'propositionally'. They simply show it. And (as in all knowledge) they can be said to know more or less intelligently in a way that is not measurable on IQ tests.

One must not make too great a divide between the two kinds of knowledge. Cyclists would be able to explain what they knew practically about balancing – pressing hard on the pedal or leaning over at corners. Furthermore, if the cyclists were competitive, they might receive advice based on the 'knowing that' of a coach. Such 'knowing that' might arise from a scientific knowledge of athletes' successes. Cyclists might use such knowledge to improve their practice. It informs the practical knowledge; it is internalised through practice; it eventually is no longer consciously remembered. There is a fusion of intellectual and physical activities which characterise the architect, technician, builder or designer. This crucial distinction is educationally significant for several reasons.

Very often practical knowledge is logically and temporarily prior to propositional knowledge. Children learn to act practically before they formulate in words what they are doing. Being able to explain or to give an account arises from reflections upon actions performed. Propositional knowledge is rooted in a world of practical engagement with material and social realities. This is clearly seen in those inventions that have transformed our lives and our societies, as theory arises from intelligent and reflective practice. The invention of the steam engine arose from the practical expertise of mechanics as they perceived the relation between temperature, volume and pressure. It was Brunelleschi, a clockmaker by training, who erected the magnificent dome in Florence.

Where schools feel less constrained by covering a syllabus, the teacher is able to show practically the relation between theory and practical engagement, as in the following example from Robert Mattock, whose family has grown roses for over

100 years and who captures this in his account of work with boys in a school which prides itself in its academic successes. They were involved in the hybridisation of roses, not for any academic purpose – it was not on their examination programme.

> I showed how to cut off the male part of the plant (the anthers and the stamens) to leave the female stigma. The boy arrived back with a flower full of pollen and we brushed its pollen on the stigma of the other. That I explained was invention. We had to make the decision of which pollen to use, based on what we wanted to create. Back to the gardens, I explained that looking after the plant we had hybridised, the cultivation of the plants was the job of the craftsman. The craftsman takes his time, he is meticulous in his attention to detail and it is his experience, not that of the inventor, that permits the successful outcome of the hybridisation, the new plant, for which he might justifiably feel proud. It is that pride in his work that enables the craftsman to incentivise himself to do the best he can. It is that pride in his work that enables the craftsman to respect not only his work but that of others. Mutual respect for each other's work is a sound, practical basis for mutual respect for each other's cultures, particularly for a school full of boys from across the world.
>
> (Mattock, 2009: 14)

Despite the importance of such practical learning, educational systems give priority to propositional knowledge in syllabuses, examinations and league tables to such an extent that there has been a massive decline in those areas of the curriculum which had focused on the practical – carpentry, design and making, cooking, rural science, horticulture, mechanics. Michael Crawford points out, in the context of the USA, that 'it was in the 1990s that shop class [for example, practical workshops for woodworking, automobile repairs, and metal fabrication] started to become a thing of the past, as education prepared students to become "knowledge workers"' (Crawford, 2009: 1), and that in California, three-quarters of high school shop provision has disappeared since the early 1980s.

But the problem and the prejudice are deep and old. As Dewey says:

> There is very little space in the traditional school room for the child to work. The workshop, the laboratory, the materials, the tools with which the child may construct, create and actively inquire, and even the requisite space, have been for the most part lacking.
>
> (Dewey, 1910: 101)

There, in words reminiscent of many policy makers who show disdain for the practical and the 'non-academic', he points to those educational authorities who dismiss such practical pursuits of interests as mere 'fads' and 'frills'. Education, surely, is about the transmission of knowledge!

Much the same can be said of England and Wales where a National Curriculum divided the curriculum into ten subjects, the assessment of which was, in the main, through written tests (as though practical know-how can be assessed through written examinations). Even the attempt to bring more practical and occupationally related subjects into schools for those who would thereby be better motivated, namely, the General National Vocational Qualifications (GNVQ), eventually bit the dust because, in order to be academically respectable, practical learning resorted to a pale reflection of more academic studies. The present proposal in England for an EBac of six subjects, setting the new 'standard' for school and learner success, omits areas of practical learning and creative arts. Consequently, the highly popular Design and Technology is now being dropped by schools as they focus upon the EBac subjects. There has, therefore, been a massive reduction both of the British equivalent of the American practical workshops in schools and of the training places for future teachers of practical subjects.

Consequently, by failing to recognise the value of such practical knowledge, we are in danger of demeaning its value – and thereby the value of those people whose working lives are characterised by practical engagement with material things – engineers, plumbers, electricians, mechanics of different kinds, and especially those whose work may in one sense be less demanding but still can be engaged in intelligently, responsibly, creatively. They include the street cleaners and the bin men – the fathers and mothers of the learners to whom the headmaster in Chapter 3 referred so dismissively. If we are to talk about secondary education for all, then we need to recognise the dignity of meaningful labour, carried out intelligently and responsibly, howsoever modest, as a legitimate end product of education. St Benedict had it right: *laborare est orare*.

Finally, to continue with Crawford's thesis: 'The disappearance of tools from our common education is the first step towards a wider ignorance of the world of artefacts we inhabit' (Crawford, 2009). Emphasis on 'propositional knowledge' to the nigh exclusion of the practical leaves students in a state of ignorance which, much more than its serious impact on economic utility, cuts them off, in a world of abstractions, from the direct understanding of the material stuff we depend on and which impacts on us – on the food that we eat and the clothes that we wear.

Recognition of this is reflected in a Steiner school where the objective in the art class was to design and create artefacts from wool. Every aspect of the process had to be experienced. To do this the learners needed to clean and card the wool, to weave, to dye and to spin it. But the dye itself had to be obtained from the berries which were in the trees and fields. The final product could not be separated in their minds from the practical processes of producing the stuff, with all the trial and error which that entailed. Along the way, they learnt about the properties of the wool and the dye and the potential of machinery to transform the wool into something that could be turned into clothes. Theory (the nature of the materials, the human effort which historically was necessary for survival, the cultural artefacts through which personality was expressed) was embedded in the practice.

In the wider vision of learning, there is need to recognise the central place for practical learning – the 'knowing how' in different contexts – not simply for its usefulness but for the understanding it gives of the material world, for the basis it provides for more theoretical understanding, for the recognition of excellence, and for deep satisfactions the attainment of those standards brings.

There is much evidence to show this. In England and Wales, 14–19 partnership schemes provided a substantial part of the curriculum for 14–16 year olds in colleges of further education. They had access to facilities and expertise in technical and craft-based learning. The evaluations of such programmes are proof of this wider vision of learning (Higham and Yeomans, 2010). Jacky Lumby draws from the survey and interviews with several thousand 15–17 year olds how the sense of mastery and its connection to self-esteem are conveyed strongly, as illustrated by one young learner: 'We done plumbing, like just tightening joints and work on toilets, work on the sinks an' all that, and it was really fun; it was real practical work and you get to use proper tools and everything' (Lumby, 2011: 257).

Education for all requires a more significant place for practical learning and knowledge – not to be confused with vocational skills or learning for the so-called non-academics, but as rigorous and worthwhile learning in its own right. Many young people would not be disengaged from education if the workshops that Michael Crawford speaks of had been kept open and if quality of learning were not confined to what can be tested through the written word. We need to recall a tradition well recorded by David Willetts, Minister of State for Universities and Science. Referring to Joseph Chamberlain's founding of Birmingham University in 1900 so that science and craft could come together and contribute to the local economy, he declared:

> His was a radical vision. . . . it offered departments of brewing, mining and commerce as well as law, medicine and theology. It was a bold departure from the Oxford model. People were immediately suspicious of such utilitarian course and critics dismissed this place [University of Birmingham] as a 'Bread and Butter' university. But this is a perfectly legitimate role for a university – after all more than half of the students are obtaining a degree which is, in effect, a licence to practise a trade or profession.
>
> (Willetts, 2010)

Are we not still governed by those who disdain such utilitarianism, who see not the challenge of bringing science and craft together, who still disdain such efforts as belonging to the 'bread and butter' institutions?

Nonetheless, we practise within particular understandings of the world of material things, of cause and effect, of social relations, and of values. Such understandings are inherited through public traditions of knowledge and wisdom that have evolved over generations. *Education for all* requires access to those traditions of thinking, criticising and valuing.

Realms of meaning

Language matters. How we practise within the world depends not only on what is external to us but also on the language that we have inherited and which organises experience into particular kinds of things and relationships. But the flip side to this is that our minds can be bewitched by the lazy use of language, especially where there is a failure to make distinctions or where distinctions are made so as to treat 'unlike' as 'like'. This is clearly the case where 'practical learning', as outlined above, is equated with 'vocational learning', and where policy makers create the division between 'academic' and 'vocational' courses.

The subtitle is taken from the book by Philip Phenix in which he talks of education as 'the means of perpetuating culture from generation to generation', thereby widening one's view of life and counteracting the provincialism of customary existence (Phenix, 1964: 3). That culture, as referred to in Chapter 4, provides the ways in which we have come to understand the physical, social and moral worlds we inhabit. These ways embody the concepts or ideas through which we organise experience and the well-tried modes of enquiry through which we examine and pursue our understandings of those worlds. They do, in other words, make meaningful what otherwise would be disconnected experiences.

Other philosophers have, in relation to education, said similar things albeit in different ways. Oakeshott, as noted in Chapter 3, speaks of the distinctive voices of poetry, history, science and philosophy in our making sense of the world. Paul Hirst (1974a) argued for different forms of knowledge, each form being distinguished by its key ideas or concepts, its mode of verifying the truth and its disciplined enquiry. The American philosopher, Joseph Schwab, argued that 'to identify the disciplines that constitute contemporary knowledge and mastery of the world is to identify the subject matter of education' (Schwab, 1964: 11). Therefore, one might speak of logically different kinds of judgement, different modes of enquiry and different ways of manifesting those insights, though not necessarily only in words or literally. Music has its own language, and metaphor reveals, in poetry and in drama, different ways of seeing.

A wider vision of learning would ensure access to these different realms of meaning. It has been frequently argued that too often specialisation from the age of 16 narrows the understanding of young people. Those who study the humanities and the arts do not develop their mathematical or scientific understandings, and vice versa.

It is important, therefore, to delineate in very broad terms the different 'realms of meaning' through which we make sense of the world and into which, in different degrees of sophistication, all young people should be initiated.

Arts and humanities

In recent years the arts and humanities were 'disapplied' in England from the required learning experiences from the age of 14, mainly so that those who were so inclined might devote more time to 'vocational studies'. It was as though the less academic or the disengaged were not capable of benefiting from them. They were seen not to be relevant, or their benefits were seen to bear little relation to future lives. But hark the following example.

The Birmingham Royal Ballet (for an event called Bally-Hoo) provided opportunity and training for young people, disengaged from education and in many cases in troubled situations, to participate in the ballet *Romeo and Juliet*, an engagement with a classical ballet that might at first sight seem remote from their interests and experience. But think again. As the Chair of the Arts Council argued: 'it was an inspired choice of story: star-crossed lovers, dysfunctional families, gang warfare, macho games, self-harm, drug abuse and knife crime; it had them all'. Through participation in ballet (and one might speak equally of all the performing arts) so the young people were able to get deeper insight into human relationships and emotions, which are encapsulated by those arts, and which have a universal as well as a personal dimension.

Evidence from this and other involvements in the performing arts suggests a transformation of how young people come to see themselves, their situations and future possibilities. Success lies not in providing a basis for future ballet dancers and actors, but in the powerful insights which they provide. Nearly all who took part, despite their previous disengagement from education, were still, three years later, engaged with the performing arts in some way or other. A connection had been made between their cultural worlds, cut off from what formal education offered, and the so-called elite culture of Shakespeare and Prokofiev.

Literature, the arts, drama provide a voice through which young people are able to explore matters of central importance in their lives. They illuminate aspects of the human condition through which the learners gain insight into their own personal and social situations. The key disciplines within the humanities – history, geography, religious studies, philosophy – provide the disciplined explorations of what it means to be human, how we became so and how we might become more so.

This is illustrated in the once influential Humanities Curriculum Project (HCP), inspired by the work of Lawrence Stenhouse. HCP arose in response to the concerns in Britain in 1965 over the raising of the school-leaving age (Schools Council, 1965). What sort of curriculum would ensure a defensible *education for all*, including those who previously would have left school at 15? HCP used the distinctively human studies as resources upon which the learners drew as they explored issues of deep personal and social concern – social justice, relationships with parents, the exercise of authority, racism, poverty, relations between the sexes, violence whether personal or political. Discussion was central, but discussion carefully chaired by the teacher who would insist that views expressed were related to evidence to be found in literature, history, sociology, theology and other areas of the arts and humanities. For example, in discussions about war, the text of St Augustine on 'the just war' would be read, the feelings of the 1914–18 war poets listened to, historical accounts of the genesis of war explored. Evidence (of different kinds) was crucial for views expressed. Discipline was required in terms of reference to evidence, heeding alternative views, respecting those who differed (see Stenhouse, 1975: *passim*).

Here is a different relationship between learner and teacher. The latter is not 'transmitting knowledge', although such knowledge lies there in the texts and evidence provided. Rather, the accumulated knowledge and insights we have inherited become the resources upon which the learners draw to understand more deeply their human condition.

Mathematics

The report *Making Mathematics Count* points to the distinctive contribution mathematics makes to experience and how we understand the world. The basic argument here is in terms not of utility but of significance to how we think. It

> provides a powerful universal language and intellectual toolkit for abstraction, generalisation and synthesis. It is the language of science and technology. It enables us to probe the natural universe and to develop new technologies that have helped us control and master our environment, and change social expectations and standards of living.
>
> (Smith Report, 2004: 11)

Mathematics thus represents a distinctive 'realm of meaning'. But such meaning, at different levels of abstraction, has also its obvious utility for what is referred to as the 'knowledge economy', for the advancement of science, technology and engineering, for the workplace and for everyday functioning.

Physical sciences

The physical sciences (physics, chemistry, biology, geology) constitute an account of the material world in measurable terms, which can be tested against experience. Such a realm of meaning lies embryonically in the explorations of the young child who anticipates future experience in the light of what has been observed in the past. But, of course, the advance of such observations into systematic study, hypothesis forming, generalisations and theory gives rise to new concepts through which experience is organised and causality established. Scientific explanations, employing the language of mathematics, have grown as communities of scientists pursue their investigations, test provisional hypotheses, and refine previous explanations. Knowledge grows through criticism.

Within the physical sciences, distinctions are made between different kinds of explanation, focused on different aspects of the material world – the organic and inorganic – and understood through their own distinctive theoretical concepts. Physics, for example, reveals the material world in terms of 'particles' interacting within 'fields of force'. At the deepest level such interactions need to be grasped in terms of 'atoms', and those in terms of 'electrons', 'neutrons' and 'protons'. Such development of 'meaning' has taken place over generations of scientific experiment, and is then reflected in much less theoretical understanding as it enters into our daily lives. As such it is part of that culture we have inherited and to which we have access at different levels of abstraction and representation. To be educated is to absorb that understanding and thereby to move gradually away from an understanding of experience based solely on immediate appearances.

Social and personal explanations

Explanations of the material world are, however, logically different from those of the personal and social worlds. By 'logically different' is meant that different kinds of explanatory concepts are employed – those not open to measurement, such as 'intention' and 'motivation' at the personal level, and 'rule-following' and 'social relations' at the level of society. The importance of a person's 'subjective meanings' enters into accounts of what is observed, demanding different kinds of enquiry and verification. It is necessary to get 'inside the mind' of the other person. But that 'inside the mind', though detected from observable behaviours, is not reducible to them and needs to be interpreted in terms of intentions and motivations, and in terms of the social rules which persons have internalised.

There are, as in the physical sciences, distinctions to be made in the studies of people and their societies – reflected in psychology, anthropology or sociology. And there are border disputes as to whether explanations should have recourse to the physical sciences (as in certain schools of psychology). The work of B. F. Skinner (1968), for example, highly influential work on theories of learning, sought explanations entirely within the 'behavioural sciences' and 'behaviour modification'.

Jerome Bruner, however, showed how these different disciplines can be integrated into addressing the three questions relevant to *education for all*: 'What makes us human? How did we become so? How might we become more so?' (Bruner, 1966). 'Man: a course of study' provided an active and cooperative exploration of what it means to be human, drawing upon the relevant social disciplines of knowledge. Popular in both the USA and Britain, it found little space finally in England under the emphasis on the 'knowledge transmission' of 'National Curriculum delivery' following the 1988 Education Act.

Assessment for learning

Integral to this wider vision of learning is the continual assessment of knowledge, understanding and skill, and of what needs to be done to deepen and to extend them.

An essential distinction here is between *assessment for learning* (AfL) and *assessment for accountability* – a distinction that policy makers do not seem able to grasp, even though it has been pointed out to them often enough. But, in not recognising the distinction, the assessments used for the one are used inappropriately for the other. Assessment for accountability usually gives the overall performance of a school system or a school. It shows parents, government and other 'stakeholders' how pupils and schools (and, by implication, teachers) have *performed* on certain tests. That sort of assessment we shall examine in Chapter 12.

The Assessment Research Group (1999) defined 'assessment for learning', on the other hand, as 'the process of seeking and interpreting evidence for use by learners and their teachers to decide where the learners are, in their learning, where they need to go and how best to get there'.

The trouble with confusing AfL with assessment for accountability is that the kinds of assessment for the latter are substituted for the former, and provide little or no help in the advancement of learning. Indeed, they impoverish it, since 'learning to understand' turns into 'learning to perform', where the 'assessment tail' of imposed performances wags the 'curriculum dog'. There is an important distinction to be made between learning and performing.

AfL requires a responsiveness from the teacher to where the learners are in their struggle to understand or to create. That responsiveness is shown in the questions asked of the learners, interpretation of learners' understanding, probing beneath the surface, recognition of different ways in which problems are pursued. But that requires much flexibility on the part of the teachers, a readiness to deviate from detailed lesson plans. As research showed,

> what teachers need is not rigid lesson plans but frameworks of key ideas that will enable them to maintain the 'flow' towards learning goals whilst adapting the lessons to take account of pupils' ongoing struggles or leaps forward in understanding.
>
> (Mansell and James, 2009)

That is not easy. Teachers' ideals run up against the reality of the need to raise pupils' performance.

Crucial, therefore, to AfL is for the teachers to have a good grasp of the key ideas (the distinctive 'realms of meaning') which shape and direct the overall direction of learning. That direction will be pursued at different paces and with many deviations *en route* as the teacher assesses the distinctive learning needs of the young people. Moreover, as the learners gain understanding and confidence in their progress, where that is clarified for them, so too they will gain greater autonomy – greater insight into how they learn best. A crucial element in AfL is helping the pupils to think about how they best learn through acquiring a language for describing and evaluating their learning.

Objections will no doubt be raised about the unreliability of teacher assessments without the use of standardised tests and public measures. These can, of course, help, but such tests and measures can never capture the subtlety of young people's learning, and the many ways they are motivated. The teacher, suitably trained, can. And groups of teachers across schools and colleges can provide the supportive framework for moderating teachers' judgements. It requires a shift in the role of the teacher from the lonely expert in the classroom, transmitting knowledge, to one within a community of other teachers and the learners themselves, as they work together in the furtherance of learning. (More on this professional role of teachers will be given in Chapter 11.)

Interim conclusion

What has been written above does not aim to set out the different components of the curriculum – the 'subjects' of the timetable. That is postponed until Chapter 10. Rather, it argues for a wider vision of learning which recognises the different ways in which we understand the world and the need for all young people to enter more deeply into those 'realms of meaning' and practical knowledge if they are to act intelligently and benefit from the accomplishments of civilisation. The main task of the teacher is to make the connections between the two cultures – that of the learners and that made available through the broader and public culture we have inherited – or between, in the words of Dewey,

> first, the narrow but personal world of the child against the impersonal but infinitely extended world of space and time; second, the unity, the single wholeheartedness of the child's life, and the specialisations and divisions of the curriculum; third, the practical and emotional bonds of child life and an abstract principle of logical classification and arrangement.
>
> (Dewey, 1902: 126)

8 Learning – a wider vision
Taking experience seriously

Learning from experience

Young people come to school, not as empty vessels to be filled, not with minds as blank slates on which someone else's wisdom is to be printed, but already with a diversity of experiences which shape how they think and what they value. Even where experiences are limited, these affect their interpretation of what they then come to experience in school. What comes out of the mouth of the teacher is not quite what goes into the ear of the learner.

This is not an empirical point, but intrinsic to what it *means* to have an experience. 'Experience' is not something that just happens to one – an imprint on the passive mind, undigested 'sense data' upon which theory is built, a 'filling of the bucket . . . in which perceptions and knowledge accumulate' (a metaphor used for describing the classic empiricist view of experience – Popper, 1972: 341). In rejecting this, we are rejecting what Karl Popper referred to as 'the commonsense theory of knowledge' (ibid.: 63). Rather, an experience is already theory laden – that is, embodying a particular way of seeing the world and of giving significance to the situation. Two people experience the same situation in slightly different ways because of the different expectations, born of previous experiences, with which they confront the world and perceive it.

Beard and Wilson (2002: 1) aptly quote Benjamin Disraeli in their book on experiential learning. 'Experience is the child of Thought, and Thought is the child of action – we cannot learn men from books.'

Education is a 'transformation of that experience' – widening and deepening it, subjecting it to critical appraisal, reflecting on the understanding implicit within it, sharing it with others. But that requires, in the wider vision of learning, a serious place for the learner's experiences.

That is why Dewey set out, in 1897, the following five core principles in his 'pedagogic creed', on the basis of which he was so critical of traditional theories of knowledge and thus of learning. This is reflected in the titles of several of his books: *Experience and Education*, *Art as Experience*, *Experience and Nature*, and in several chapters in *Democracy and Education*. The problem with traditional education was that it:

- was disconnected from the experiences that the students brought from their homes and communities;
- was disconnected from the manual and practical activities through which they are engaged with experience;
- ignored the interests that motivated young people to learn;
- treated knowledge as purely symbolic and formal – organised in textbooks and 'stuck on' without connection to experience or existing ways of understanding;
- maintained discipline through external authority rather than through the engagement of young people.

(Dewey, 1897)

However, experiences can be more or less significant, more or less open to deeper understandings. Indeed, they can, as Dewey argued, be 'mis-educational', that is, deadening the mind, as when a learner becomes bored by what happens. How often is interest in literature killed by the experience of it in preparation for examinations? On such occasions, the transmission of knowledge often becomes an experience of learnt formulae, not of drama, literature or poetry as that is intended in the text.

Furthermore, the experiences might be extremely limited, not providing the basis for further worthwhile experiences. Many young people are out of touch with the natural world. An Ofsted Report (2008) argues that 'being in the natural environment and "playing" has proven benefits for children, helping them to learn crucial skills and ways of understanding the world', whilst at the same time such experiences are increasingly being denied to young people because of their cost, or through fear of litigation following 'risk assessment', or through their lack of immediate relevance to the curriculum to be covered. The Field Studies Council announced that in recent months 12 field study centres closed, some of which had hosted children for more than 50 years, and that a further 62 are under threat. In 2010, there were 9,000 fewer visits to York's National Railway Museum, 6,000 fewer to London's Science Museum, and 2,000 fewer to London's Natural History Museum.

A wider vision of learning for all young people requires a reversal of such a policy wherever it occurs. Preaching social mobility, whilst closing off the very experiences that enrich the lives of young people, is hypocritical. Where such experiences are limited, they need to be expanded.

Alternative sources of experience: the Youth Service

This book is being written under the shadow of the riots which took place in major cities of England. One wonders how much those young people were disengaged from an education which related so little to the personal and social experiences that shaped their lives. For many the most significant learning experiences were to be had, not in formal education, but in the youth centres where a different set of relationships was established. As the National Youth Agency said of the Youth Service in evidence to the Select Committee:

Its distinctive characteristics include the voluntary engagement of young people, young people's active involvement in developing provision, the use of informal education as the primary method of youth engagement and an approach to provision that is responsive to young people's preferences.

(HoC, 2010: 9)

According to the National Youth Agency, approximately 28 per cent of all 13–19 year olds are in contact with some form of youth service, many of them from the most desperate of backgrounds in terms of family breakdowns and potential abuse. As one young person said, giving evidence to the Select Committee:

I felt that no one cared, but the youth centre, no matter what age you are when you walk in, never turns you back. It got me interested in music again after suffering from my drug addiction . . . it was a full-on, life changing experience for me.

(ibid.: 15)

However, the youth centres have suffered worst from the cuts to the education budget. In Greater London, a borough of considerable poverty and disadvantage has closed eight of its 13 youth centres. In other local authorities there has been a 100 per cent closure. Thereby is removed a vision of learning from those who are most in need of it.

Work-based learning experience

At the time of writing, work-related learning has been a legal requirement for all 14–16 year olds in England. But the practice often does not measure up to the theory. The recent Wolf Review of Vocational Education urges that this legal requirement should be dropped because of what it sees to be its generally poor quality (Wolf Report, 2011: 131).

Work-based learning requires, first, selected experiences that have the potential for growth in skills and understanding, and, second, mentors, teachers or trainers who match those possibilities to the learners. Often this is not the case. A survey of employers by the Confederation for British Industry in 2010 found that only 37 per cent of companies were satisfied with the work experience they offered (CBI, 2012). More positive steps need to be taken to ensure the wider vision of learning. But there are examples of where and how this can happen.

Example 1

The Centre for Engineering and Manufacturing Excellence (CEME) in Dagenham brings together employers, public sector partners, colleges, schools and universities as part of the London Thames Gateway Regeneration Scheme. World-class engineering facilities and expertise serve over 20 schools in the locality, thereby enriching the Diploma courses in engineering, providing routes for young people through school, apprenticeships and foundation degrees alongside the re-skilling of workers in neighbouring engineering and manufacturing businesses (including Fords). The pupils benefit from working with skilled technicians, using state-of-the-art tools and machinery, on complex engineering problems (www.ceme.co.uk).

Example 2

Scotland's *A Curriculum for Excellence* called for more 'skills for work' options for young people to help progress to further qualifications and work, aided by acquisition of generic employability skills. One hundred and fifty pupils took part in Glasgow Education Services' Culinary Excellence Programme. This comprises training sessions in a professional kitchen and a front-of-house setting and culminates in a lunch or a banquet. It includes lunch service for senior citizens, and visits to a fruit and vegetable market and to the prestigious Gleneagles hotel. Strong relationships are built between schools, colleges, hotels and restaurants. In 2010, eleven 4- and 5-star hotels, a restaurant and Glasgow Metropolitan College worked with linked schools. Much followed from this. For example, pupils worked on a cross-curricular project with the drama department, organising a 'Dinner, Drink and Drama'. The Skills for Work pupils advised drama pupils what to eat to help their performance; they in turn taught the Skills for Work pupils about body language and how to serve in a confident manner (Findlay, 2010).

There are, however, dangers here of falling into the trap of seeing the relevance of such work experience as 'vocational' and thus only for the 'less able', not capable of or motivated by the so-called academic curriculum. Rather, however, such work experience during the compulsory years of schooling should be seen as part of that wider vision of learning opened up by a more practical context.

There are now radical accounts of schools becoming more thoroughly trans-formed by the workplace context. 'Studio Schools' provide an alternative approach to formal education suitable for young people looking for a more entrepreneurial option or alienated by traditional pedagogy. There is a strong emphasis on practical work, teaching the curriculum through interdisciplinary enterprise education.

All these cases, however, relate to making the workplace accessible to those still at school, not as vocational training, but as a more practical aspect of general education. The quality of workplace learning becomes more acute when it comes to post-16 education and training, especially in the case of apprenticeships, but that must be postponed until Chapter 14.

The voice of the learner

Experience has both a public and a personal dimension – 'public' in the sense of *what* is experienced (e.g. the knowledge transmitted) and 'personal' in the sense of *how* it is experienced. One must not exaggerate the one at the cost of the other as often happens. The public nature of the experience (for example, the 'high culture' referred to in Chapter 4) can be transmitted without reference to the personal experiencing, and thus appear boring and irrelevant. Likewise, the personal nature of experience can be treated so subjectively that it is disconnected from the public understandings that might transform it.

Essential to making that connection must be listening to, and taking seriously, 'the learner's voice'. This has been well researched by Rudduck and McIntyre (2007) who speak of the maturity and capabilities of young people, often exceeding the assumptions of their teachers, and of the learners' desire for more active and collaborative learning.

Indeed, that is what good teachers do. The teacher of English enables students to articulate their thoughts and feelings through writing and discussion. We saw how, in Bally-Hoo, ballet *gave a voice* to young people as they articulated through dance (that is, 'made public') what was extremely personal. Listening to the learners' voices meant also giving them the language through which they might speak.

For that reason the much neglected Bullock Report (1975: ch. 10), *A Language for Life*, stressed the role of the teacher in respecting and attending to 'student talk' in the development, internalisation and communication of ideas. Students' talk became increasingly central to the learning experience encouraged in English classes, particularly in classrooms with a large number of pupils from different language communities. The use of storytelling and narrative was encouraged. It is the everyday form, by which we think, learn and communicate. Storytelling has to be taken seriously. David Holbrook's *English for Maturity* and *English for the Rejected* helped form this role of English in a generation of teachers.

But of course that can bring problems. Chris Searle enabled the young people at his school in Hackney to find a voice in their poetry and narratives which were then made public through *Teaching London Kids*, a widely circulated journal, published and printed by the young people themselves. That, however, was finally banned because the 'student voice', articulating the problems of racism and social dislocation which they faced, provoked a backlash from the authorities (see Searle, 1975).

However, the learner's voice requires an emphasis on the group. Classroom groups, carefully nurtured, come to share interests, including identification of common concerns, respect for differences in opinion, and openness to critical appraisal by others. Cultural development arises, not from the direct transmission of knowledge, but from the serious social interactions taking place in the light of evidence and of experiences brought to the discussions by the learners themselves. Such serious social interactions require, in the words of Stenhouse, a

> new climate of relationships with adolescents which takes account of their responsibility and is not authoritarian. Education must be founded on this co-operation, not on coercion. We must find a way of expressing our common humanity with our pupils, and we must be sensitive to the need to justify the decisions of authority to those affected by them. . . . In short, we need to transform our adolescent pupils into students.
>
> (quoted in Plaskow, 1985: 45)

In enabling that social interaction to take place within groups as they come to recognise shared interests and concerns, the teacher is able to relate those interests and concerns to the broader and deeper analysis of them which is to be found in the richness of the aesthetic, scientific and humanistic traditions.

Conclusion

If you start with broad aims of education, you inevitably arrive at a wider vision of learning. Too often educational aims are conceived narrowly, ignoring the importance of practical learning in its many forms for everyone, neglecting the deeply significant experiences which young people bring to school and college, failing to see the relevance of the different cultural resources (the different 'realms of meaning') to the lives of all young people. The perceived irrelevance of formal education to many is as much due to the failure of education's vision as it is to the incapacities of the young people themselves.

If there is to be education for all, then there must be:

- a wider understanding of what it means to become more fully a person;
- a recognition that all are able to appreciate to some degree the different voices through which we learn to be human;
- the capacity of all to live flourishing lives with a sense of dignity and personal worth; and
- the propensity to participate actively within the wider community.

Much of that vision is blinded by a narrow focus on what can be easily measured and by a 'transmission of knowledge', which ignores the practical ways of understanding, doing and making, and which is disconnected from the experience and concerns of young people. To remedy that requires more than a more intensive 'transmission of knowledge'. It requires rethinking what it means to learn in its different ways and to meet different aims. It requires less disdain for the practical and experiential. And it requires, above all, a questioning of an examination and testing system which militates against worthwhile learning.

But there is more to this wider vision of learning, for if we are concerned about each person, then we must realise that part of 'being a person' lies in relations to others. That wider vision must include a 'community of learners'. To that we now turn.

Postscript: can learning be enhanced by neuroscience?

Education for all, we are often told, cannot ignore the lessons to be drawn from neuroscience. That is about understanding the mental processes involved in learning. A report from the Royal Society (2011) explained the ways in which the brain's functions are affected, although it issues a cautionary note about claims made by some commercial interests which, at this stage in research, mistakenly point to lessons to be drawn from neuroscience research.

Nonetheless, we know that the brain changes physically from the development of skills and through constant practice and adaptation, and that these changes revert when practice ceases. The intensive training and concentration of London taxi drivers affects the actual size of the brain relevant to memorisation and spatial sense.

Furthermore, neuroscience enables us to be aware of, and to understand, specific learning difficulties, such as dyslexia, and behavioural difficulties such as ADHD, which otherwise might be seen simply as 'bad behaviour' to be treated with appropriate punishments. An increasing number of young people have physical and mental disorders, such as 'foetal alcohol syndrome' and genetic problems, which previously had not been recognised and which limit the ability to learn. These can now be identified through brain scans. Again, a poor grasp of number sense is an underlying cause of arithmetical disability. Computer games have been designed to give learners practice in understanding numbers that adapt to the learners' current skill level.

With such awareness, a better use of digital technology can provide the interactive modes of addressing some of the problems. And thus, 'experimental design that gives rise to neuroscience insights can often be adapted to support remediation and transferred to technology based platforms, such as lap-tops and mobile phones' (Royal Society, 2011: 15). Such possibilities must be taken seriously since the failure of so many to learn might well have physical causes which neuroscience will eventually be able to explain.

9 A community of learners in an age of communications technology

On-line learning – a path to the future?

Joel Klein, now Chief Executive of Wireless Generation, was keen, when Chancellor of New York City Education, on Innovation Zone (iZone). This offered whole programmes of 'on-line learning'. It was expected that, by 2011, 80 schools would take part in the experimental programme, half of which would adopt the 'virtual school model'. This would include:

- on-line Advanced Placement classes;
- credit recovery courses (as in one school which had a lot of failing students);
- combined on-line and face-to-face meetings;
- software for the instructional needs of those with learning problems or advanced learners.

Why, some asked, do we need schools? It would be so much cheaper to learn directly from expertly structured lessons on-line. Or why do we need so many teachers when very sophisticated lessons can be tailored and delivered to individuals' needs? According to Rupert Murdoch's interview in the *London Times*, 'you can get by with half as many teachers by using his computers' (quoted in *Private Eye*, no. 1294, 5 August 2011, p. 5).

It happens to be Mr. Murdoch's News Corp that has bought Wireless Generation and employs Joel Klein. This computer company produces the software which, it is claimed, can replace textbooks and, indeed, aid teachers. It also provides ARIS – Achievement Reporting and Innovation Systems – which can track student attendance, grades and progress, and which has been bought by New York schools. Murdoch hired Joel Klein to help him expand into education and now to superintend Wireless Generation.

Interesting responses emerged on various blogs. Who is doing the virtual tutoring which no doubt would be contracted out to unknown tutors – possibly from an 'offshore outfit' and never faced or known personally?

Is such scepticism valid? Certainly at a time when public services are increasingly contracted out to private 'for-profit' companies, the impersonal and unseen private tutoring at the cheapest possible rate needs to be examined carefully. More serious, however, is the underlying assumption that interpersonal interactions with others (the teacher and fellow learners) are no longer necessary where 'personalised learning' is made possible by modern advances in communications technology.

The error lies in the failure to see the crucial importance of the 'community' in learning. In pursuing this line of argument, I start with the contrast between the individual and the group, stressing the key, but often forgotten, importance of the group in each person's growth of understanding. The group is a community writ small. It is the embryonic 'community of learners' which is integral to quality learning.

All this, however, is not a rejection of communications technology. Far from it. Its advances open up immense opportunities, as I shall explain. But it is important not to be so seduced by its advances that learners become divorced from their partners in learning.

Forget not the 'group'

Despite the constant assertion of individual autonomy as an educational aim, the interrelationship with, and indeed continued dependence on, others is essential to being and to grow as a person. What the philosopher John Macmurray referred to as 'the form of the personal' included the relationship with other persons: 'Against the assumption that the Self is an isolated individual, I have set the view that the Self is a *person*, and that personal experience is *constituted* by the relation of persons' (Macmurray, 1957: 12).

No one is an island. Growth of self-awareness from the earliest days arises from the growing awareness of 'the other' with whom one interacts; one's actions require appreciating others' *re*-actions; furtherance of one's wishes requires cooperation from others; growth of understanding requires the critical scrutiny of one's beliefs in the light of others' comments and observations, because 'the context of all knowledge is the interpersonal world in and through which each of us comes to consciousness of ourselves as agents already and necessarily engaged with other persons who are acting towards us' (ibid.: xvii).

We are by definition 'groupies' – often maybe not very successfully and maybe reluctantly. But we cannot avoid being members of groups through which we get a sense of solidarity, acquire ways of seeing and valuing the world, and receive support for, or resistance to, our endeavours. Learning to live and work fruitfully in groups is essential to quality learning.

It was in recognition of this that Stenhouse stressed the importance of the group within the classroom in the promotion of young people's learning. He argued that teachers too often underplayed it, and that, in neglecting the dynamics of the group, they often failed to achieve their goals. It is through interactions within the respective groups that cultural understandings and values are transmitted. Stenhouse referred to Talcott Parsons' analysis of culture: 'this induction is achieved through partaking in a process of social interaction' (Stenhouse, 1967).

What are the lessons for the organisation of formal learning?

First, it is important to create such a group – a cultural togetherness – out of the different cultures brought into the classroom. Such a classroom group would come to share values and interests, including the identification of common concerns, respect for differences in opinion, shared procedures of enquiry, openness to critical appraisal of others, the relation of evidence to the conclusions provisionally reached. Cultural development would arise, not from the direct transmission of knowledge, but from the serious social interactions which take place in the light of evidence and in the light of the experiences brought to the explorations by the learners themselves. Hence, in contrast with so much educational theory and practice,

> the class or working group rather than the individual pupil must be our starting-point. The essence of the classroom situation may best be captured by asserting that the group is prior to the individual, that individuals are well educated because they take part in groups and share experiences which have an educative quality.
>
> (Stenhouse, 1967: 6)

In other words, it is important to create a 'community of learners', and the more diverse the membership of that community, the richer the social interactions. Does not the lower 'half our future' suffer from the increasing social segregation in our society?

Second, such serious social interactions require, as argued in the last chapter, a 'new climate of relationships with adolescents which takes account of their responsibility and is not authoritarian. Education must be founded on this co-operation, not on coercion' (quoted in Plaskow, 1985: 4).

Third, however, in enabling that social interaction to take place within groups as they come to recognise shared interests and concerns, the teacher is able to relate those interests and concerns to the broader and deeper analysis of them which is to be found in the first sense of culture outlined in Chapter 4 – in the richness of the aesthetic, scientific and humane traditions which, on a wider scale, have evolved through critical engagement of different people and generations. Let us, for the want of a better phrase, call them 'communities of intellectuals'.

Community of intellectuals

A rather dramatic intervention by an undergraduate in the debate in Congregation of the University of Oxford, concerning the proposed 'new system' of student fees and the danger that such would create in widening access, went as follows:

> This is a clear sign of the fundamental danger of the new system in turning this place into one of consumers and producers of knowledge. I believe we are not consumers and producers but a community of intellectuals, engaged in the common task of investigating the world around us and understanding the human condition.
>
> (*Oxford University Gazette*, 16 February 2011)

The 'new system', incurring so much debt despite the long period for repayment (and then only when a certain level of salary had been reached), would not only deter potential students of lowly means, but would transform the language of higher education and the consequent relations between the university and its students. These latter become 'clients' or 'customers', and what the university has to offer is a 'commodity' which, if bought at £9,000 per year, would be expected to give 'worthwhile returns' on this initial and large 'investment'. It was this changed relationship that the undergraduate was highlighting and objecting to.

But what is a community of intellectuals? It could refer to a group of people engaged together (or at least interacting with each other) in the pursuit of academic activities. It would be a critical group, interested in ideas, following the evidence, open to argument and criticism. Such would, at least ideally, be the 'dons' dominion'. What it would not be is an *aggregate* of individuals, each working on his or her particular research project, or (worse still) seeking the most competitive price for selling their product to willing customers.

However, though often the case, it would not necessarily be a community defined by space. This is especially so where technology widens the sense of community to include people at considerable distance from each other. But in many ways, it never has been defined in terms of space. Subject associations, such as the Historical Association, become communities of intellectuals, furthering scholarship, teaching and research, and drawing upon each other for criticism and evidence.

Furthermore, the communities that the undergraduate was referring to, go beyond the constraints not only of space but also of time. In learning science or history, the young person is heeding the voices within the conversation between the generations. The community of scientists straddles the generations and not simply the different locations where they engage in their research and teaching. To learn is to begin to belong to a different community, a tradition of research, scholarship and criticism.

This might, at first, seem a far cry from the classroom. But is it and should it be? The teacher of the arts, humanities and sciences is enabling the members of the group to tackle problems that call upon the artistic, practical and academic cultures we have inherited. Those cultures embody not just 'content' but the spirit of criticism and distinctive modes of enquiry. The classroom community is the forum in which such critical enquiry, informed by the cultural achievements of the wider intellectual community, is played out.

The evaluation of Learning Futures (2010) describes this sense of community amongst the teachers in the schools in which different pedagogical approaches were being tested.

They described the need for a community of collective teacher responsibility for change with other schools across the Learning Futures programme, where there was time for dialogue and space for reflection. They felt that as a group they were more than the sum of the individual parts and were part of a social movement for change.

Learning in communities

There is a further dimension to this sense of community, namely, the development of positive cooperation within the group and the acquisition of the appropriate values and virtues – crucial, one would have thought, not only to being open to ideas and critical discussion, but also to preparation for future civic responsibilities.

Let us remind ourselves, in our account of educational aims, of the importance of enabling young people to develop a sense of a community and of having the propensity to participate in it. In *Democracy and Education* (1916: 83), Dewey refers to 'education' as a 'social function, securing direction and development in the immature through their participation in the life of the group to which they belong'. *Practising* democracy would seem to be crucial. One learns how to do things by doing. Therefore, creating that sense of community was, for Dewey, essential for the development of democracy. And the foundations needed to be laid at school.

> As soon as a community depends to any considerable extent upon what lies beyond its own territory and its own immediate generation, it must rely upon the set agency of schools to insure adequate transmission of all its resources . . . Hence, a special mode of intercourse is instituted, the school, to care for such matters.
>
> (ibid.: 19)

An example would be Kohlberg's 'just community school'. Lawrence Kohlberg, at the Center for Moral Development at Harvard University, had mapped out the stages of moral development, based on the central understanding of justice and fairness in the deliberations about what one ought to do. By trying to solve moral dilemmas, students would develop their capacity to think according to 'principles', ultimately those that they would be prepared to make universal principles of practice. One major problem, however, was that young people could score high on the moral thinking tests without necessarily following through that thinking in practice. It was necessary that those principles should be embedded in the institutional context of the learners. There is little point in teaching the principles and understanding of justice if the daily experience of the young people is that of injustice. Kohlberg and his colleagues, therefore, established what was called the 'just community school' in which the students themselves played an active part in the decisions and deliberations which affected them. As Kohlberg said:

> In summary, the current demand for moral education is a demand that our society becomes more of a just community. If our society is to become a more just community, it needs democratic schools. This was the demand and dream of John Dewey.
>
> (Kohlberg, 1982: 24)

In the same way, the Crick Report (1998) was an important landmark. It recommended 'citizenship' as an obligatory element for all young people. In so doing, it followed the arguments put forward over many years for political education in schools. If it is crucial to the well-being of each that our communities, central and local, should be democratic, then it is similarly crucial to have the future generation educated in democratic principles and to be so motivated as to put them into practice. Central to education should be an understanding of such basic concepts as 'political authority', 'democracy' and 'justice', as well as the ability to apply such concepts in the appropriate contexts. Crick referred to the acquisition of such concepts as 'political literacy' (Crick and Porter, 1978).

There are inevitable difficulties. Eric Midwinter, working in inner city Liverpool in the 1970s, questioned the prevailing benchmark of a successful school as that which enabled young people to *escape* from their deprived communities. He pointed to the oddness of educational success lying in the escape of a small minority from their very family and community background. Rather, success should be measured in terms of how that education provided the consciousness whereby that community might be transformed into something better. He argued, 'as a theoretical goal we had defined the community school as one which ventured out into and welcomed the community until a visionary time arrived when it was difficult to distinguish school from community' (Midwinter, 1975: 160). For Midwinter, the students who were engaged in such community activities became a community of learners.

Recently, and not on such a scale of community involvement, we have seen the development of 'restorative justice' as a way in which schools, working with the community police, enable young people who have committed anti-community offences, to confront the victims of their behaviour – an example of a broader vision of learning which embraces a greater 'moral seriousness'. Family Links, too, has pioneered ways in which young people are enabled to develop those social skills whereby they come to empathise with others in their group. But this requires the understanding and the cooperation of the parents, and so these are engaged with the school and the teachers in the development of the relevant skills and social awareness. The learning community is extended through the links established between school and family (www.familylinks.org.uk).

Learning enhanced by communications technology

Communications technology, with almost universal access to smart phones, iPads and iPods, has transformed not only access to education but also the very nature of relationships at the heart of it. Obvious uses lie in the much greater and easier access to information and resources through the internet – not only for students. The *Guardian*'s education resources network gives access to 70,000 pages of lesson plans and interactive materials, all free.

This can give rise to excessive claims for the enhancement of learning. Learners become less dependent on the 'authority' of the teacher. Rival sources of information enable them to challenge what the teachers say. The expertise lies in the internet, rather than in the classroom. If you want to know anything, then google it.

There is, of course, much truth in this, especially where teaching is seen as 'the transmission of knowledge', but the argument is less persuasive where one sees the growth of knowledge and understanding, not so much in the acquisition of facts and formulae, but in the initiation into a community of learners such as that described above. To be educated lies in learning to take part in a conversation with others who are pursuing the same interests and struggling with the same problems. It is a matter of opening the minds of young people to ways of seeing things which they had not previously envisaged. It means acquiring new ways of understanding. It requires the acquisition of concepts and skills under the critical supervision and correction of the good teacher. Let us, therefore, always be cautious of excessive claims for the personalised programmes facilitated by e-learning and tailored to the needs of the autonomous learner.

However, let us also be cautious of drawing too firm a line between e-learning, on the one hand, and the initiation into a community of learners, on the other. Indeed, the two should work together.

One example would be that of *Notschool.net*, one of Ultralab's most successful research and development projects. Its 'on-line environment' meets the needs of young people, many of whom are not in school ('the phobic, ill, disaffected, sick, pregnant and the excluded'). It has shown how they have renewed their confidence in learning, and gained certificates to recognise their learning progress. But *Notschool.net* initially established a virtual community of 100 young people who were given the opportunity to develop their self-esteem and be reintroduced to learning. This was achieved through the support of mentors, buddies, experts and the use of new technology. Working with Local Education Authorities throughout the UK, the project expanded on its success to offer a similar experience for more of the estimated 50,000 young people who could benefit. It created a community of learners.

A second example is that of NISAI. Located in London's Harrow, it provides a 'virtual academy', serving over 400 young people unable to attend school for a variety of reasons (medical, school phobia, exclusion, in custody, etc.). It has a virtual classroom, virtual chill-out room, secure social network, daily teaching and supervision by qualified teachers and via the internet, leading to public examination. It is now rapidly expanding its services throughout Britain. Although it places young people at the centre of their own learning process and thereby provides personalised, tailored programmes designed around the individual's needs, the development of a community is central to the teaching. From the very beginning, students take part in live on-line training sessions with an NVA specialist teacher where they learn to use the virtual classroom and the learning community site. Group work is essential. The lessons are fully interactive on-line. The students collaborate with other on-line classmates around the UK. Group learning activities are central. For many young people, this technical capacity to interact with others outside mainstream schooling provides not only a productive learning environment but also much needed safe social networking, forums and blogs for enrichment and peer-to-peer interaction. It aids reintegration very often into the mainstream – indeed, a vibrant learning community. According to Andrew, aged 18, an ME sufferer:

The NVA brings me as close to the classroom experience as I can imagine and is without a doubt the first thing I'd recommend to people who couldn't go to school or college. The hardest part of not going to school is not being able to see my friends and people my own age. Since joining the NVA I've made friends and it's great to talk to them in the classroom and in other areas.

(NISAI, 2010)

A third example is provided by a government project, that of the Gifted and Talented Young People's Programme (GTYP). Networking with other learners, not only the teachers, is most important for those who otherwise might be isolated. This is important with young people, identified as 'gifted and talented'. GTYP pioneered e-learning communities through which the learners were able to converse with each other across the country in addressing problems which they were asked to tackle. In many cases, these young learners were reluctant to show their intellectual interests in class and valued the anonymity of an on-line community (Nuffield Review, 2009: 25).

A final example is that of the use of mobile phones. There is fear of the ubiquity of mobile phones in schools and their classrooms. But some argue for (and demonstrate) the positive way in which such devices might be used to enhance education for all. Dr Anne Looney, Chief Executive of Ireland's National Council for Curriculum and Assessment, reports on the use of mobile phones, lent to students of the Irish language, in which they had to communicate with each other and with their teacher only in the Irish language. Significant progress was recorded with considerable increase in their level of engagement in spoken Irish (Looney, 2010: 97).

All we can note, in this brief reference to the potential of communications technology, is that it opens up enormous opportunities, not only in making revolutionary access to resources for learning, but also in changing the relationships between learner and learner and between them and the teachers. Used properly, it enriches that community of learners. Especially for those excluded from mainstream education and social intercourse, but also for those in mainstream education, it opens up further opportunities for achieving education for all.

In one sense of course (to be elaborated in Chapter 11), the teacher becomes less of 'an authority' in the subject matter to be taught, for the teacher can more easily be challenged by reference to the facts and to the analyses which now can be found on the internet. But that leaves the teacher free to engage with the learners from a deeper understanding of the cultural resources upon which the learners draw in their thinking and deliberations. To re-iterate the words of Stenhouse, quoted above, it can create a 'new climate of relationships with adolescents which takes account of their responsibility and is not authoritarian'.

But, more than that: does not such ready access to resources in aid of learning and to other learners, mentors and supporters through various networks, signify that the provision of formal learning needs to be radically rethought? Are the schools of yesterday appropriate for the schools of tomorrow? Consider the 'Hole in the Wall Learning Project' which installed computers with internet connections in Delhi slums for local children to discover. From these the children started to learn English, mathematics and computing and now, so successful has this been in promoting 'self-activating learning' that there are 500 such PCs installed in walls across India and Africa. And now the project is working with 12 year olds in Tyneside.

But beware the dangers

There are inevitably dangers, many of them obvious. But this is particularly the case where social networking is concerned. On-line social networking, made possible by Facebook and Twitter, can be a weapon of abuse and worse. In the words of a 15-year-old girl: 'At my school we hear words 'shit', 'sket' and 'slag' every day. It's got so it's not worth challenging it, it is not worth arguing about because it just doesn't change anything' (*Guardian*, 16 April 2011).

'Sket' sites – pictures of girls posted by vengeful ex-boyfriends – on network sites, circulated on smart phone message systems, sometimes request marks out of ten for the 'sket' or bitch. Much is influenced by violent male attitudes in music and film. As the domestic violence coordinator for Blackpool Advocacy noted, 'We are noticing more disclosures of girls of 13 and upwards who are in quite violent and abusive teenage relationships', and this is seen to be partly due to the 'learning' arising from the social networking made possible by modern technology (see D. Conlan, domestic violence coordinator for Blackpool Advocacy, *Guardian*, 16 March 2010). Tender UK and ROTA (Race on the Agenda) interviewed girls in Liverpool, Birmingham and Manchester, revealing how verbal disrespect can escalate into horrific abuse and sexual assaults on girls as young as 13.

Therefore, such technology provides not only greater opportunities for enhancing learning, but also challenges which need to be faced by schools and colleges.

Conclusion

Secondary education for all requires a shift from seeing learners as a lot of autonomous individuals for whom learning is heavily personalised. The group matters, and the skilful teacher will utilise the group in encouraging learning for all. Properly orchestrated interactions within the group enhance learning – as critic of tentative opinions, as partner in the search for understanding, as source of experience and knowledge. The more diverse the group the richer can be those interactions.

More than this, however, is the need in such group participation to acquire those virtues which are essential for living harmoniously together, for disagreeing without being personally aggressive, for cooperating in shared tasks and concerns – in other words, for learning to be community minded and democratic in the resolution of problems.

Such a community of learners is particularly important for those least successful in school – Newsom's 'half our future'. No longer excluded from the company of others, their views come to be articulated and respected. And, as the examples show, e-learning and communications technology can help in that. But it must be realised that belonging to such groups must be seen as a mode of entry to the wider community of learners, reflected in the 'conversations between the generations of mankind'.

10 Bring back curriculum thinking

Translating ideas into practice

It is one thing to argue for a broader vision of learning – a vision that introduces young people to different realms of meaning, to practical thinking, and to the moral dimension of a fully human life. It is quite another to translate such a vision into the year-by-year, day-by-day planning of young people's learning.

Too often governments do not think so. The National Curriculum in England grew into a 500-page document of what should be learnt and how. That 'curriculum' (which was smaller when first published in 1988) set out in detail the aims, targets, content and assessment in ten areas of experience. These ten areas were remarkably like the traditional subjects that most people who had been to a grammar school would recognise. However, they were supplemented by cross-curriculum themes, which dealt with matters of social and moral importance but which could too easily slip through a curriculum focused on subjects. Such themes could indeed be integrated with science, history or literature. But, as political fashion changed, so did these themes. Government agencies constantly 'reform' the curriculum – for instance, introducing 'vocational subjects' for some and freeing them from much of the erstwhile 'national curriculum'.

Then a changed government had different views of the aims of education. The government in England, upon election in 2010, proposed a six-subject English Baccalaureate (EBac) (English, two sciences, mathematics, history or geography and a language) as the core curriculum for all and removed the 'equivalences' that had been established between the General Certificate of Secondary Education (GCSE), normally taken at 16, and 'vocational' subjects. Suddenly the world changed dramatically. For example, many of England's 164 grammar schools appeared not so good on the new measures of standards (namely, Grade C in the GCSEs that constituted the EBac). 'Good schools' as measured on previous standards became failing schools; and much acclaimed academies could no longer be acclaimed. Less than a fifth of pupils in some grammar schools would have qualified for the EBac on 2000 GCSE results (*TES*, 4 March 2011), and the annual league table of school performance shows that just 15.6 per cent of pupils in all schools would have got EBac in 2010 (*TES*, 11 March 2011).

Little justification was given for this innovation except for statements about the need for greater 'academic rigour'. But surely there is need for deeper curriculum thinking than that. Why, for instance, two sciences for all rather than the integrated science which many schools had adopted for those motivated by practical concerns? On what grounds should there be choice between history and geography? Why should subjects, which enhanced the practical learning argued for in Chapter 3, not appear in the EBac? Understandably there was a protest from the Design and Technology Association as engineering-related knowledge was demoted and as schools dropped Design and Technology (D&T) in order to transfer their energies to subjects that gain brownie points within the EBac. For example, as Richard Green, Chief Executive of the Design and Technology Association observed,

> Because of the way the EBac. works, many schools are now readjusting their curriculum lower down the school to concentrate on EBac subjects earlier on – and since these do not include DT, it's not being prioritised . . . But it makes no sense to have the Department of Business, Innovation and Skills talking about a shortage of people with creative skills in the next decade, while the Department of Education moves towards a more academic curriculum that cuts DT out.
>
> (*Guardian*, 14 June 2011)

Pronouncements by government too often lack any curriculum thinking.

Scotland, on the other hand, is bent on full-scale reform of the curriculum in its *Curriculum for Excellence*. There is felt to be a need for a 'transformation of education'. That transformation is encapsulated in four 'capacities', namely, 'confident individuals', 'effective contributors', 'successful learners' and 'responsible citizens'. These capacities require: acquisition of skills for life, learning and work; numeracy and literacy; health and well-being. These capacities are spelt out in terms of a large number of 'outcomes' and 'experiences', and these in turn are to be understood within 'curriculum areas' under the headings of 'expressive arts', 'languages and literacy', 'health and well-being', 'mathematics and numeracy', 'religious and moral education', 'sciences', 'social studies', 'technologies'. For example, within the sciences the concepts related to 'planet earth' – forces, electricity and waves, biological systems, materials, and topical science – are suggested, together with 'can do' statements expressing the objectives. These 'can do' statements express not only key concepts which have to be grasped at different levels (for example, 'friction', or 'magnetic, electrostatic and gravitational forces') but also the four 'capacities'. Thus, by 14,

> By investigating how friction, including air resistance, affects motion, I can suggest ways to improve efficiency in moving objects.

And

> I have collaborated in investigations to compare magnetic, electrostatic and gravitational forces and have explored their practical applications.

The focus upon key ideas within curriculum areas is admirable, as shall be argued below, but the subsequent translation of these into 'outcomes' presupposes a questionable understanding of 'curriculum'.

Different meanings of curriculum

Curriculum as a means to an end

That 'questionable understanding of curriculum' has a long history and is beguiling, tied to the 'logic of action' briefly introduced in Chapter 3. We need to think carefully about the meaning of 'curriculum', lest it too gets hijacked by an ideological view which, though on the surface seemingly obvious, does in fact distort the very nature of learning.

Several decades ago, 'curriculum' became the focus of academic study. No doubt this arose from the resurgence of *education for all* and the need for greater systematic thought about 'the science' of teaching and learning. A key book was Ralph Tyler's (1949) *Basic Principles of Curriculum and Instruction*. This set out the principles of what came to be called 'rational curriculum planning', namely: first specify aims; second, translate these into objectives or 'intended learning outcomes'; third, choose the content and teaching method which (it can be shown) lead to these outcomes; fourth, measure whether the outcomes are the intended ones; finally, evaluate the whole process in the light of the measurements. Do the aims, objectives, content or method need to be revised?

By the 1970s, educational objectives had become big business.

> In the United States some school systems have contracted out sectors of the educational system to profit-making learning system companies whose profits depend on their capacity to achieve objectives prespecified in terms of children's performance on standardised tests.
>
> (Stenhouse, 1975: 69)

The privatisation of public education to for-profit organisations is not so recent after all.

This model led, inevitably, to a greater precision in the specification of outcomes. Measurement required such precision, and therefore outcomes needed to be written in behavioural terms, namely, what can be observed and measured with accuracy. In the 1960s, Mager (1962) and Popham (1969) in the USA became the architects of the 'science' of curriculum planning in terms of behavioural outcomes. As Denis Lawton said,

> By the early 1970s there was a powerful movement amongst US curriculum theorists demanding that the only meaningful interpretation of objectives was to emphasise behavioural objectives. Numbers of educationalists appeared at curriculum conferences with lapel badges and car stickers with slogans such as 'Help stamp out non-behavioural objectives'.
>
> (Lawton, 1989: 11)

Not long afterwards, as often is the case, the American fashion entered Britain, especially in trying to make formal education more relevant to economic needs. It all seemed so rational. A prime example was the specification of competencies ('can do's') to explicit standards. Jessup, whose book on 'outcomes' was seminal to the development of the National Vocational Qualifications, gave two examples of an 'element' within the broad occupational area of 'catering and health care', namely: 'maintain a standard of hygiene in food preparation areas' and 'assess the physical conditions of patients by inspection'. In each case, there followed a long list of performances which each person would be able to do in specific conditions. These were the *units of competence*, grouped together under the *elements of competence* (Jessup, 1991). The consequent long lists of units and elements would enable the check-list assessors to judge the overall competence of a person for that job – or, indeed, for progression to higher education.

This takes us back to the 'logic of action'. If I want to go to the shops and if bus no. 32 takes me to the shops, then it makes sense to get bus no. 32. The bus is the *means* for reaching the intended *end*. The efficacy of the means is easily ascertained. It is an empirical matter (observation) to show that catching that bus gets me to the shops. Translating this simple piece of logic into educational contexts, one might say that going through certain exercises is the proven means of achieving the desired outcome. Thus might arise a 'science of the curriculum' – the discovery through empirical investigation of 'what works'.

However, something disagreeable might follow. The learners get bored through constant preparation for the tests (the outcomes). They have 'hit the targets', reached the intended 'end', and yet they are put off any further education. Indeed, the very 'means' for reaching the defined 'educational ends' seem, surprisingly, to have been mis-educational. They cause boredom and disengagement. The achievement of the behavioural objectives does not lead to deeper understanding and readiness to continue with their learning. They have 'hit the target', but not really understood (see Smith Report, 2004 and ACME Reports, 2011 a and b). Here is a 'theory of curriculum' disconnected from a 'theory of learning'.

Curriculum as an engagement between learner and teacher

To learn anything of significance is not like that. I want us to go back to the chapter on culture, and the importance of entering into those traditions of understanding, making and creating that we have inherited and through which we make sense of the world. We enter those different 'realms of meaning' in different ways and via different journeys. It is often a struggle where, at first, we only dimly understand, and where we are open to correction or refinement in that understanding. Moreover, having entered into that world of ideas and practices, learners gain increasing capacity to form their own judgement. And that judgement or interim conclusion might not be what is specified by the 'curriculum creators'.

The curriculum, therefore, is not the means to a fixed outcome, but the engagement, assisted by the teacher, with a body of knowledge (theoretical and practical) through which learners come to understand and act intelligently within the physical, social and moral worlds they inhabit.

Such a curriculum is characterised more by content (key ideas and modes of inquiry) than by outcomes. And such content can be grasped at different levels of meaning – what Jerome Bruner (1960) referred to as the 'spiral curriculum'. By spiral curriculum, Bruner meant constant revisiting of these key ideas, through which experience is organised. Those ideas can be represented at different levels. As learners grow in understanding, so they move from practical ('enactive') ways of portraying those ideas, to more 'iconic' ones and finally to the abstractions of a symbolic mode of understanding. Take the example of 'leverage' – a most important idea within classical mechanics. Small children soon gain a practical (or 'enactive') grasp of how to play on a seesaw – gaining in skill as they shift their weight along the plank. Later they are able to visualise ('iconically') and express in a concrete way the general principle. Later still they can formulate general principles more abstractly, possibly mathematically and thus 'symbolically'.

Thus the first thing in any curriculum proposal is to identify those key ideas that can be understood at different levels and without which one cannot see things from a particular point of view. The criticism from the ACME (2011a) working party at the Royal Society is that, in pursuing a curriculum model in terms of outcomes, young people fail to grasp the underlying conceptual structure of mathematical understanding. They learn the formulae for the test but do not either understand its significance or know how to apply it to the world around them. Hence, the report maps out the key ideas (for example, 'ratio', 'proportion', 'scaling') and the logical connections between those and more advanced concepts. To understand from a mathematical point of view is to grasp a conceptual structure, rather than single concepts in isolation.

The curriculum, therefore, specifies the key ideas which constitute a mode of knowing or making, and which can be grasped at different levels and through different routes. The imaginative teacher tests out those different routes, provides different exercises depending on the perceived learning needs of the student, engineers different experiences, and creates different applications for the learner's tentative thinking.

To that extent the curriculum is what Stenhouse (1975: 5) referred to as 'a proposal', indeed a hypothesis, to be tested out in different classrooms and with different learners. As such it is open to refinement in the light of experience. And that is why the curriculum is not something to be handed down to teachers for 'delivery' (whatever Sir Michael Barber's Delivery Unit might think) but a specification or proposal of how the learner might proceed if he or she is to enter a way of thinking and practising. And that proposal has to be sufficiently clear that it can be tested and refined by the teacher, who therefore is the curriculum creator (not deliverer), though within a given framework of key ideas.

The problem with the idea of curriculum defined in terms of specific outcomes and of the means for attaining those outcomes is that it fails to understand the nature of knowledge and the nature of learning – namely, that struggle to enter into a world of ideas with its own distinctive mode of thinking about the world. As

Philip Jackson (1968: 167) observed, 'the path of educational progress more closely resembles the flight of a butterfly than the flight of a bullet'. Or, according to Hirst (see James, 2012), reminiscent of Wittgenstein and indeed Dewey's map, 'understanding a form of knowledge is far more like coming to know a country than climbing a ladder'.

In so arguing and in promoting *education for all*, there is a need to examine the nature of 'subjects', for it is these which too often have fallen victim to the widening of access to all young people. Too often they are associated with 'academic learning', suitable for a minority – the rest being better off with practical activities, projects and vocational preparation. I believe this to be a false antithesis.

The importance of subjects

A typical secondary school timetable would be divided into periods, each period filled with a distinctive subject – mathematics, sciences, literature, and so on. The learning which goes on in those periods would lead to public examinations in those respective subjects. Indeed, the curriculum is often seen as a collection of subjects, and (as in the English and Welsh National Curriculum established in 1988) each subject would be spelt out in terms of a content to be learnt and attainment targets to be reached.

Often such a division of the curriculum appears defective insofar as matters of importance might be neglected. They do not fit into the traditional collection of subjects. 'Citizenship' is a good example. If one aim of education is to nurture the future citizen, then there should be a place for that on the curriculum. The National Curriculum overcame that problem by adding to the ten subjects 'cross-curriculum themes' such as 'economic awareness', 'enterprise', 'citizenship', 'personal and social relations', 'health education', 'information technology'. These could be taught in isolation (thereby becoming 'a subject' examined in public examinations) or integrated into different subjects. For example, aspects of 'citizenship' could be taught in 'history'; parts of 'health education' in the science curriculum.

That view of the curriculum as a collection of traditional subjects is criticised by those, on the one hand, who see subjects as but the 'social constructions of people in positions of political control', a position influentially argued in the 1970s in a collection by Young (1972), and those, on the other hand, who (not bothering about such philosophical niceties) undervalue the role of subjects in favour of themes, interests or relevance. Reference has already been made to William Kilpatrick and his 'project curriculum' – knowledge growing through the pursuit of a project. The Royal Society of the Arts, in its Opening Minds Project, taken up by several schools, stresses 'competencies' rather than the content within traditional subjects and 'themes' within which these competencies might be acquired.

In both cases, however, there is rarely a clear analysis of what, at their best, major subjects represent. It is the argument of this book that to underrate the significance of subjects is to deny to all young people access to that culture which enables them to make sense of their lives.

Why is this?

Subjects, as such, are convenient ways of organising the process of learning. There is so much to be learnt, so much to understand, that a convenient way of packaging it all and putting it into the timetable must be found.

There are, however, logical reasons for packaging what is to be learnt in particular ways. There are different kinds of knowledge, different kinds of enquiry, each kind employing different key ideas or concepts, explaining events in different ways, applying different tests of what is true. Biologists, for example, see the field system differently from the medieval historian and will pursue different kinds of investigation. The results of the enquiries by biologists or medieval historians are written down in books and articles, argued about by fellow scholars, made the basis of yet further enquiries. These constitute Oakeshott's 'conversation between the generations' and they become the material or resources from which teachers might draw in order to initiate students into similar ways of understanding the world and of pursuing enquiries. The aim is to get the learner on the inside of a disciplined way of thinking that provides a fruitful but by no means finished way of understanding experience and of taking an active interest in it.

Pupils, therefore, need to be initiated into this differentiated structure of knowledge. This is best achieved through those subjects that provide focused introductions to these distinctive ways of thinking and practising. At least, it is argued, the subject matter of these different ways of thinking should provide the content or resources for a curriculum even when it is organised around integrating inquiries or interests.

The danger, however, is to take the product or abstractions of others' enquiries and to present them as propositions to be learnt, as formulae to be remembered, dead because they have been disconnected from the form of inquiry to which they belong. To refer once again to Dewey, often wrongly accused of a so-called anti-subject child-centred education, he criticised 'traditional education' where that commonly consisted of transmitting bodies of knowledge, inert ideas that could be memorised for examinations but which meant very little. Rather, the subjects embody 'the wisdom of the race' and it is the job of the teacher to make the connections between this wisdom on the one hand and the child's present world and thinking on the other.

Dewey illuminates this distinction by reference to the *psychological* and the *logical* aspects of learning – the state of mind of the child, on the one hand, and, on the other, the organised bodies of knowledge arising from different traditions of enquiry. The former is like the explorer finding his way; the latter is like a map left by previous explorers to help him on his way but open to refinement in the light of further experience (Dewey, 1902: 136). The world from the train window is more than a funny-shaped field with a lonely church in the middle – it is the remains of a medieval village with its early enclosure and field system. But to see that requires a grasp of geographical and historical understandings.

However, the relation of subject (in this organisational sense) and subject matter (in this logical sense) is often tenuous and needs to be established by the teacher.

Putting theory into practice

The problem, as many perceive it, is that many young people seem unable to enter these different forms of enquiry, and the subject teaching which purports to do this becomes a turn-off. The learners are disengaged. They do not see the subject matter to be relevant to their dominant interest. Or, more seriously, they have not the capacity to grasp the key ideas. Access to our cultural heritage (in the eyes of some as instanced in Chapter 1) would seem to be restricted to a minority.

On the other hand, by simplifying the subject matter (by relating it to the interests of the learner and ensuring its relevance) in order to make it accessible to all, so it then fails to do justice to the 'logic of the subject', that is, to the acquisition of those key ideas and theoretical concepts that enable progression to higher levels of learning. And even those who seem to do well in a subject often have little understanding but have succeeded in memorising the propositions and formulae transmitted from the teacher's rostrum.

It is important, in envisaging *education for all*, to challenge such doubts and to see the curriculum, though shaped by a framework of ideas that we have inherited, as adaptable by the good teacher who sees different ways of entering such a framework. A good place to start is science education.

Science for all or only for some?

A significant report on science teaching addressed the claim that (to quote a member of a House of Commons committee – HoC, 2002) science teaching was 'so boring that it put young people off science for life'. There was a need to distinguish between the importance of scientific understanding for all (so that everyone can grasp the significance of science and scientific reports which affect our lives) and the deeper grasp of science as a preparation for those who wished to become scientists. The former is frequently referred to as 'scientific literacy'. The distinction is explained by the Council for Science and Technology (1998) thus:

> The term scientific literacy is used here to cover a basic understanding of the scientific ways and means for knowing and thinking critically and creatively about the natural world, along with the inherent uncertainties and limitations of the new scientific knowledge from leading edge research . . . For the minority of these pupils who subsequently pursue further science-based education and careers, there is, of course the additional need to become scientifically literate by mastering the relevant units of scientific knowledge and techniques in their chosen field during their education.

Subsequently, the Nuffield Foundation in partnership with the University of York produced a more flexible structure for 15–16 year olds which provided different pathways. It included:

- 'core science', taken by all, which introduced learners to (a) key explanatory ideas such as 'genes', 'radiation', 'nutrition' and (b) general processes and practices of science including political and sociological aspects;
- either 'additional science' for those who wished to acquire a deeper grasp of the key ideas, or 'additional applied science' which focused on work-related scientific processes, as in health care or agriculture, for those who wished to progress to more technical careers;
- 'triple science' (physics, chemistry and biology) which included modules from 'core science' and 'additional science' as well as more specific and deeper understanding of the science within these respective scientific disciplines.

Fundamental to this more flexible framework is the linking of the 'logical' and 'psychological' aspects of a subject (Dewey, 1916: 219–223) – the 'logical' being the ideas within the corpus of scientific knowledge we have inherited ('the map left by previous explorers') and the 'psychological' being the most effective routes into those ideas, namely, the ways in which they can be seen to relate to the experience and interests of the learner. A good teacher, as Dewey argued, can deepen a child's knowledge of key ideas in science through the activities of cooking or gardening.

A warning shot, however, is sent across the bows of those who make too sharp a distinction between the scientific understanding necessary for personal needs and the science required for specialisation at a higher level. One should look more deeply at the place of scientific knowledge in the general education of all. As Donnelly argued:

> The central argument for the position of science at the core of a statutory curriculum lies in introducing children to *science as our best available account of the world, understood materialistically* (that is, to scientific knowledge). Such substantive scientific knowledge is frequently described, disparagingly, as 'facts' and 'content'.
>
> (Donnelly, 2005)

That sentiment was strongly re-iterated by Sir Martin Rees: 'It is a cultural deprivation not to appreciate the wonderful panorama offered by modern cosmology, DNA and Darwinian evolution . . . [these] should be part of global culture' (*Guardian*, 19 September 2011).

The curriculum, therefore, is the connection of this framework of ideas (identified by those who are proven experts in the respective scientific disciplines) with the pedagogic skills of the teacher who constantly tests out ways in which the young people might be introduced to those ideas at different levels of difficulty.

Can everyone be a mathematician?

Two recent reports from the Advisory Committee on Mathematics Education begin their curriculum thinking with an identification of needs – the 'bottom-up' approach of identifying the needs of all learners to engage successfully in their lessons, and the top-down approach of identifying the needs of higher education and employers. The two approaches are interesting because very often the problems are seen exclusively in the top-down approach, thereby failing to involve so many young people who become disengaged.

Let us start with the 'bottom-up' approach. According to the first report on the needs of the learner:

> By the end of the secondary school, learners' perceptions of mathematics are often closed tasks and correct answers. They show increasing negativity towards mathematics, and associate their failures in the subject with low self-worth, even though they show an increasing understanding of the importance of the subject for their futures.
>
> (ACME, 2011a: 8)

However, a range of methods, which show the open-endedness of mathematical enquiry, its functional use and its application to the real world (for example, 'bringing abstract ideas into the manipulable world'), increases motivation and engagement even of those deemed low-attaining (Watson and De Geest, 2008; QCDA, 2010; Drake, 2011). On the other hand, such emphasis on enquiry, function and use in the real world does not diminish the essential importance of the framework of ideas which makes this distinctively mathematical thinking. The curriculum requires a mapping of the 'big mathematical ideas' and the progression from the early and limited grasp of these to the later and more abstract grasp and application of them. The early ideas of 'large and small', of 'relative size' or of 'correspondence between quantities', employed in everyday life, can be refined gradually into the key ideas of multiplication and division, and later into complex ideas of measurements or into the manipulations in algebra. We are back to Bruner's spiral curriculum.

Let us turn to the top-down approach. What mathematics is needed in higher education or the workplace? A range of courses in higher education require an understanding of mathematics. These are taken by roughly 40 per cent of undergraduates – in the sciences and in some of the social sciences, including, for example, economics, criminology and psychology. But 'during the last 20 years, concern has been expressed about the inadequacy of the mathematics skills possessed by undergraduates' (ACME, 2011b: 15). There is a lack of deep understanding of those key ideas which enable the learner to understand the physical and social world from a distinctively mathematical point of view – for example, through mathematical modelling and elementary probability. Thus higher education should be partnered with school and college teachers in identifying those key ideas, modes of inquiry and skills (as used to be the case), which provide the framework for the curriculum and for the assessment of learners' achievements.

Similarly in the preparation for the world of work. Obviously for higher level jobs, the university degree is crucial. But many non-degree level jobs require a mathematical understanding, if only to interpret the instructions from above. The ACME report gives many examples.

Therefore, we have this dual problem: at the lower end of the ability range, a large group of learners who do not enter into the world of mathematics at all, and, at the higher level, those who are demonstrably competent (they do well in their examinations) but who are without the understanding required for their higher studies or for the problems arising at work.

The solution lies, first, in agreement on that framework of ideas – the 'map of the territory' bequeathed to us by previous explorers – and, second, in the connection between that and the early and embryonic understandings of the young learner, dominated no doubt by the need for relevance, interest, functionality and application to the world he or she understands. The art of the teacher lies in that of inhabiting both these worlds and making a bridge between them. That is at the heart of curriculum and its development. It is not something to be delivered.

Why should Design and Technology be a 'Cinderella subject'?

It remains a mystery how and why the practical know-how, described in Chapter 7, is treated with such disdain – not part, for instance, of the latest proposals for the Baccalaureate. In China, conscious of the needs of industrial expansion, the equivalent of D&T is compulsory for all young people up to their school leaving. It is impossible to understand the nineteenth-century dominance by Britain of industrial innovation without reference to the genius of the many who had little formal education but who demonstrated an understanding of the material world through practical engagement with it (see Dyson, 2010).

Sir James Dyson, highly successful industrial designer, puts the problem well.

> It took me years to realise that DT was my subject, because at my school 'woodwork', as we called it, was for thickos, and I was a bright boy, so the assumption was that I wouldn't be interested in it. This is the perception I am fighting to change – because if DT had had the profile it deserves back then, I'd have cottoned on to it a lot sooner than I eventually did.
>
> (quoted in *Guardian*, 14 June 2011)

Several attempts have been made to ensure that D&T, in various forms, is recognised as an essential part of *education for all*. A memorable one in England and Wales was the launch of the Technical and Vocational Education Initiative (TVEI) by Prime Minister Margaret Thatcher in 1982 'in response to growing concern about existing arrangements for technical and vocational education for young people expressed over many years, not least by the National Economic Development Council' (quoted in Dale *et al.*, 1990: 12).

TVEI was piloted and extended under the control and direction of the then Manpower Services Commission (MSC), but fell victim to yet more bureaucratic change when the MSC was disbanded and the National Curriculum established in 1988. For a brief period it was highly popular and flourished in schools and colleges. Why was this?

There are three reasons. First, there should be closer relation between what is learnt in school and the skills and dispositions that are needed economically. Second, a form of learning based on doing and making and technical know-how is an important ingredient in general *education for all*, where mathematics and science are fused together in practical problem-solving. Third, its curriculum model was precisely what is argued for in this chapter, namely, that of a broad framework of principles applied by teachers within the context of local needs and possibilities. 'Curriculum' was not a list of specific outcomes to be 'delivered' but the creative attempts by teachers, working in partnership with employers and trainers, to make concrete the general educational principles of TVEI.

Such initiatives, however, are not dead, albeit lacking the formal backing of government bureaucracy. A new initiative by the James Dyson Foundation has established a network of 'DT Ambassadors' who spend time in businesses to see how their subject can develop the knowledge and skills that their industries require.

Arts and humanities

Chapter 7, in promoting a 'wider vision of learning', gave examples of the role that the arts and the humanities might play for all young people, and indeed for engaging those who might well have been turned off formal education. The argument is persuasively put in Ken Robinson's 1999 report *All Our Futures: Creativity, Culture and Education*. The arts (dance, music, drama, poetry, painting) intensify our aesthetic appreciation of experience, revealing significance in them previously unrecognised, and increasing sensibility. They get at parts of the brain too often untouched by so-called academic education. They bring alive an interest where previously there was a sense of boredom. They relate to the interests and experience of all young people. They cannot be classified in the crude duality of 'academic' and 'vocational'. (The aesthetic is the opposite of anaesthetic which puts you to sleep.)

In similar fashion Elliot Eisner strongly argues for the distinctive cognitive understanding of experience provided by the arts – an understanding of reality which is different from that expressed in propositions and measurements. They embody a distinct 'realm of meaning'. 'The interaction of the senses enriches meaning. The arts are not mere diversions from the important business of education; they are essential resources' (Eisner, 1986: 67).

This is not the place to enter into a long account of the curriculum content of the arts and humanities. Just the opposite, in fact, because here *par excellence* we have an example of the curriculum as, on the one hand, a broad framework of principles and key works on which the teacher might draw, and as, on the other hand, a 'laboratory' where the teacher (skilled and knowledgeable in the arts) tests ways in which the learners are enabled to appreciate and to find meaning in them. Each teacher of the arts will do this differently. No directions, thank you, from central 'creators of curriculum'. The artistic achievements we have inherited are, in the words of Eisner, the 'essential resources' upon which the knowledgeable arts teacher draws.

Similarly with the humanities. The traditions of literature, history, geography, social studies and religious understanding, through which we have been enlightened on what it means to be human, become the resources on which the learners might address matters of deep concern. This was illustrated by the HCP, already referred to (Stenhouse, 1975: *passim*).

However, there is a danger, in so understanding the curriculum, of neglecting the need for the initiation into the distinctive mode of thinking and inquiring as that is embodied in subjects. An interesting case is that of history. Is the study of history important in a general *education for all*? If so, to what extent should there be a detailed specification of what all young people should study and know? Who is to define the great events in the past with which everyone should be familiar? Different people, in positions of power, seek to dictate the history content that should be taught. Should we in England be concerned that in 2010 more than 100 state secondary schools entered no students for history in the GCSE; that students in independent schools are twice as likely to study history at GCSE; that England is the only country in Europe that does not make history compulsory post-14, or that 30 per cent of comprehensive schools spend less than one hour per week on history up to the age of 13? There may well be different periods and aspects of history which the teacher chooses to focus on, but at least (so it is argued – see *Education Guardian*, 29 March 2011) they need to be able to place what they focus on within a coherent long-term narrative. That could well be part of the requirements embodied in the statement of general principles.

Interim conclusion

The above four examples (from science, mathematics, D&T, and the arts and humanities) are not to be seen necessarily as subjects on the curriculum. Rather, they are what Phenix referred to as 'realms of meaning' through which we view and understand experience. *Education for all* requires all young people to enter these realms. The curriculum is the place where the teacher communicates the riches of those different realms to the learners who are struggling to understand the world they are living in. However, in order to penetrate deeply those different realms, it surely is necessary to find time to focus on the key ideas and modes of enquiry that constitute the different realms of meaning – and that is why we need subjects.

On the other hand, be wary. There are many problems we need to address in life which 'an educated person' should have thought about seriously – problems to do with environmental pollution, climate change, racial and gender discrimination, democratic participation, increasing poverty side by side with increasing wealth. The answers to such problems require an integration of different forms of thinking, as well as deliberation within moral traditions. They need to take seriously the experience of all learners and the opportunity to reflect critically on that experience. Not all learning can fit comfortably within a curriculum framework made up almost exclusively of distinct subjects. Learning to be a good citizen may indeed benefit from a historical perspective – the rough and stony path, for example, whereby we have reached our understanding of democratic governance. But it requires, too, the sort of learning that arises from participation in a just and democratic community. Kohlberg's 'just community school' was a reaction to the failure of moral thinking by itself to transform moral behaviour (Kohlberg, 1982). Some schools, therefore, widen their curriculum framework to include such communal involvement. For example, Phoenix High School, serving an economically disadvantaged area of south London, presents ways in which the students are able to address real problems (such as the prevailing gang culture), to effect change within their communities and to have their ideas tested and interrogated.

Conclusion: curriculum framework rather than a national curriculum

Curriculum is too often confused with a detailed list of objectives, content, means for attaining those objectives, and assessment as to whether those objectives have been reached. Such a model (and the National Curriculum was an example) is attractive to governments which wish to control what is learnt. Hence, there is the widespread development of the science of 'deliverology' and the identification of teachers as 'deliverers' of the curriculum.

My argument is that such a model has little to do with how people learn or with the nature of that which has to be learnt. It embodies a mistaken theory of learning and a mistaken theory of knowledge.

Instead of a detailed curriculum there should be an agreed 'curriculum framework' which sets out the ideal of a *general education for all*.

That would include the different 'realms of experience' which all young people should be enabled to enter into at different levels of understanding. Such a framework would spell out the key ideas and modes of enquiry, based upon what we know from the traditions of enquiry we have inherited and from their constant refinement within the on-going 'conversation between the generations'. Neuroscience, for example, poses new questions that were not asked a generation ago. Biochemistry brings together two distinct disciplines and so enables us to pursue new questions about the environment.

It would include, too, those practical capabilities through which we are connected with the material world, not just in a dispassionate and abstract sense, but as acting and creating within it.

Furthermore, communication skills, including the use of technology, transcend subject boundaries but are essential for personal, intellectual and moral growth. Who now refers to the Bullock Report *Language for Life*? Though published in 1975, it is as valid today as it was then in its criticism of a narrow view of language development, neglecting the oral skills of communication and not recognising the power of language to transform the society in which we live (Bullock Report, 1975: ch. 10).

However, within such a broad framework of ideas, the curriculum becomes the creation by the teachers who, on the one hand, are knowledgeable within the respective disciplines of enquiry and, on the other hand, are experts in pedagogy – or the different ways in which the learners might enter into and value these different forms of understanding and enquiring. As Stenhouse said, 'there is no curriculum development without teacher development'.

To this, therefore, we must turn.

11 Bring back teaching

Introduction

> I owe Mr. Fazackerly – the D and T technician at my school – a huge debt of
> gratitude. Without his help and enthusiasm, I would never have got started.

These are the words of the UK finalist, no less, for the Dyson Award in 2010. He
had been a student at a comprehensive school and not been seen to be academically
gifted. But he valued the school's well-equipped D&T department. By 15 he was
competent to use the equipment in all the workshops. Leaving school at 16, he
studied Industrial Design at the Royal College of Arts and then at Imperial College
where he gained a double masters. The Design Award was gained for an ingenious
set of recyclable wheels and handles used for moving heavy objects.

There are countless examples of where the insight of a teacher opened up a
different world to the learner, and whose expertise enabled that learner to enter that
world, to succeed (indeed to do brilliantly) and to find fulfilment in it. That requires
not only pedagogical skill on the part of the teacher, but also an educational vision
of the kind of learning which too often (as illustrated in the last chapter) is treated
with disdain – not to be part, for example, of the new English Baccalaureate.

But what is a good teacher? Much has been written about teaching – pedagogical
skills, knowledge of the subject matter, moral qualities of care for the pupils, insight
into ways in which pupils are motivated. Yet Gabriel Moran claims that all these
together do not get at the essence of being a teacher. In the introduction to his
book, *Speaking of Teaching: Lessons from History,* he asks

> Why is there almost no discussion of the activity of teaching in works of
> philosophy and education? Why does the topic of teaching seem to be avoided?
> My question may seem preposterous. Are there not libraries filled with books
> on teaching? . . . What is seldom asked is: What does it mean to teach? What
> is the meaning of the word 'to teach'?
>
> (Moran, 2008: vii)

In some respects Moran is wrong. Paul Hirst asked precisely that question in
1971 (see Hirst, 1974b). But in another sense, for reasons I shall explain, he is right.
Moran's question needs to be asked again and again, just as questions about the

aims of education remain of perennial interest. Our understanding of teaching is tied to our understanding of education and its aims. *Lessons from history* show how differences about the aims of education are reflected in different understandings of what it means to teach.

A conceptual interlude

Hirst gave a useful conceptual analysis of what it means to teach (as opposed, say, to social working or to keeping the children happy). Such an analysis of teaching has to accommodate many different activities which, on the surface, do not look alike. What brings these diverse activities together as *teaching* activities is the intention to get the students to learn something. Therefore, teaching consists in taking the appropriate steps for the student to learn x (e.g. 'osmosis' or 'democracy'), and that in turn means respecting, first, the nature of x (e.g. the logical aspect of thinking biologically) and, second, the ability and motivation of the learner (the psychological aspect of learning x). (See p. 105 for an explanation of the distinction between the logical and psychological aspects of learning.)

This might seem trivial, but it is worth pondering. It is interesting to note that university teachers are called 'lecturers', as though lecturing is a kind of teaching. But is it necessarily so? Take, for example, the lecturer who year after year reads her lecture notes to obedient audiences of undergraduates. Is she teaching? No account is taken of the learners, of their readiness to understand, of their previous experience with which to connect her words of wisdom. She is lecturing but not teaching. Or take the teacher who is given a class in biology even though he understands nothing of the subject. Teaching notes are downloaded from the internet and followed but without any understanding. Key ideas are to him mere words. Queries from the learners are responded to with encouragement to find out for themselves. No doubt in so doing the teacher is demonstrating praiseworthy skills. But he surely is not teaching. There needs to be a connection between what the teacher does and says (intentionally) and the learning that is achieved by the pupil.

The teacher, therefore, has to have a range of expertise: first, the subject knowledge which is to be 'imparted'; second, an understanding of the learners (how they best learn and are motivated); third, the pedagogical skills to bridge the gap between that subject knowledge and the present understanding and motivation of the learner.

All that is a purely conceptual point, but there remain important differences between how teaching is understood. These arise not just from the 'grammar of the word', but from their roots in different educational traditions, and are to be examined and criticised within those traditions. Some traditions seem non-educational – indeed the very antithesis of what education is about. Other traditions place the teacher on a pedestal – as the custodian of what is worthwhile in a culturally hostile world.

Where one stands with regard to this concept of teaching profoundly affects our hope or despair in promoting *education for all*. Let me illustrate this in the next four sections.

Teachers as deliverers

The tone was set in England by the Labour Government's White Paper, *21st Century Schools: Your Child, Your Schools, Our Future*. As Beverley Hughes, the Children's Minister, declared: 'It is fundamentally a deep cultural change. It is about changing boundaries of professional behaviour and thinking in a completely different way' (DCSF, 2008).

So, what are the clues to the 'deep cultural change' which creates new 'boundaries of professional behaviour'? The language gives the clue. 'Performance' and 'performing' are mentioned 121 times, 'outcomes' 55 times, 'delivery' 57 times. Libraries get no mention in the twenty-first-century schools, and books only one – in the section on IT. The following statement sums it up perfectly. 'It is only the workforce who can deliver our ambition of improved outcomes' (see Warwick Mansell, *TES*, 17 June 2008).

So, the teacher (or 'the workforce') is a 'deliverer of improved outcomes' or a trainer of those who have to hit targets – not the thinker of what those outcomes might be. Here we are back to 'the logic of action' (see Chapter 3) – expertise in what is the most likely means of delivering outcomes which are decided elsewhere. As Peter Abbs so well describes the situation we are in, 'teachers become the technicians of subjects, not the critical guardians of a long culture; nor the midwives of the creative potentialities of living children' (Abbs, 1994: 4).

Indeed, teachers become redundant as information technology systems 'deliver the product' more cheaply and effectively. To repeat the reference to Rupert Murdoch, 'You can get by with half as many teachers by using his computers' (*Private Eye*, no. 1294, 5 August 2011, p. 5).

Such a conception of teaching prevails in many schools, is taught in school management or leadership courses and shapes how many teachers see their professional role. The word and its meaning have been subsumed under an impoverished language of 'delivery', reflecting a different and mis-educational framework. But it was not always so. Nor need it remain.

Teachers as guardians of a culture

I want to contrast this narrow 'technician' understanding of teaching with a very different one.

> The teacher, particularly the teacher dedicated to liberal education, must constantly try *to look toward the goal of human completeness* and back at the natures of his students here and now, ever seeking to understand the former and to assess the capacities of the latter to approach it . . . The teacher's standpoint is not arbitrary. It is neither simply dependent on what students think they want . . . nor is it imposed on him by the demands of a particular society or the vagaries of the market . . . He is, willy-nilly, guided by the awareness, or the divination, that there is a human nature, and that assisting its fulfilment is his task.
>
> (Bloom, 1987: 19; author's italics)

The teacher within this tradition is not the 'deliverer' of government or business directives, but is the *custodian* (often in opposition to such directives) of the values, embedded in the culture we have inherited, through which we have a vision of 'human completeness'. The teacher is there to preserve and pass on that vision of human achievement in knowledge, understanding, aesthetic appreciation, and practical creativity. In the words of Oakeshott, 'man [*sic*] is what he learns to become: this is the human condition' (Oakeshott, 1975: 17). And that 'learning to become' is achieved through coming to appreciate the voice of poetry, the voice of science, the voice of philosophy.

This distinctive moral perspective of teaching is illustrated in the work of a teacher, Fiedl Brandejs. Visitors to Prague should enter the ancient synagogue, now a museum to the victims of the Holocaust. They will see some remarkable poetry and paintings of children aged 10–16, very few of whom were to survive. The children had been deported to Terezina, a garrison town about 50 kilometres from Prague. The conditions were appalling, and there was a daily coming and going of prisoners – to destinations that could only be guessed at. Fiedl Brandejs managed to keep the children together in a makeshift schoolroom. A brilliant art teacher, she insisted upon high standards of technique, perspective, use of colour. Art had standards, and these had to be rigidly applied. These children saw what the adults did not see – butterflies outside the windows, rainbows in the sky, green fields beyond the gates, merry-go-rounds on which children played, dinner tables for family and friends, autumn leaves blown by the wind. On the other hand, their poetry gave a different picture – fear, sadness, unbelief at the inhumanity of their conditions (see Jewish Museum Prague, 1993).

The human spirit grew through their poetry and painting. These embodied that struggle to make sense of their situation and their lives. That was made possible by a teacher who did not see herself to be doing anything other than being a teacher. She was, through the medium of the arts, enabling those young people to make sense, to refine their feelings, to embody the human emotions of hope and sadness, love and fear. She remained an educator to the very end, and this educative achievement was extended to all. There were no grades for the best poem or painting. There were none rejected as ineducable. Each person's work was a struggle to understand, helped by a teacher who was able to draw upon the resources of art and poetry at her command.

Remember, once again, the words, given in Chapter 1, of the high school principal in her letter to the newly appointed teachers in her school: 'My request is: Help your students become human. . . . Reading, writing, arithmetic are important but only if they serve to make our children more human.'

This distinctively moral role of the teacher is crucial in a liberal society, supporting a critical tradition based on evidence and argument, whereby young learners might be liberated from those powerful forces (politicians, snake-oil sellers, profiteers). Yet one sees this role gradually eroded in an impoverished concept of teaching, even in a government 2010 White Paper entitled *The Importance of Teaching*.

Teachers as curriculum thinkers (not deliverers)

Not long ago, though no longer in the bureaucratic memory, this vision of teachers as the creators, not deliverers, of the curriculum prevailed. The raising of the school-leaving age from 15 to 16 in 1971 with a view to a 'general education for all' required radical rethinking of what education was for. That rethinking required a partnership between teachers and the wider community. For that purpose, the Schools Council was established. As the civil servant, Derek Morrell, the first Secretary of the Schools Council, argued in his Joseph Payne Memorial Lecture, reflecting upon the need for such a Council,

> Education has become much more than a system for maintaining an elite from one generation to another, or for conferring status on those who seek, or are lucky enough, to be educated beyond basic literacy and numeracy. We now consider that our educational purposes include the development of individuals to their full potential: increasing the amount of talent available within the community: the development of intelligence, quality in personal relationships, and indeed in the whole life of our society.
>
> (Morrell, 1966: 7)

To this end, Morrell argued for links between what schools offer and the communities of experience (home, neighbourhood, local occupational groups) from which the learners come. This should meet the 'urgent demand for help in thinking about the nature of the human condition, and the purpose of life itself' (ibid.: 9). That, for Morrell, meant shifting the curriculum emphasis from the *impersonal* to the *personal*. The classroom thus becomes a place where this dialogue takes place between the learner (trying to make sense of experience) and the teachers (with a deeper and wider cultural understanding) – where, in the light of that inherited wisdom within literature, the arts or sciences, the teacher 'shares his humanity' with the pupils.

A new and distinctive role of the teacher, in this response to social change and to the pursuit of *education for all*, was the central concern of the Schools Council. Teachers should no longer be seen as 'deliverers of the curriculum' or 'the transmitters of knowledge', but the mediators of the best of what we have inherited in our understanding of the human condition (through the arts and humanities, through sciences and mathematics, through moral and religious traditions). School teachers need to have not only a deep understanding of those different traditions but also the pedagogical skills to relate them to the modes of understanding, experiences and concerns of the learners themselves. To that end, it was seen necessary to 'consider the role of the teacher in relation to the actual conduct of research . . . problem solving research, shading into development work' (ibid.: 22).

Morrell's vision required of the teachers an active role in curriculum development. This, in turn, required knowledge of the subject or practice to be taught, respect for the experiences and concerns of the learners, exploration with other teachers of pedagogy and shared systematic enquiry into problems faced. There flourished for a decade or so, mainly in the many Teachers' Centres sponsored by the Schools Council, research-based curriculum development in the humanities, the arts, sciences, technology and mathematics – the HCP, Nuffield Sciences, Geography for the Young School Leaver, Design and Technology, and many others. It was a period when teachers were in the driving seat, where development depended on their research and cooperation.

Few in England have now heard of the Bullock Report, *Language for Life*. Much of it was influenced by the work of James Britton and his colleagues at the London Institute of Education (Britton, 1970). It was a call to teachers of English to see the indispensable role of language for young people as they come to understand themselves and the society in which they are growing up. The emphasis on speaking and listening (where 'the pupils' own exploratory talk has much more scope') stands out starkly in the world where academic prowess is assessed almost entirely in the capacity to write. The National Association of Teachers of English became missionary in the promotion of social understanding through the medium of English – spoken as well as written, listening as well as speaking. There was a deep commitment to *education for all*, to 'pupil talk as a valuable means of learning' and to the teacher as the key agent in that mission (Bullock Report, 1975: 189).

Teacher as creators of a democratic social order

Much of what is said above would have Dewey nodding in agreement. But there was something distinctive about Dewey's understanding of educational aims which translated into a distinctive concept of teaching. Being a member of a community, and learning how to contribute usefully to it, were the essence of being human – and thus the criticism of a schooling which, far from contributing to community cohesion, militated against it. Dewey's most comprehensive educational writing was called, significantly, *Democracy and Education*. There he refers to 'education' as 'a social function, securing direction and development in the immature through their participation in the life of the group to which they belong' (Dewey, 1916: 81).

It was an essential task, therefore, for teachers to create a community within the school where teachers and students could grow through working with others and through learning to take account of the beliefs of other people. Segregation from people of different backgrounds was the very antithesis of education. And the development of a sense of community within the school would gradually extend beyond the school and into a sense of citizenship.

This emphasis on teaching as an essential component in the development of a democratic order reflected the social and economic conditions of the time. Thousands of immigrants from all over the world were arriving in the United States from different economic, ethnic and social backgrounds. The common school had a key part to play in developing from such disparate communities a common culture and mode of understanding. For Dewey, 'education is the fundamental method of social progress and reform' (Dewey, 1897: 32) and, indeed, in one extravagant moment he described the teacher as 'the true prophet and usherer in of the kingdom of God' (quoted in Moran, 2008: 69).

Kohlberg saw that no amount of exercises in moral reasoning (whereby the learners would reach a cognitively higher level of moral judgement) would lead to better or changed behaviour. That integration of thinking and doing required the appropriate moral ethos. Personal virtues are nurtured in virtuous communities. It was in Dewey's democratically run community school that Kohlberg found inspiration for his own 'Just Community Schools'.

> In summary, the current demand for moral education is a demand that our society becomes more of a just society. If our society is to become a more just community, it needs democratic schools. This was the demand and dream of John Dewey.
>
> (Kohlberg, 1982: 24)

This particular understanding of teaching – its essential duty in preparing young people for a democratic social order – stands in stark contrast with one in which the teacher focuses mainly or exclusively on the personal good, individual achievement or government-dictated targets. It would treat with abhorrence the current managerial practice of concentrating on borderline cases in national tests in order to raise the profile of the school.

A profession or an unexpected proletariat in the new technocracy?

The 'new proletariat' referred to by Abbs (1994: 6) is the modernised teaching profession, reshaped to *deliver* the curriculum and to be assessed in terms of productivity, where the product is the measurable output. If there is to be *education for all*, teaching needs to be reclaimed from performance management and seen as the way in which a new generation is introduced to those cultural resources that enable them to live life more fully and to contribute to the wider community of which they are to be part. With a wider vision of learning, that ideal can and should be extended to all young people. The teacher is the key person in this, the custodian of that which is worth learning and the agent of social reform through the distinctive values of the school.

Until the 1970s, Her Majesty's Inspectorate (HMI) was fiercely independent of politicians and government. No minister, not even the prime, would dare to speak about education without the script being approved by the Chief Inspector. HMI, through their carefully gathered evidence from around the country ('the ears and eyes of the Minister'), protected the independence of the profession.

By 'profession' I mean four things: first, a body of people with its own distinctive expertise and knowledge-base, gained from training, education, experience and continuing professional development; second, independence of judgement based on that expertise – fiercely critical of interventions that diminish the lives of those they serve; third, an ethical position in which service given to 'clients' is based on the interests of the client, not on personal profit; fourth, a collective voice on matters of concern to the profession, reflecting that independence of judgement.

In the recently attempted 'reforms' of the National Health Service in Britain, we have seen that independent and critical voice through such professional bodies as the British Medical Association and the Royal College of Nurses, based on their considerable expertise and experience. Within the educational service, which is being transformed equally radically (hence the title of this book), such a voice is deafeningly silent. There are not the equivalent representative and professional bodies to resist the political pressures to deliver what the government dictates.

Is teaching a profession? There is the distinctive expertise. There is, too, in the vast majority of teachers, a service to the learners which is not shaped by the prospects of personal profit. But there is no collective voice. The Teaching Council Act in 2001 established a council to set and maintain the highest professional standards in the interests of the teachers, students, their parents and the wider school community, and have a code of professional conduct. Ten years later, that has been abolished.

Furthermore, the independence of judgement is forever dismissed by government and its servants, whether that be on the correct way to teach reading, on curriculum content, on assessment and testing regimes or on qualifications structure. A large-scale survey of teachers in the summer of 2011 showed that just over half the sample had thought of leaving teaching, of whom 60 per cent referred to excessive government interference in schools as the reason and 90 per cent complained of teacher bullying by senior management, parents, students or colleagues (*Guardian Teacher Network Survey*, 4 October 2011).

> If there is a single message that sings out loud and clear, it is a plea from teachers to be treated as professionals, rather than infantilised by short-termist government and political philosophies.
>
> (Berliner, 2011)

Therefore, the meaning of teaching which needs to be reclaimed is that of an 'educator' and professional. The key characteristics of such a teacher are:

- understanding and love of that which is to be taught – the subject matter, craft skills, ideals and virtues;
- understanding of the different ways in which young people learn, are motivated, have aspirations, are influenced and become disengaged;
- pedagogical expertise to bridge the gap between the subject or craft knowledge of the teacher and the level of understanding and motivation of the learner;
- ethical disposition to serve the best interests of the learner.

Such a teacher is demeaned where he or she is required to *train* young learners into doing well at tests, hitting targets and meeting government demands unrelated to defensible educational aims, or where it is assumed that better performance will depend on better rewards. And the profession is demeaned where appointments are made to 'headship' of people who have never taught but evidently have good management skills gained from business – chief executives, no longer head *teachers*.

Preparation of teachers

In England, though not in Wales, there are presently two different qualifications for teaching. One is the QTS for teaching in schools. The other is QTLS for teaching in further education. Such a distinction makes less sense as schools and colleges teach the same young people in the many partnerships that have been created and as schools, pursuing a wider vision of learning, need teachers who have the background and skills normally found in colleges of further education. Clearly there is a need for one profession and a single qualification across schools and further education. The present two-tier system stands in the way of the wider vision of learning required if there is to be secondary education for all.

There is an obstacle. Having a degree is a requisite for qualified teaching status. Further education, by contrast, employs over 25,000 instructors who have no degree but the necessary vocational qualifications and experience. Surely we must not be so hung up on degrees that we cannot recognise the equally rigorous practical training which has led to such qualifications. Equivalences between university degrees and high-level vocational qualifications plus relevant experience must be recognised for teaching purposes if young people are not to be deprived of the kind of teaching essential for secondary education for all.

Preparation for teaching cannot be adequately covered in the initial training. Experience and the systematic reflection on experience are crucial. Therefore, the reclamation of teaching from being mere trainers and deliverers requires systematic professional development, organised by teachers themselves or through their professional associations such as the Historical or Geographical Association. But the teachers, not government or its quangos, are best placed to know what professional development is needed. To that end it is important for teachers to be able to work together, to imagine ways forward together and, together, to test out the results of their thinking. Professional development most effectively arises from the teachers themselves. Once, such mutually supportive professional development was assisted in England by a network of Teachers' Centres. Now, no longer.

And the role of higher education in all this?

There has long been a suspicion amongst politicians that education departments in higher education have been part of the perceived problem – promoting child-centred views in the 1960s and 1970s, teaching theory disconnected from practice, engaged in research which had little or no impact. Therefore, we are presently seeing a shift away from higher education in the initial training of teachers. In England, at the time of publication, there will be 100 designated 'teaching schools'. Eventually there will be 500. Teaching schools will work in partnership with other schools both for initial training and for continuing professional development. But beware – the present introduction of 'Teach First', imported from the United States, will enable the government to control teacher training directly. Is that what we want?

Although these teaching schools have university partners, they are in the driving seat, and courses in universities are closing down. Is this a good thing?

Where teaching is seen as a craft, then certainly much of the preparation needs to be at the 'chalk-face', not in the university halls. But teaching is more than a craft.

It embodies a vision of what is worthwhile. It therefore requires a constant questioning of that vision in the light of the social context of the learners, of knowledge of the subject matter, and of critical appraisal of the underlying aims of the system and school. If higher education does not retreat into ivory towers, it can and should contribute to those teacher- and school-based deliberations.

The Oxford University Internship Scheme pioneered school/university partnerships in the initial training of teachers. It was based on a profound respect for the experience and craft knowledge of teachers and in effect turned the schools into what are now referred to as 'teaching schools'. The university role was a humble but major one, namely, to train the mentors in the schools, to provide the framework in which the professional tutors and the subject specialists in the schools could meet together, and to ensure the critical and wider perspective gained from a research tradition (see Benton, 1990).

It may well be that, in 'bringing back teaching', this might be the model for the future.

Conclusion: bring back teaching

Teachers are vital to the preservation of what is essential to civilised living and to our understanding of what it means to be human – in a world which too often is inhuman and diminishes the dignity of the most vulnerable. Secondary education for all depends on the capacity of the teaching profession to question what this means for all – those presently disengaged and disadvantaged as well as those motivated and able. To this end, the following are essential.

First, teachers should be respected as professionals, freed from ever-increasing government interference in curriculum and pedagogy, and thus, as in the health services and professions, have an agreed professional body with a representative voice on educational matters.

Second, there should be established a national forum in which the teaching profession can address the values, aims, curriculum, qualifications, etc. in the light of professional experience, teacher-based research and research evidence. Bring back the Schools Council – or nearly.

Third, there should be a united profession with a single qualification for schools and further education.

Fourth, continuing professional development should be part of the teaching contract, but organised by teachers, located in Teachers' Centres, shared across schools and colleges, and research-based.

Fifth, the language of teachers as 'deliverers' should be banned.

12 Testing, testing, testing
The death of education

Campbell's Law

Campbell's law stipulates that 'the more any quantitative social indicator is used for social decision-making, the more subject it will be to corruption pressures and the more apt it will be to distort and corrupt the social processes it was intended to monitor'. Campbell warned us of the inevitable problems associated with undue weight and emphasis on a single indicator for monitoring complex social phenomena. In effect, he warned us about the high-stakes testing program that is part and parcel of *No Child Left Behind*.

(Berliner and Nichols, 2007)

The above quote referred to the USA. But the takeover of education by the testing industry is becoming universal. Achieving high scores in tests becomes increasingly important for schools and national systems because of the consequences of the comparisons made within the growing number of league tables. Unfortunately, those who run our educational systems have not heard of Campbell's Law.

Testing, testing, testing – a case of Campbell's Law

England provides an exemplary case. But the lessons from it (the distorted vision of education emerging from the testing industry) are of universal significance. Therefore, the message to everyone is 'Beware'.

Prior to 1988, there was no public testing apart from national examinations, normally taken at 16 at the completion of compulsory schooling and at 18 for a minority who, in the main, wished to progress to higher education. However, all this changed in the 1980s. English children are now possibly the most examined and tested in the world. Why did this happen? Why were the examinations at the end of compulsory schooling, and at 18 not sufficient?

A bit of history

The post-war settlement, following the 1944 Education Act, put teachers firmly in charge of the curriculum and teaching. Ministers had no powers in that regard.

They were not allowed to penetrate what the Minister, David Eccles, referred to as the 'secret guardian of the curriculum'. But there was growing disquiet about standards (as reflected in national comparisons) and about readiness to progress into employment and higher education – especially as there were fewer opportunities for unskilled workers. These concerns found outlets through many channels, both official and unofficial, as shown in Chapter 2. However, the nail in the coffin of teacher autonomy was the 'William Tyndale affair' – the school which became infamous for its extreme 'child-centred approaches'. This became the subject of the Auld Report (1976). It was increasingly felt within government that, in investing so much money in its schools, it needed to monitor how effective that investment was. Could the teachers be trusted? Were we really getting value for money?

The 1988 National Reform Act ushered in a National Curriculum which provided the pegs on which to hang national assessment in ten subjects at three 'key stages' (KS), namely, ages 7, 11, 14. The final Key Stage (16) was covered by GCSE examinations. Very soon league tables appeared based on the results of Key Stage tests and of the results of GCSE and A Level examinations. At GCSE, only the core subjects counted in the tables – English, mathematics and science. In this way it was felt that the performance of the system as a whole could be assessed, improvement over time measured, and individual schools' progress (or regression) monitored. Weaknesses could be identified, remedial action instigated, good teachers rewarded, failing schools identified and either closed or spurred on to improve.

But that is only half the story. *Pre-vocational* courses were introduced in the 1970s, providing opportunities for 'applied learning' related to 'occupational sectors'. These were intended to be more relevant and motivating for those who were disengaged from the traditional academic pathway. Hence, City and Guilds of London (CGLI) 365 courses were introduced – superseded by the Certificate of Pre-Vocational Education (CPVE), superseded by the Diploma of Vocational Education (DOVE), superseded by the GNVQ, superseded in 2008 by the 14–19 Diplomas which, according to the DCSF, 'could become qualification of choice for young people' (DCSF Press Release, 23 October 2007). Well, not quite. Come a change of government, the Diplomas were, within a short period of three years, on their way out. At the same time there were the BTEC courses leading to National and Higher National Certificates.

It is important to remind those who feel they have followed the story so far that this is by no means all of it. Despite the plethora of examinations and tests and the constant 'reforms', many people ('stakeholders' as they are called) believed the right things were not being examined. Universities argued that the highest grade at A Level did not discriminate sufficiently for their purposes – hence, the introduction of an A* grade. A Level was criticised for going modular, with the opportunity to retake the AS modules if first time round assessment was unsatisfactory. Independent schools disliked the modular GCSEs and so the Awarding Body OCR introduced the IGCSE (International GCSE) which was linear rather than modular. 'A Level' was seen in some independent schools as a qualification for lower ability pupils (*TES Magazine*, 5 March 2011). They offered parallel qualifications –

International Baccalaureate (IB) and Cambridge Pre-U for the more able and the A Levels for the others. Mathematicians believed that those aspects of the subject that are valuable were not being tested, namely, problem solving and the opportunity to demonstrate reasoning ability. But also concern was expressed that, with three competing awarding bodies, any attempt to stiffen up the assessment would result in losing clients in a competitive market (*Mathematics Today*, December 2009).

Creating a unified framework

With such a vast array of examinations, tests and qualifications, it was felt necessary to create a framework which brought them all together. Indeed, given the globalisation of education and work, such a framework should, as far as possible, be within an even larger framework of international awards and equivalences. The 'industry' grew.

Such a National Qualification Framework (NQF) required *equivalences* between different awards. Then it would be possible to construct league tables not only on the basis of GCSEs and A Levels, but also on success in the 'equivalent' pre-vocational courses. For example, in 1997, the Intermediate GNVQ was deemed equivalent to four GCSEs graded A to C. Later, when the GNVQ disappeared, the BTEC Ordinary National Certificate and the new National 14–19 Diplomas were made 'equivalent' to four GCSEs. Hence, future league tables would be based not on GCSE results alone but on GCSE *equivalent* results – though 'equivalence' has rarely been mentioned when the percentage of young people obtaining GCSEs is published or when schools go shooting up the league table.

That opened the game to some interesting manoeuvres. One school, and others followed, saw the chance of gaining many more GCSEs through the 4 to 1 equivalence with GNVQs. One school's record improved rapidy to 100 per cent GCSE A to Cs by putting all learners in for the GNVQ Information Technology (equivalent to four GCSEs). The head teacher got a knighthood (Mansell, 2007: 116).

However, according to the Wolf Report, 'the perverse incentives created by performance measures combined with indiscriminate "equivalences" have resulted in large amounts of sub-standard education in which young people take courses that were in no sense truly vocational or useful' (Wolf Report, 2011).

But in what way can very different awards be regarded as equivalent – four GCSEs in engineering, physics, chemistry and mathematics, say, with a Diploma in Health and Social Care? The equivalence cannot be in subject matter. Is it in time spent or on the difficulty level? But that would be nonsensical. Difficulty level lies in the complexity of the concepts, in the skills needed, in the ability of the learner. Someone might find practical know-how easier than academic study. And, vice versa, the academically inclined might collapse when confronted with a practical or technical problem. To take an analogy, one cannot say which is better, an orange or a piece of meat. They are different. So much of the NQF was nonsense, distorting the monitoring of standards.

It gets worse. The NQF became the Qualifications and Credit Framework (QCF) in 2009, bringing together *all* vocational qualifications, including National Vocational Qualifications (NVQ). These differed from the pre-vocational in their relation to 'competence in the workplace', in measuring 'can do' in occupationally specific areas, and in recognising smaller steps of learning, thereby enabling students to build up qualifications bit by bit. Credits could accumulate over a long period. Therefore, grades inflated and 'equivalences' had to be renegotiated. Edexcel's Level 3 BTEC National Diploma in Health and Social Care under NQF became, under QCF, an 'Extended Diploma', equivalent to three A Levels. BTEC National Certificates became Diplomas, equivalent to two A Levels. BTEC National Awards became Subsidiary Diplomas, equivalent to one A Level. How could employers and university admission tutors digest all that? More seriously, many pupils were to take sub-standard qualifications as a result of the explosion in schools of the number of 14–18 vocationally related courses, with GCSE equivalences (rising from 1,882 in 2003 to 462,000 by 2010).

Moreover, at the whim of the Secretary of State, it can change again. Michael Gove declared that the standard for deciding between succeeding and failing schools, and for determining the place in the league tables, should now lie in the percentage of learners obtaining a new EBac – that is Grade C in six subjects of English, mathematics, two sciences, history or geography, and a language (which could include Latin), in place of the previous standard of five subjects (unspecified apart from mathematics and English). No reason was given why practical subjects such as D&T or the arts should be excluded from Mr Gove's idea of general education. 'Equivalences' between GCSE and pre-vocational qualifications were scrapped. Instantly schools seen to be good (even excellent) under the old criteria, became failing schools under the new. As the head teacher of a prestigious independent school remarked, referring to the omission of Edexcel's IGCSE from the EBac, 'government tables have always been misleading because they generally call for measures at the whim of Ministers, but this year they are downright silly' (*TES*, January 2011).

Consequences of such ministerial whim were immediately felt. Design and Technology, as has already been pointed out, is dropped by schools as they concentrate on subjects that raise their profile in league tables. The arts suffer also and musicians have launched a national campaign to persuade ministers of the importance of studying music at school – the arts being omitted from the EBac.

Much of this can only be described as tragic. False hopes were given to young people who were persuaded to pursue qualifications which have a life-span of two or three years. But no award has value which is as transient as the succession of these short-lived pre-vocational courses, not recognised by employers or higher education. What employer would know the value of a *curriculum vitae* which refers proudly to the CGLI 365 or CPVE or DOVE or GNVQ?

More important, however, for the present argument is the burgeoning testing industry, its 'corruption of social processes' which Campbell's Law predicted, and its detrimental impact on 'education for all'.

The corruption of social processes – the beginning

An industry has been created, exposed in great detail by Warwick Mansell (2007) in his book *Education by Numbers: the Tyranny of Testing*. Testing has swollen out of all proportion. Indeed, the examinations and testing referred to above are only part of the overall picture. So much hangs on the results of these tests as they appear in the public league tables (for example, parental choice, head teachers' pay, teachers' promotion, school closure, designation as Specialist Schools, even the occasional knighthood) that increasingly much time and effort is spent preparing students for them.

For example, the government introduced a 'National Strategy' for secondary schools, a main task of which was to improve the 'outputs' as measured on tests. Advisers were appointed from Capita to oversee the government's drive to improve standards. The *Invitation to Negotiate* (the contract that Capita won and which was part of the Public Service Agreement targets) stated the purpose of the National Strategies.

> The ultimate objective of the National Strategy is to make improvements in the practice of teaching and learning in the classroom, and through these improvements to raise pupils' attainments as measured by national curriculum tests. The central purpose of the contract [is] increasing the [test] attainment of pupils.
>
> (DfES, 2003, quoted in Mansell, 2007: 11)

To this end, the National Strategy provided a 328-page pamphlet with 'booster classes' aimed at those at age 14 who were seeking to reach Level 5 in English. This showed 'exactly how teachers should gear their teaching to the precise requirements of the tests' (Mansell, 2007: 59). It provided 14 areas of competence central to the marking scheme, the characteristics looked for at Level 5, the things to memorise crucial to the assessment. And this refers to but one particular group within one Key Stage in one subject!

The consequence has been a devotion to test practice. Typical of the many teachers interviewed by Mansell was the following:

> I don't feel my Year 9 have learnt anything of value this term. I have done practice reading papers, writing papers, targeted writing for writing papers, and put immense pressure on them.
>
> (ibid.: 59)

A London school curriculum 14–18 coordinator, with reference to Year 9, said:

> Most schools seem to be doing two to three mock tests per child before the real thing. Year 9 is totally dominated by test preparation.
>
> (ibid.: 58)

It is not surprising, therefore, that the Annual Report of the Chief Inspector of Schools said, with regard to Key Stage 3 in English,

> Many teachers spend too much time preparing pupils for the tests in most schools. The whole of the Spring Term, and often time before and after, is devoted to explicit test preparation, especially as to the set Shakespeare tests.
> (Ofsted, 2005)

But should not this be expected? As the Report of American National Research Council, 2011, declared,

> programs which impose sanctions and offer rewards on the basis of test results encourage teachers to teach to the test – originated in the debate started by *No Child Left Behind* which required students to pass a state-wide standardized test.

But what, after all, do the tests show? This is an important question to ask for two reasons – the costs incurred and the effect on the quality of learning.

Pause: What do the tests show?

First, is the cost worth it? Could not the money be better spent on teaching? As long ago as 2005 the annual cost of examinations and testing was £610 million – and that does not take into account the time spent by teachers preparing for the tests (PWC, 2005, referred to in Mansell, 2007: 3). The costs have risen since then – now in the region of £1 billion. Ofqual warned that the huge hike in costs cannot continue; there had been an 83 per cent increase in the exam fees paid by secondary schools between 2003 and 2009 (*TES*, 17 December 2010). In 2011 Ofqual reported that exam bills had doubled in seven years; £302 million had been spent by secondary schools in England in 2009/10, a rise from £154 million in 2002/3. This was almost twice the rate of schools' total running costs. Several schools spend much more than £100k per year. This is caused partly by modularisation, a larger number of re-sits, and increased variety of qualifications (Ofqual, 2012; *TES*, 27 May 2011).

Second, with regard to quality of learning, superficially the testing and examining would seem to have shown an incredible improvement in standards, frequently quoted by politicians who want to show success. Thus, the percentage 'progress' in Key Stages and in GCSE and A Level has been as shown in Table 12.1 (figures extrapolated from Mansell, 2007: 5).

But how far can one trust these statistics? To what extent is this a case of Campbell's Law: 'the more any quantitative social indicator is used for social decision-making, the more subject it will be to corruption pressures and the more apt it will be to distort and corrupt the social processes it was intended to monitor'?

Table 12.1 Percentage 'progress' in Key Stages and in GCSE and A Level

		1965	2006
GCSE grades A–C		20%	59%
A Level	A Grades	9%	24%
	Pass	69%	96%

		1995	2006
Key Stage 2	English	49%	79%
	Maths	45%	76%
	Science	70%	87%
Key Stage 3	English	55%	72%
	Maths	58%	77%
	Science	56%	72%

Corruption of the social processes – getting worse

The consequences of 'teaching to the test' have been noted several times in the course of this book – evidence from reports on mathematics, the sciences and chief inspectors. Exams might be passed, high scores on tests attained, progression up league tables ensured, but have the students learnt anything of value? Have they got a grasp of the key ideas and concepts upon which they can build further and deeper understanding?

The ways in which 'social processes', which testing was intended to monitor, get distorted, are several, recorded at length by Mansell.

First, the *Times Educational Supplement*'s on-line discussion forum every Spring gives examples from teachers worried about the pressure to 'distort the social processes', made possible through the importance of course work in the overall assessment. For example,

> I'm busy marking GCSE course work at the moment. I know full well that vast amount of it is cut-and-paste (some had even left hyperlinks) but I am going to have to pretend I have not noticed. If I failed this whole cohort, I would be in trouble, so I won't make waves, I'll go along with cheating.
>
> (Mansell, 2007: 76)

Second, 'assignment frames' set out the structures within which answers should be given. Detailed 'frames' of what to write often appear on school and local authority websites related to the examination boards' detailed specifications for the different grades. Effectively they are told what to write by their teachers. The examination boards are aware of the problem, but not its solutions. Thus, Edexcel on its English GCSE: 'teachers' guidance to candidates stretches what is acceptable to the limit (and beyond) by providing over-detailed essay plans. [These] specify what should go in each paragraph, including the points to be made and the quotations to be used' (Mansell, 2007: 72).

How far can one go before this moves to cheating, especially where the specifications for getting good grades are so explicit and where textbooks are published by people connected with the examination boards, setting out in detail what needs to be said and done for a good grade? For example, Edexcel produced, in 2006, a new GCSE mathematics course. This, however, was accompanied by a textbook written by Edexcel for teachers 'so that you can be sure of a complete match to the new . . . specifications'. But this is now universal. Each examination board produces or sponsors textbooks for each GCSE and A Level subject – teachers, thereby, know exactly what the examinees need to write to meet the specifications of the examination and to meet the demands of the marking scheme. And there is profit to be made by Pearson, the private owner of Edexcel, which sells textbooks seen to be important reading for getting grades in the public examinations which it administers.

'How far can one go before this moves into cheating?' The question above was posed in the penultimate draft of this book in November 2011. In December we read of examiners for the Welsh Joint Examinations Board suspended over 'secret advice' to a gathering of teachers. One had been recorded by *The Daily Telegraph* saying, 'We're cheating. We're telling you the cycle [of the compulsory question]. Probably the regulator will tell us off'. Similarly the chief examiner for Edexcel's GCSE Geography said that teachers should pick her board's exam because 'you don't have to teach a lot' (*Daily Telegraph*, December 2011).

Third, inevitably, under such pressures, schools enter for re-sits candidates who receive poorer grades than predicted. Over two-thirds of one sample took re-sits (mainly at AS Level), with a higher proportion from the independent schools whose generally richer parents can afford the considerable extra costs. Again, where a successful plea is made for 'special consideration' such as illness, a 5 per cent mark-up can be awarded. Applications for 'special application' have risen in one examination board from 30,000, in 2000, to 80,000 in 2009, suggesting how pupils and teachers might be abusing the system in order to boost results – helping the school to climb the league table. According to Ofqual, there were 329,000 GCSE 'special consideration' papers across all examination boards in 2010. Again, independent schools were more likely to submit requests (Ofqual, 2011).

Fourth, focus of attention on the borderline C/D grades is rife, as is shown in evidence to the Parliamentary Select Committee, and elsewhere (HoC, 2003; Gillborn and Youdell, 1999). The victims of this are, of course, those in the bottom percentiles of unlikely 'passes'. Not really *education for all*, then.

Why was this allowed to happen? How can intelligent people see that such a use of tests, such detailed specification of grade criteria, such high-stakes testing, far from improving quality of learning, narrows the curriculum to 'what counts', impoverishes learning experience, atrophies the intelligence, and turns young people off further learning?

Accountability – and control

There are two reasons: one, good in intention, poor in implementation; the other, poor in intention, good in implementation.

Good in intention, poor in implementation

Any public service of such significance for people's lives and the public good needs to be accountable. The gradual realisation of this was described above, namely, a move from a post-war system with next to no accountability to one in thrall to what Mansell calls hyper-accountability. What is easily measurable becomes the dominant aim. There is a logical error here of immense practical importance. Marilyn Strathern of Cambridge University put it well. 'Where a measure becomes a target, it ceases to become a good measure' (Mansell, 2007: 50). To use the analogy already employed, smiling might well be an indicator (a measure) of happiness, but it is not itself happiness. To train someone to smile is not the same as training them to be happy – it is an indication of happiness but neither a necessary or nor a sufficient condition of it.

There are alternative models of accountability which avoid the perverse effects of constant testing. The National Assessment of Educational Performance (NAEP) based in Denver, Colorado, developed a stratified, randomised light sampling procedure for assessing the performance of learners across the USA. Over a period of time, using the Rasch model, longitudinal comparisons could be made about the rise or fall of performance against agreed standards across the curriculum. By 'stratified' I mean that the sample would take in, and discriminate between, categories of learners according to age, gender, ethnicity, social class and location. Within such categories, selection would be made at random across all schools. Sampling was 'light' in that only a few young people from any one school would be selected and only a small part of the overall work of the student chosen. In this way, one could get an accurate picture of what was happening in the different federal systems across the curriculum without distorting the learning. The information from such sampling would not enable league tables of school or individual performance to be developed. There was no point in teaching to the test!

In Britain the Assessment of Performance Unit (APU) was established in 1975 to monitor standards in schools. Initially its main purpose was to acquire knowledge of disadvantaged children with a view to diagnosing their special difficulties. Later, however, it was concerned with developing a model for monitoring standards in general. For that purpose, the APU was modelled on the NAEP. The total learning experience of formal education was divided into six broad areas of development, in each of which were item banks of questions, the answers to which would give evidence (but not proof) of standards reached. Light, randomised and stratified sampling, conducted annually, provided a picture of the system as a whole, against which individual schools could assess their own performance. As with NAEP, such was the light sampling that no conclusions could be drawn from the APU surveys themselves about particular individuals or particular schools.

The APU was killed off with the onset of universal testing following the introduction in 1988 of the National Curriculum and assessment.

Poor in intention, good in implementation

The second reason why all this was allowed to happen was (and remains) that such testing is a very effective tool for controlling education, and this has been achieved with remarkable success. In contrast with the post-war arrangement, the Secretary of State can, in setting the targets on which schools are to be publicly judged, determine what is to be learnt and, indeed, how it is to be learnt. The professional judgement of the teachers is by-passed. They are not to be trusted.

The consequences of such ministerial meddling are unpredictable. For example, when modern languages were 'disapplied' from the National Curriculum at 14, the number of students studying a foreign language soon reached a record low. Entries for French GCSE halved from 319,000 to 154,000. As already mentioned, the definition of EBac in six specified subjects immediately had an effect on the otherwise highly popular Design and Technology.

The intention (namely, ministerial control, in by-passing professional judgement) was wrong, but the implementation extremely successful – and thereby deeply detrimental to 'education for all'.

Problems of control: who should take charge?

Assessment is necessary – both for helping the teacher to see how a student might improve, and for monitoring what is happening in the system as a whole and in particular providers. But assessment has become an industry which, far from helping and monitoring, comes to control what the students learn and how the teachers teach. Assessing becomes a substitute for educating. Therefore, the control of the assessment industry is all important.

First, however, is it out of control because of the sheer problems of scale? The testing and examining industry is enormous. Sixty million items are submitted for assessment each year (*TES Magazine*, 18 March 2011). The likelihood of error is considerable with dire consequences for the examinee. In 2011, over 9,000 A Level students had their grades changed on appeal as a result of inaccurate marking or clerical errors. In the same year, AQA's on-line marking system meant that 3,000 papers were only part-marked, and 600 pupils were given the wrong overall grade. In 2011, 100,000 students across all schools were affected by mistakes in the examination papers – both printing errors and questions that could not be answered (*TES*, 24 June 2011).

Second, the GCSE and A Level examinations are awarded by five major examination boards (OCR, AQA and Edexcel and the Welsh and Northern Ireland Boards). They also are responsible for general vocational awards which used to be independent – those of BTEC, Royal Society of Arts and City and Guild of London Institute. The boards were once closely tied to universities. The universities, working in partnership with schools, were in control. They determined the content of the courses leading to A Level examinations, bearing in mind what was needed by those progressing to university.

Much of the independence of the boards was lost when agreement by government (or its agent, the Qualification and Curriculum Agency) was required for the *specifications* for the award of grades in GCSE and A Level examinations. The more detailed these specifications became the greater the control over assessment, and therefore over learning, by government and its agency.

Such independence was not lost in theory. The boards are able to respond, as indeed had been their wont, to aspirations in schools and colleges. Much innovation in the past had arisen from partnerships between boards, schools and universities. OCR's Pre-U and IGCSE arose from the dissatisfaction within schools (particularly in the independent sector) with the 'reforms' of the GCSE and A Levels. But such independence was limited by the refusal of government to fully recognise these awards for funding and league table purposes.

Therefore, Cambridge Assessment (2011) has called for greater involvement of university academics in setting the content of the A Levels in order to guarantee standards and ease the university admissions process. As they argue, the increasing role of government in setting examination standards has created a 'divorce' between exams and their main users.

> The best international qualifications (IB, Pre-U, IGCSE) are such because they have a minimum of state intervention, with producers and users of the qualification creating a community of ownership and practice that takes upon itself the responsibility for maintaining the integrity of the qualification.
>
> (*TES*, 24 June 2011)

On the other hand, the boards are in competition with each other. Schools understandably look across the boards to see which is more likely to give higher grades in each subject. It is a market.

The latest version of pre-vocational courses, the 14–19 Diplomas, were developed through the respective 'occupation sectors', reflecting the concerns of employers, with minimal involvement of the major awarding bodies or the teaching profession, and subject to the detailed specifications of the government's agency, the QCDA (successor to the QCA).

We are seeing, therefore, a disconnection of the all-important testing industry from the professional responsibility of those who teach and the experts in examining, a failure to ask basic questions about the very aims of education which should determine the appropriateness of the tests, and an ever-increasing control by whims of successive Secretaries of State.

Conclusion: neither education nor for all

What has all this testing got to do with educating young people? Let us return to Chapter 2 where we raised the question: 'What counts as an educated 19 year old in this day and age?' Is an educated person one who has been trained to pass tests, to mouth the answers he or she has been told to come out with?

Education, it was argued, was about acquiring those qualities which make us distinctively human, namely, knowledge through which we are able to understand the physical, social and moral worlds we inhabit, the practical knowledge through which we are able to act intelligently within the world, the dispositions or virtues through which we appreciate the moral responsibilities towards others and the universe, and the sense of and participation in one's community. Such a person acquires a sense of personal worth, a considered appreciation of what is of value. It is this positive vision and capacity which a genuine education aims to produce.

It was argued, too, that such educational aims require a wider vision of learning than what prevails – deeper understanding through the grasp of key ideas and concepts, appreciation of the different voices which make up the conversation between the generations, practical and technical activities too often neglected, engagement with matters of social concern.

Furthermore, it was argued that all individuals, not just those privileged with wealthier parents or high intelligence, were capable of acquiring those qualities to some extent. There are inevitably limitations, but none needs to be excluded from reaching a certain rung on the ladder of learning – from entry into the different forms of understanding. Respect is owed to every learner's struggle to understand, to partial understandings still to be refined, to the different ways a sense of personal worth is achieved.

In what ways is that denied or destroyed by the testing industry?

First, that industry focuses on what is easily measured – not the deeper understanding, the wider appreciation, the joy in learning, the pursuit of what is true, the deeper meanings that engagement with scholarship and the arts brings about. Thereby it is not only limited in its aim, but (because of its impact on policy and practice) also curtails and impoverishes learning. Examples have been given – demotion of the arts, exclusion of practical knowledge from the experience of many, failure to address the moral concerns that confront individuals and society.

Second, it creates a sense of failure amongst those who, however hard they struggle to understand, get little recognition or reward. No wonder many disengage from education. To them it does but re-enforce a sense of inadequacy. They inevitably turn to other pursuits in order to get recognition and satisfaction. As Richard Williams, Chief Executive of Rathbone, wrote:

> [T]he process of qualifications reform in recent years has perversely diminished rather than enhanced opportunities for young people with significant learning and personal support needs. This is particularly true for those young people who are hard to reach, difficult to engage in learning, and who are neither apprenticeship ready nor able to cope with life in a large institution such as a sixth form or FE college.

> (Williams, 2010)

There are, of course, many examples of schools and colleges which attempt to recognise and celebrate these achievements against the grain of the testing industry. To help them in this task, the awarding body ASDAN opens up wider learning opportunities for all young people, especially in relation to the development of valued personal qualities, employability related skills and aspirations, and wider social commitment. It provides nationally recognised qualifications for validating successful learning in these areas, and challenges dominant conceptions of education which tend to focus, almost exclusively, on so-called 'academic achievement'. Recognition of what ASDAN stands for and has achieved is reflected in the exponential embracing of its awards by schools, colleges and voluntary organisations.

The way forward, therefore, must be as follows.

First, cut back the assessment industry. It shapes rather than reflects learning, thereby narrowing what is to be learnt, impoverishing the quality of learning, and disengaging many young people who, despite their best efforts, are constantly proclaimed as failures. Wales discontinued Key Stage testing in 2005, Northern Ireland in 2000. It can be done.

Second, do not confuse assessment for accountability with assessment for learning. Provide the former with the kind of light, stratified sampling (referred to on page 79).

Third, hand overall control of examining and testing to an independent body representing school, college and university teachers, examination boards and representatives of employers. Government should have a voice but not a controlling one.

Fourth, teacher assessment, carefully monitored and conducted in the light of broad educational aims, should play an essential role in the assessment of young people – noting the achievements and qualities, not just the failures.

Fifth, get rid of league tables – and thus the need to teach to the test.

Sixth, learn the lessons of history. Many of these solutions have been tried successfully before – in the Schools Council, the APU, the monitoring of teacher assessment for the defunct Certificate of Secondary Education, and 'Pupil Profiles'.

The expansion of the testing industry has inevitably led to the sorry state we are in. The failure to distinguish between aims and performance indicators means that the indicators become the aims. The sheer quantity of assessments and tests requires such large workforce that there can be little or no room for professional judgement. It is inevitably pursued through tick-box audits on an industrial scale. And that, too, leads to widespread breakdown.

In all this, Newsom's 'half our future' suffers most.

13 'Know thyself'

The need for guidance

The need for a lot of advice and guidance

Why, one might ask, should there be a whole chapter devoted to 'Information, Advice and Guidance' (IAG) which, howsoever useful for some, would seem peripheral to the main educational function of the school? Are not the progression routes spelt out clearly through the different well sign-posted pathways – academic and vocational? Well, not really, but even if they were, the case for IAG as part of *education for all* is still overwhelming.

In the words of Socrates, 'Know thyself'. 'Knowing thyself' is a central aim of education. However, such self-knowledge does not take place in a social or economic vacuum. Young learners need to understand themselves in relation to the adult world they are entering into. What sort of life, and engaged in what kind of occupation, will enable the young person to flourish and to find personal fulfilment? That requires knowledge of the range of occupational possibilities and of the relation of those possibilities to the interests and aptitudes of the learner. This, in turn, requires not simply information but also the sensitive relating of that information to developing self-knowledge. It requires an expertise on the part of teachers, who need to be knowledgeable about both what is possible and the qualities and aspirations of the young learners themselves. It is a teaching job, not simply one of information giving.

Never has the need for education and guidance in respect of future aspirations and possibilities been so great, as possible choices multiply. At the age of 14 choices are made about subjects to be taken – which affect further possible choices at 16, which affect further possible choices of higher education courses at 18, which affect the kind of career or employment one is finally in a position to choose.

How can many young people see their way through all that at 14 or indeed 16?

Take, for example, access to university courses in England. There are over 8,000 possible combinations of three A Level subjects. The wrong combination (selected in ignorance) denies access to the desired subject (engineering, say) at a university of first choice. Different universities make different A Level demands for the same degree course in terms of A Level subjects and subject grades. Without the right advice, wrong choices are made early in one's schooling (see Andrews, 2008). The Browne Report (2010) on higher education recommended that every school should be required to give all pupils individualised careers advice if they are not to be misled in their subject choices and preparation.

That, however, concerns only the pathways into higher education. A more appropriate pathway for many young people would be into training schemes and apprenticeships. But there may be little or no acquaintance with such schemes in the family or school. Wrong advice is given to take up vocational courses in further education which subsequently are found to lead to nowhere. The 'churn' amongst those who proceed at 16 to Level 1 or Level 2 vocational courses at a college of further education is high – creating disillusion and wasting money. One survey claimed that one-third of 550 young people felt schools had not given enough information about their post-16 options and one-quarter felt they had not been given enough information about courses in their local college (AoC, 2004).

The present context of a recession makes the task even more urgent with 20 per cent of 16–18 year olds and 15 per cent of 16–25 year olds not in education, employment or training and looking for work at a time when there remain skill shortages at technical and associated professional levels in important growth sectors, especially in science, technology, engineering and mathematics related careers (Careers Professional Task Force, 2012). Careers advice is not the only solution but young people need to be aware of which courses lead to worthwhile qualifications.

What, then, are the problems?

The first problem lies in the lack of teachers who are knowledgeable about the different pathways into higher education, apprenticeships and training programmes. That is inevitable, given the sheer complexity of the university and employment scene. Teachers themselves would not have the extensive knowledge about university entrance, local employment possibilities or apprenticeships. As the 2010 Ofsted Report concluded, even Personal Advisers in the Connexions Service 'were also facing the pressures of keeping up-to-date with a wide range of developments so that they could provide well-informed and impartial advice' (Ofsted, 2010b: 9).

The second problem is that advice is often not impartial, serving the school rather than the student. That is the inevitable consequence of an increasingly fragmented and competitive system, where schools have to market themselves against their competitors. It is in the interest of schools to keep some young people even where, given the small size of their post-16 cohort, the student is denied the range of opportunities available in another school or a neighbouring college. On the other hand, it is also in the interests of the school, with an eye on league tables, to advise some students to move into a vocational course at the local college, even though the course undertaken proves to be unsuitable and not providing the base for further progression. Impartial IAG is essential if the good of the learner, not the institution, is to come first. Again, quoting from the Ofsted Report: 'The IAG given were not always sufficiently impartial about the options available to young people at the age of 16, for example, where secondary schools had their own sixth forms.'

The urgency of such developments is reflected in a letter from one school:

> A 15 year old girl attends a college open evening, puts in an application, goes to an interview with her parents and is offered a place. The college then asks for a reference from her school, prompting the head teacher to demand to see the girl. Why is she planning to go to that college instead of staying in the school's sixth form? Doesn't she know that it has no pastoral support? And it's up to the students as to whether they work or not? The girl persists. Invited to meet staff again and other prospective stunts at the college's fresher day held towards the end of Year II, she dutifully asks permission to attend. Mysteriously, a new event appears in the school's calendar for the same day: a library day when all leavers are required to return books to the departments and the school library.

This example shows what happens when the interests of an institution override the needs and wishes of young people.

With large numbers of schools moving out of local authority control or acquiring academy status, and with small sixth forms multiplying, one would have thought that an all-age careers service, with a presence in every school and college, was an absolute necessity. Instead, despite several false dawns from previous administrations and bold statements by the government, we seem to be further than ever from protecting young people's freedom of choice. The government is committed to expanding apprenticeships, intending to develop that route into university education. It is determined to enhance progression into technical training. But, who will advise school students about these options when they conflict with a school head's desire, at a time of falling rolls, to build up the sixth form?

The third problem is that mixed sex schools are not doing enough to promote girls' confidence and ambitions. Work placements tend to be in stereotypically female occupations such as hair salons. Little information is given about starting salaries, career prospects and earning potential irrespective of gender. This is not *education for all*.

In response to these problems, the importance of IAG (especially the information-giving bit) is recognised, at least in theory. The government in England has established a new All-Age National Careers Service with the intention of revitalising the professional status of careers guidance practitioners and creating professional standards. The Matrix Standard is the unique quality framework for the 'effective delivery' of IAG on learning and work.

However, the money and the organisation are shared between two Departments of State (DfE and DBIS – Department for Business, Innovation and Skills). The small change left for schools hardly ensures that the new statutory duties will provide independent careers guidance from the all-age service or from private providers. At the time of writing, one-quarter of Connexions have closed; leaving two million 16–19 year olds with nowhere to go for careers help. A sixth of career advisers say that no young people in their area will be able to receive face-to-face advice. One local authority has closed its entire careers service except for a website and telephone line. Another will be providing advice only for pupils with special educational needs. Yet another has scrapped its face-to-face advice (*TES*, 24 May 2011). The government just doesn't get it.

These difficulties can be met only if there is a highly professional and knowledgeable IAG service available to all young people across schools and colleges. This would be both integrated into the general curriculum from an early age and set apart for specific and expert advice.

In what sense might this be a curriculum matter, and as such part of general education from the age of 11? (see Andrews, 2008).

How to live one's life fruitfully, with a sense of fulfilment and enjoyment, is part of that general education described in Chapters 7 and 8. Getting to know how one's life might be lived in terms of the values to be pursued and of the kind of life one wants, must be part of general education. Such questions can be asked and discussed from an early age, open to further questioning and exploration. Even 'vocational preparation' is not training 'set apart'. As Dewey saw it:

> A vocation means nothing but a direction of life activities as renders them perceptibly significant to a person, because of the consequences they accomplish, and also useful to his associates. The opposite of a career is neither leisure nor culture, but aimlessness, capriciousness, the absence of cumulative achievement in experience, on the personal side, and idle display, parasitic dependence upon the others, on the social side.
>
> (Dewey, 1916: 307)

From the start, therefore, need we not to be encouraging all young people to have that 'direction of life', to see 'the consequences' of their aspired-to 'life activities', to have the sufficient sense of achievement (not failure) and self-worth as to be rendered neither aimless nor idle and parasitic? Such 'direction of life's achievements' is surely 'progression' within the broader context of educational aims.

Conclusion

What is the way forward?

First, no one school can go it alone. It is no good transferring responsibility for careers guidance to individual schools. The promised all-age 'help-line' and website hardly do the trick. Schools do not have the capacity or funding to employ the range of expertise. Neither do they have the capacity and resources to gather the detailed national and local information on employment possibilities, career prospects, the hundreds of possible pathways into higher education or the false trails that might alas be followed, though no doubt helped by the several on-line services (for example, Babcock's Lifeskills Careers resources or Careersoft with its comprehensive information on UK degree courses). An effective, informed and impartial IAG requires a strong body of careers advisers in partnership with neighbouring providers – a service to be shared. The quality of careers advice, work experience and employer engagement should be key components in the Ofsted assessment of schools and colleges.

Second, educational support, as distinct from mere information giving, is recommended from the start of secondary school – exploring through discussion, on the basis of experience and evidence, what the young people would like to do, opening the imagination to the range of possibilities, coming to understand one's own potential and limitations in relation to different futures, raising questions about the social and moral context of different ambitions. The NFER 1996 longitudinal study of two cohorts of young people (over 14,000 took part) from Years 9 and 10 highlighted the importance of an early start to careers education – gaining the exploratory skills (using computerised databases, paper sources or people), developing self-awareness and good self-image, obtaining sound factual knowledge of courses and routes open to them (Morris, 2004).

Third, a key element of the educational input would be appropriate work experience. A YouGov Poll of nearly 1,000 19–24 year olds pointed to the importance of work experience in helping them decide on a career. But the distribution of positive responses varied significantly across types of school. Those attending independent schools benefited most (81 per cent); those attending grammar schools 59 per cent; those attending comprehensive schools, 54 per cent. Once again it is the lower 'half our future' who least benefit in an education intended for all (see Education and Employment Task Force, 2011).

An impartial, professional and data-driven IAG, shared by collaborating schools, is crucial if there is to be *education for all*, not just for the more privileged in our society. That is part and parcel of a general education that aims to help all young people to live fulfilling and useful lives.

14 Progression
Should we take employers and universities seriously?

Progression

In the much more mechanical approach to educational policy, 'progression' is a deceptively simple concept. It means moving from Level 1 to Level 2 – and (forever) numerically upwards. In so doing, those who 'progress' help government to hit its targets. At times one might be excused for believing, a little cynically, that such targets are hit as a result of inexplicable changes to the progression routes (as would seem to be the case with apprenticeships – see below). At what stage does 'progression' become 'regression'?

'Progression' is like 'reform' or 'education'. It is an evaluative term. It presupposes that there is some 'improvement' – from ignorance to understanding, from social disharmony to social cohesion, from disengagement to involvement and commitment. Indeed, 'progression' in education cannot be separate from what we believe to be the aims of education. Broaden those aims and you open up further possible progression routes.

For instance, where teachers struggle (with some success) to capture the interest and attention of disengaged young persons, there is progression. Even when such success is not registered on the ubiquitous 'levels', there is progression. That is why we need to beware of the narrow and measurable 'progressions' according to which such achievements go unrecognised.

'Learning to labour' – is it really 'progression'?

The Labour Market

Willis's book (1977) of this title gave a different understanding of 'progression' from that which is implicit in government-speak, although it might provide a more accurate picture of reality these many years later. Despite the ambition to achieve 'world leadership' in 'world class skills' for yet more growth, there still will remain many unskilled labouring jobs. Indeed, we have what is referred to as growing 'hour glass economy' – demand for employees both at the professional and high-skill end and at the unskilled end, though these are increasingly filled with low-paid immigrant labour. Is successful preparation for such lowly jobs 'progression'? Perhaps, but only if such 'preparation' embraces a broader educational framework within which young people acquire the skills, interests and confidence to find personal fulfilment, a sense of worth, the capacity to contribute to the broader society.

That broader education clearly includes numeracy and literacy. The Moser Report (1999) identified Entry Level (EL) 3 numeracy as the standard necessary to function at work and in society in general (for example, able to add or subtract money using decimal notation or being able to work with fractions). But subsequently it was found, according to the Leitch Review, 2006, that 21 per cent of working-age people lacked EL3 number skills. According to the CBI (2010), all young people should continue with numeracy and maths in post-16 education and training. But there is a lack of valued pathways post-16 that would allow all learners to continue studying mathematics up to age 18 (ACME, 2011b).

The prospects for young people seeking work are, and will be for some time to come, bleak, particularly if lacking such basic skills. Entry to the labour market is difficult, let alone progression through it. Nearly 20 per cent of 16–18 year olds are not in education, employment or training (the NEETs). Particularly hard hit are those from the black communities. The unemployment rate for all black people aged 16 to 24 has risen to 47 per cent in the final quarter of 2011 – an increase of 70 per cent in three years (*Guardian*, 10 March 2012, reporting on the latest figures from the Office of National Statistics). The Audit Commission reported the long-term effects of a lost generation socialised into benefit dependency, creating multiple barriers to participation in society. For those not aspiring to higher education, preparation for and entry into the labour market is essential.

At the same time, the increasing demand for high-skilled workers would seem to require what was referred to as a 'skills revolution', with ambitious qualifications targets and a 'world class skills base' by 2020 (Leitch Review, 2005). The 'revolution' lies in a much increased supply of qualified people from within the education and training system. To that end, the previous government had intervened considerably in education and training, in the belief that a better educated and trained workforce would be the way to stimulate economic growth, especially through the creation of a Unified Qualifications Framework and the setting of improved targets for higher levels of vocational qualifications (see Chapter 12). There was a lot of 'performance management' (see Payne and Keep, 2011, for an extensive analysis).

But it is no good proceeding with an expansion unless the employers respond to such a supply-led revolution. Their involvement is essential. They provide the opportunities for work-based learning. They must produce the demand to meet the supply. They must fund at least part of the training. They are best informed of future needs within the respective occupational sectors.

Has the message got across? According to the UK Commission for Employment and Skills (UKCES), the weakness lies as much on the demand side as it does on the supply.

> The relatively low level of skills in the UK; the limited extent of skills shortages; the potentially relatively low demand for skills relative to their supply taken

together, imply a demand side weakness. The UK has too few high performance workplaces, too few employers producing high quality goods and services, too few businesses in high value added sectors. This means that in order to build an internationally competitive economy, the future employment and skills system will need to invest as much effort on raising employer ambition, on stimulating demand, as it does on enhancing skills supply.

(quoted in Payne and Keep, 2011: 2)

The point is: first, that there remain low-skilled jobs which employ over 20 per cent of the workforce and which are set to increase in future; second, that Level 2 qualifications acquired by many do not generally qualify for much (even progression to Level 3); and, third, that employers have been reluctant to fund, even in part, the further training of young people (as reflected in the poor record of *Train to Gain*, a government initiative which struggled to secure employer and individual co-funding).

Therefore, progression to the labour market for many may well mean the low-wage, low-skilled employment of which there remains much. At least it is a rung (a low one, perhaps) on the ladder of employment. And it should not be treated with disdain. Low-skilled employment is preferable to remaining on benefit. Earning a living gives a sense of dignity. It establishes the habits of working and provides a platform from which more rewarding employment might be sought. However, the provision of valuable but low-skilled employment requires close partnership between schools, colleges and local employers. That must be part of the expanded duties of a school system which seeks education for all.

Nonetheless, much hope is placed by successive governments in a reformed apprenticeship route into employment, developing both the supply of and demand for the higher level skills.

Apprenticeships

'Apprenticeship' evokes images of the craftsman who has, over a long period, acquired a set of skills which meet high standards. These skills have been acquired through the example, teaching and correction of a 'master craftsman'. It takes place within a community of craftsmen – the 'guild' of old. The standards of excellence which distinguish that community are internalised. The true craftsman dislikes a shoddy job. The knowledge gained through practice and training reflects a unity of thought and action, an integration of hand and brain.

That at least was the medieval concept and practice, well described by Sennett (2008) in *The Craftsman*. The apprentice would, at the end of seven years, present his *chef d'oeuvre* to the Guild, demonstrating the complex skills acquired. The former apprentice would be judged fit to practise.

Of course, this is the medieval ideal. But there are many features of it which we have inherited in learning to become engineers, gardeners, plumbers or electricians – the mastery of a range of skills learnt on the job over a period of time, subject to criticism and example from the 'master craftsman', underpinned with a growing theoretical knowledge. Such an apprentice internalises the standards of excellence related to the practice. The long training ensures a depth and adaptability of knowledge gained from experience. When I was a boy, to have got one's 'City and Guilds' was a badge of honour. Apprenticeship was and remains a 'brand name'.

An enhanced apprenticeship scheme is seen by successive governments to be central to the 'skills revolution' – to the attainment of a world-class skilled workforce. It is also seen as a route for young people from school to employment, denting the number of young people in the NEET group. Indeed, there has been a lot of policy intervention in the last couple of decades. 'Modern apprenticeships' in 1994 were aimed at stimulating more work-based learning – a reconstitution of the traditional idea of apprenticeship to meet modern conditions. These consisted of an NVQ at Level 3 ('fit to practise') plus a Key Skills Certificate in literacy, numeracy and information technology. But completion rates were low (see Brockmann *et al.*, 2011, for a comprehensive account of these developments). By 2001, the Modern Apprenticeship could be completed at Foundation as well as Advanced level. Further evolution in 2004 created Higher Apprenticeships at Level 4 and Young Apprenticeships from the age of 14. This was seen as a progressive route from school to a highly skilled workforce, and indeed one-eighth of Advanced level apprenticeships progressed to higher education, according to the research from the University of Greenwich (*TES*, 4 November 2011). Finally, this was all brought together in 2009 in an 'apprenticeship framework' across occupational sectors, aimed at increasing yet further the number of apprentices.

But something went wrong. The re-branding of the ancient term 'apprenticeship' (as described above) leads to lack of confidence in the term, howsoever the 'new definitions' boost the statistics of 'starts' and 'completions'. Level 2 becomes the norm although in no way does it provide 'fitness to practise'. The relation between apprentice and employer is severed – over 60 per cent of the so-called apprentices in the construction industry were college based. The extension of 'apprenticeship' to a range of occupational sectors such as retailing redefines the concept. Employers took advantage of the funding available within the 'framework' to provide further training for existing employees – many apprentices over 25 were already in work and enrolled on apprenticeships lasting as little as 12 weeks.

Finally, the 'framework' became extremely narrow in terms of general education, in sharp contrast with that maintained in Germany's 'dual system' which requires a background in general and civic education and is within broadly defined occupations. Roughly 50 per cent of school leavers enter the programme, in contrast to the 10 per cent in work-based learning in England, only half of which are in what are referred to as apprenticeships (and most of these not progressing beyond Level 2). Brockmann *et al.* contrast England's 'skills based approach' (the performance of prescribed tasks without reflective use of knowledge) with the 'occupation based model' of Germany's dual system (with its general and civic education and developed through social partnerships).

What does all this mean for progression – at least according to the House of Lords Select Committee (HoL, 2008)?

First, progression remains only for the very few. Second, non-completion rates are high (Advanced Apprenticeships declined from 77,000 in 1999 to 50,000 in 2002). Third, places for apprenticeship declined (of the 50,000 applications for places in construction, only 7,000 were placed with an employer in 2007). Fourth, the 'framework' is constantly being watered down to meet the targets for 'starts' and 'completions'. Fifth, they are seen increasingly to be for those not capable of the academic route. In a nutshell, apprenticeships are being dumbed down as the standards of quality are lowered to attract employers and, indeed, to find places for young people. Level 2 apprenticeships would not be recognised as such in other countries.

The brand name of apprenticeship must not be compromised in solving a social agenda of getting otherwise unemployed young people into employment. That is a different problem, requiring different solutions.

What needs to be done?

The original brand of apprenticeship needs to be restored, namely, progression (mainly for those leaving school) through work-based learning, with integration of practice and underpinning knowledge. The frameworks, occupation by occupation, should arise from a partnership between employers, worker representatives, and colleges of further education – what in Germany is referred to as a 'social partnership'. Progression should lead to 'fitness to practise', meeting high standards not only of skills but also of an understanding of the wider occupational context.

To achieve this, employers need to be convinced that investment in apprenticeship pays dividends. High-level apprentices do pay their way in the second year. Excellence and completion, not quantity, should be the goal. Partnerships should extend to the schools and the IAG service so that young people know this very different route into employment, something which is rarely understood.

Hence, there is a need to explore a variety of pre-apprenticeship routes and programmes which begin to address issues of access and status. And IAG needs to be more creative in opening up understanding amongst young people and their parents, especially amongst those from black and ethnic minorities. Data from the Learning and Skills Council to the Select Committee on Innovation, Universities, Science and Skills (IUSS, 2008) show that two-thirds of learners aged 16–18 said that more careers education and guidance in school around apprenticeships would have made them more likely to apply, 92 per cent said they knew what apprenticeships were but not how to apply, and 77 per cent who were beginning apprenticeships were already with an employer.

Progression into higher education

Again our minds are bewitched by language. There is the constant temptation both to make distinctions which mislead and yet to fail to make distinctions which are necessary.

With regard to the former, just as the dualism between academic and vocational at school is indefensible, so too is that between the 'two routes for progression' – higher education and high-level apprenticeships. Apprenticeships make demands as great in terms of understanding and know-how as do the so-called academic studies, and these latter, in turn, often demand the practical expertise associated with high-level apprenticeships. Indeed, some would argue along with Sennett and Crawford (see Chapter 7), that cerebral studies, disconnected from the complex practical world in which we live, too often lack validity. In thinking of progression, we must think of many different routes, not squeezed into two contrasting ones.

On the other hand, we constantly fail to make distinctions when these are necessary. The word 'university' covers a range of diverse organisations, experiences, levels of work, intellectual demands and public perceptions. Calling all such institutions 'universities', and what goes on within them 'higher education', may be useful for certain purposes (e.g. funding) but conceals the range of progression routes to different educational goals and occupations – and conceals, too, the diverse nature of higher education in terms of its *raison d'être*.

The Robbins Report (1963) set out four aims of higher education: (i) instruction in skills suitable to play a part in the general division of labour; (ii) promotion of the general powers of the mind; (iii) advancement of learning; (iv) transmission of a common culture and standards of citizenship. Such aims are mutually compatible – 'general powers of the mind' can be promoted even where significant motive lies in the economic utility. But there may well be differences of emphasis between institutions. And that matters where students make choices as to where they want to be.

What, however, would traditionally have characterised a university is academic independence ('dons' dominion'), not beholden in the content of courses on government or corporate pressure. Now, however, students are facing higher education with much increased diversity affecting the choices they might make. A. H. Halsey (1992) referred to the 'Decline of Donnish Dominion', as they increasingly are subject to outside control through financial incentives or punishments, or as they have to shift the balance between teaching and research as a result of the constantly evolving metrics by which research performance is judged and funds distributed.

The 'donnish dominion', as a collection of scholars committed to advancement and transmission of learning, has increasingly to be responsive to the performance indicators manufactured elsewhere. The students, once neophytes entering into the world of ideas, have become customers purchasing a commodity on the assumption that it has a certain market value. And, given the marketisation of education in general and its increasing privatisation, then the universities need to sell what they have to offer through establishing the right price for the right product. In doing so, they are becoming part of an international network of universities backed by private and profit-making entrepreneurs (see Ball, 2012). They reflect different interests, different balances of learning experiences, different matriculation requirements, different standards, different openings into employment and careers. It is now a much more complex world which young people are asked to negotiate.

How does that complexity affect education for all?

First, access requires complex knowledge of the right combination of A Levels for particular courses at particular universities (and there are over 8,000 possible combinations of A Levels). The same subject at different universities could make different demands, unknown to the students at their moment of choice. Where advice on what is needed is not available, the students are at a grave disadvantage.

Second, the opportunities for those from disadvantaged backgrounds are being eroded by present government policies because of the 8 per cent cut to the number of places to be offered to students achieving fewer than two As and one B at A Level. This will mean fewer students from disadvantaged backgrounds progressing to the 'top universities'. But, with reference to Robbins' fourth aim cited above, perhaps future prime ministers and cabinet colleagues, emerging from the private sector, would benefit from engaging at university with those from not so privileged a background.

Third, there are entrance tests for particular courses at particular universities which in many cases focus upon the specific qualities required for the university course – for example, the BMAT (Biomedical Admissions Test) for some medical courses, or the TSA (Thinking Skills Assessment). Some universities have developed tests for their own specific courses, although these will often be delivered at interview and results simply enrich the other evidence presented. Such tests, external to A Levels and IB, are required for less than 2 per cent of all university courses, although the proportion is obviously greater in the more prestigious universities (over 70 per cent at one university). It would be wrong to conclude that these necessarily create a major barrier for certain categories of aspiring students. Nonetheless some of these tests are not necessarily known about where good IAG is not available, and the results of some may well be enhanced by extra help and coaching.

Fourth, university admissions systems unduly award early applicants, thereby penalising pupils from disadvantaged backgrounds. The system is weighted against late developers. Students with poor predictions at 16 were less likely to be offered places than candidates with better results at 16 but where the final results turned out to be the same. Where there are oversubscribed courses, disadvantaged pupils often apply when there are fewer offers to be made. Offers are made on predicted results and on qualifications gained at age 16. And yet students from comprehensive schools with three B grades are likely to do as well at university as those educated privately or at grammar schools with two As and a B. The conclusion drawn by the chairman of Sutton Trust, Peter Lample, was that '[t]hese findings provide further evidence that universities are right to take into account the educational context of students when deciding whom to admit – alongside other information about their achievements and potential' (Sutton Trust, 2010 – *Guardian*, 3 December 2010).

Fifth, back to mathematics: of all the acceptances for university places in 2010, 42 per cent required a significant understanding of mathematics and a further 36 per cent required some mathematical understanding, although many such courses felt it necessary to recruit those without adequate mathematics – 40 per cent of chemistry students had not studied A Level mathematics (ACME, 2011b).

The Chief Executive of Ofqual criticised universities for their unfair admissions system, which should be less of a lottery, with applicants needing to be 'clairvoyants' as early as age 13. Fee-paying schools generally had more expertise in 'decoding' what was required, giving them a competitive edge (*Guardian*, 15 December 2010).

Conclusion and way forward

Let us be careful about employing too narrow an understanding of 'progression' by which the educational system, individual schools and particular students are to be judged. What counts as progression depends on the aims of education. Of course, being prepared for ultimate employment is of vital importance from the point of view of the learner. Being prepared to contribute to the general economic welfare is clearly important from the point of view of society. There is a dearth of skills, knowledge and qualities which an advanced society needs. But those educational aims, through which progression is defined, also should include those personal qualities, that sense of fulfilment, the commitment to serving the wider community relevant to all young people, whether or not they will advance to higher education or high-level apprenticeships. Fast progress for some may be slow progress for others, but progress nonetheless.

Progression, howsoever defined, requires the right kind of learning experience as well as the guidance and insight through which young people might understand better the world they are entering into. They need help, too, in detecting the interests that are worth pursuing and the potential they have for relating to that world. 'Know thyself'.

This, as I have argued, requires:

- putting IAG at the centre of the learning experience provided by schools and colleges; there are too many misinformed decisions and selections which limit future possibilities;
- the creation of partnerships between schools, colleges and universities, so that professional expertise and impartial advice can be available to everyone;
- creation of detailed data bases, both national and local, on routes into higher education, apprenticeships and employment, together with information on career prospects, qualifications needed and financial details;
- close relation between schools, colleges and local employers so that work experience is integrated more effectively into general education and so that students, at all levels of achievement and where relevant, might find local employment;
- higher education becoming more transparent, course by course, about the necessary qualifications and also the looked-for qualities required for entry;
- development of on-line services, constantly updated, geared especially to those who, for one reason or another, have not got access to IAG in schools or colleges.

Part III

Provision of education

15 Public service or private gain?

Global reform of provision

We are facing the biggest upheaval in the organisation of education in decades.

> It is helpful to remind ourselves that we are not alone in the challenge we face
> . . . the attacks on education and public services more widely are part of a
> global education reform movement promoting policies that challenge the idea
> of universal access to free education as a basic right and calling the concept of
> public service into question.
>
> (Blower, 2010: 1)

As Christine Blower indicates, the 'reforms' of education in England, which are
recounted in this chapter, are but an instance of what is happening globally. That
is important to remember. If the analysis of this book is correct, then it applies not
only to the particular case of England but to all education systems which are caught
up in a set of political ideas concerning the relation of the state to the communities
and individuals within it.

Therefore, 'to whom do the schools belong?'

This is a question of both perennial and universal interest, raised by Brian Simon
(1985) in his book *Does Education Matter?* and much earlier (as Simon points out)
by Lester Smith, the distinguished Director of Education for Manchester in 1942
when deliberations about the post-war reorganisation of education for England and
Wales were beginning.

The answer *then* was that they belonged to 'the public' as this was reflected in
the local and democratically elected authorities. It is a public service. That was
embodied in the 1944 Education Act.

A public service

The provision of education for all is based on two principles.

The first is that all young people matter, whatever their background or ability,
and therefore that all should be given the opportunity to develop their distinctively
human capacities for personal fulfilment. Few would have such an opportunity if
the community at large did not provide it. In the 'newspeak' of the Big Society, it

is called 'solidarity'. It needs, therefore, to be a public service for the personal good of each. At the height of the Second World War, the newly formed Council for Education Advance, anticipating a new Education Bill, pressed for 'free education *under a single secondary code* for all children after the primary stage' (author's italics). This needed to be a public service rooted in a democratic order.

The second principle is that, whatever the pursuit of personal good, the good of the community to which we all belong must also be nurtured. Society at large has an interest in its schools because the health of each depends on the health of all – upon a sense of community and citizenship, to be nurtured through common experiences and a common culture.

A public service, therefore, would have the following characteristics:

- it serves the interests of all relevant members of the public, irrespective of background ('relevant' here are the young people in school and college);
- it serves the interests of the community as a whole, not just those who are directly in receipt of the services (we all have a stake in our schools);
- professional decisions are made on the basis of what is good for the learner and the community, not on the basis of profit for the provider or of social privilege;
- it is openly accountable to the public which it serves, by whatever democratic processes this might be achieved.

Such an ideal of public service no doubt develops in different ways in different societies. Some countries put the 'ownership' of schools (the implementation of 'public service') in the hands of the state, but sometimes with disagreeable results. For Germany in the nineteenth century, according to one advocate:

> Compulsory education is closely associated with military service and manhood suffrage . . . for this reason . . . the state which embraces politically the social whole, is and must be the master of the schools. Educational matters, just like other public affairs, must have a central head, if they are to be carried on systematically, and if they are to flourish.
>
> (Rein, 1900, in Simon, 1985: 56)

But, how far can a highly centralised system have either the local knowledge or the local accountability to provide a public service, rather than one which serves the interest of the state and those in positions of power?

Local responsibility

It was partly as a reaction to the German ideal of public service that the 1944 Education Act for England and Wales insisted upon much greater localism, namely, a partnership between central government, local government, voluntary bodies and the teachers. Not too much power to the centre. Again, to revert to the 'newspeak' of the Big Society, 'solidarity' needed to be supported by 'subsidiarity'. The Permanent Secretary's warning to Dr Marjorie Reeves, when she was appointed to the Central Advisory Council for Education (England) in 1946, was: 'Be prepared to die at the first ditch as soon as politicians get their hands on education' (Reeves, 2011).

The 1944 Education Act confirmed that the education service should be maintained, staffed and owned by Local Education Authorities. Since the 1870 Act, there had been local School Boards. After the 1902 Act, Local Education Authorities strengthened this local responsibility. As Brian Simon shows, so much innovation and thinking emerged, not from central government, but from the imagination and dedication of local education officers. Indeed, quoting his mother, who had been Chief Education Officer for Manchester, Simon argued that 'all experiment in education has come from below . . . from enterprising local education authorities'. Moreover, the education committees were the 'touchstone of local public opinion' and 'representatives of the local community as a whole' (Simon, 1985: 75).

Such LEAs were responsible for ensuring enough places in schools and colleges for all young people in the local community, enough teachers to teach them, complementary services such as the Youth Service, specialist advisers, legal expertise, support for special educational needs, fair distribution of resources and a fair admissions system. They were close enough to the community to know the changing needs such as those arising from demographic changes. They maintained a tradition of public service which sought the public good without appeal to private profit. The Chief Education Officers were committed people who jealously guarded that tradition. When the School Council was established in 1964, referred to in Chapter 7, the most important person to be persuaded was Sir William Alexander, Secretary to the Association of Education Committees. Seeing in the initiative an attempt by central government to shift power to the centre, he warned: 'If the Minister wanted the co-operation of the local authorities and teachers, he must set up [a council] which was representative of LEAs, teachers and other educational agencies' (Simon, 1985: 312).

Such local control, and responsiveness to local opinion, did inevitably result in different systems in different localities – two-tier (primary and secondary), three-tier (primary, middle and high schools), selective and non-selective, colleges of further education and tertiary colleges. Crossing such distinctions were community, voluntary-aided and voluntary-controlled schools. Nonetheless, it worked as a system under the watchful eye of the local authority whose job it was to maintain them all.

Decline of local responsibility

The earlier worries of teachers and LEAs were not misplaced. There has been gradual erosion of local control, and with it the professional responsibilities of teachers. Shifting responsibility to central government, which could not have the knowledge to be gained from local familiarity, required the more mechanical and insensitive accountability described in Chapter 11. The system of education is now monitored and governed in a different way.

This changing balance in the partnership between central government, local government, teachers and voluntary bodies, through which a public service was assured, has been well described by Peter Newsam (2011): the incorporation of LEAs within the corporate management of local authorities in the 1960s, the creation of educational 'quangos' which by-passed LEAs (such as the Manpower Services Committee in 1973 and the Qualifications and Curriculum Authority), the removal of further education from LEA responsibility in 1992, the creation of a National Curriculum in 1988, the provision in 1989 of opportunities for schools to opt out of LEAs as Grant Maintained Schools.

But such gradual weakening of local responsibility for education has inevitably led to a terminal illness, and the funeral will be announced very soon.

How is this the case?

The government has promoted 'free schools' and 'academies', and these are now enshrined in an Education Act. These are state-funded schools outside the control of the local authority, and exempt from the legal conditions and regulations which have to be met by maintained schools on such matters as admissions, exclusions and curriculum. They are, in that sense, independent, although they receive their funds from the Department for Education. Gone is the post-war dream of 'free education under a single secondary code for all children after the primary stage'. The new schools are subject simply to the conditions enshrined within their individual contracts negotiated with the Secretary of State. These might include many of the regulations applicable to the maintained schools within the Acts of Parliament, but (as in the case of admissions) they might not.

The 'conversion' to academy or free school status is going on apace. Soon one-third of 3,300 secondary schools will have academy status. It is not simply a matter of being encouraged to shift from local authority to academy or free school status. Any new school *has* to be an academy or a free school. Moreover, existing schools within the maintained system are encouraged or forced 'to convert' and there are financial advantages in doing so. Such schools can be proposed by a group of parents, a religious group, a business corporation, a major donor, another school or a university, irrespective of whether a new school is needed in the community. Free schools can be set up in disused office blocks or factories. They will not need to follow normal planning and building regulations. The transition is made easy; a head teacher need get only the support of governors without reference to parents, teachers and the community, and thus with minimum or no consultation. It is envisaged that eventually all schools will be either free schools or academies. Gone will be local authority responsibility for schools.

Independent schools are 'converting' to 'free schools' status. Five of the first 24 were independent schools and 40 more are expected in the next wave of free schools with an average class size of 15. And why not? They are able to carry on as before but now with state funding. Seen from the perspective of Nick Gibb, Lib Dem spokesperson for education, in his address to independent and fee-paying schools, they as academies would be able to fulfil their mission to help poorer pupils – 'spreading their unique ethos, culture and thinking to tens of thousands of people who cannot afford their fees' (*TES*, 10 June 2011). Hence, private schools are being paid now by the government just as funds for maintained schools are being cut and as parents of children at private schools find the fees more difficult.

Resistance from those who deplore the destruction of local accountability is swept aside, and increasingly, if only for financial reasons, school governing bodies feel obliged to become academics. The money given by central government to local authorities to maintain their schools is transferred from their accounts proportionately to the number of schools 'converting', thereby weakening the authorities in their provision of advisory, legal and other services.

In being freed from the legislation that governs maintained schools, each academy and free school has its own individual contract with the Secretary of State renewable every seven years. The Secretary of State has the authority to set the conditions and not to continue with the contract, should he or she be so minded, with the minimum of accountability to Parliament.

Why should we be concerned?

First, what is being created is the most personally centralised education system in Western Europe since Germany in the 1930s – each school contracted directly to the Secretary of State, the conditions of the contract not constrained by legislation. Back to Rein's 1900 lecture, quoted above, which speaks of the centralised system emerging in Germany – 'the state which embraces politically the social whole, is and must be the master of the schools'. And the military analogy offered by Rein rings true for some. The proposed Phoenix Free School in Manchester is to be staffed entirely by former soldiers showing a 'demonstration of martial values' including 'self-discipline, respect and an ability to listen'. It is proposed by the Centre for Policy Studies and is backed by Lord Guthrie, former Chief of Defence Staff. The intended head teacher is an army captain. It may be housed on surplus army land and would serve as a model for a chain of hundreds of schools (*Guardian*, 2 September 2011).

Second, as a consequence of such powers, parents and the community do not have the same legal rights of appeal or opportunities to protest, for example, in the cases of admissions, exclusions or provision for special educational needs.

Third, in this erosion of the maintained system, excluded or special needs children could be left without proper provision.

Fourth, the expansion of academies and free schools will create surplus places, thereby increasing financial costs and undermining essential local services such as home–school transport, psychological support and advisers. For example, in Oxford, an estimated £29 million 'black hole' has been created because of transfer of money from Children's Services to fund the new academies. As Keith Mitchell, the Conservative leader of the County Council (not normally a critic of the government) protested:

> We are most concerned that the previous commitment of the Department to ensure there is a level playing field between academies and other schools are not being kept which runs against the Government's commitment to fairness. By implementing these proposals the burden of the miscalculation would fall on all other parts of local authority services.
>
> (*Oxford Times*, 1 September 2011)

Finally, in the more competitive system developing between schools and the emphasis upon 'choice' in what is becoming a 'market' to 'drive up standards', it will inevitably be those people less able to exercise choice and those schools serving the most disadvantaged who will suffer. *Education for all* seems further away than ever.

By contrast, a public service treasures accountability to the community, respect for the voices of those concerned, awareness of local circumstances, and determination to serve all, not just a privileged sub-section. Problems are created for a national provision of education where local accountability and responsibility are abandoned. International evidence from PISA is that the countries that do best in terms of both quality and equity, such as Finland, Canada and Japan, rely much more on sustaining comprehensive integrating school systems (Glatter, 2010: 19).

Different kinds of partnership

The vacuum left by the demise of local authorities is quickly being filled by various kinds of sponsors or trusts created by charities, businesses, faith groups, philanthropists and even football clubs. Such trusts may sponsor a chain of academies. For example, (see Hill, 2010):

- E-Act (formerly 'Edutrust Academies Charitable Trust') has a chain of 14 academies and a free school. It has entered talks with the government to open a super-chain of 250 within five years, making it bigger than most current local authorities.
- United Learning Trust (ULT), a subsidiary of United Church Schools Trust and presently the largest single sponsor of the government's academies programme, has 20 academies.
- Edison Learning, pioneer of US Charter Schools, and owning schools in the Middle East, has established its own Collaborative Academies Trust for the 17 academies it is sponsoring and for providing advice to those wishing to set up free schools. It has rights over the 'intellectual property' arising from the Trust.
- Cognita is the UK's largest owner of independent schools in England, with a turnover of £150 million, and 50 schools world-wide. A profit-making company, it is working with parents on free school projects and advertises on the New Schools Network.
- ARK; a charity providing schools in USA, India and Uganda and backed by a City Hedge Fund (Arpad Business), has eight academies with a further seven planned.
- Harris Federation has 12 secondary and one primary academy, and aims to have 25 concentrating around London.
- Manchester City, Everton and Tottenham Hotspur football clubs have considered opening free schools alongside existing youth development programmes with greater involvement in the education of their top young players, but open to pupils of all abilities. The chief executive of the Football League said in 2010 that he could envisage schools being run by the Football League.

- VT Group is responsible for schools in Surrey and Waltham Forest. Its managing director, Marcus Watson, believes that it does not seem unrealistic for his company to be running 1,000 schools (Wilby, *Guardian*, 20 October 2011).
- Kunskapsskolan, which runs 30 state-funded schools in Sweden, plans to sponsor two academies – in Richmond and Suffolk.

There are several others.

These Trusts are, in fact, 'edubusinesses', in which educational provision, either directly or through services offered, is part of their business plan – buying business in education. Two of them (Edutrust and Ark) were trustees on the New Schools Network, the charitable body supported by government to establish academies. The trusts are beholden to different kinds of businesses and pressure groups. Where this is the case, the governing bodies of the respective schools have little power and authority. Accountability to the local community or to parents is negligible.

> [I]n some areas, school leaders report that schools that are part of the chain are choosing not to work with other local schools. Indeed, chains are apparently even starting to claim intellectual property rights for their teaching and learning model. It would be ironic if learning across an education system were stifled rather than stimulated by the arrival of chains.
>
> (Glatter, 2010: 34)

Another sort of chain is developing which is not created by a sponsor of academies or free schools, but, seeing the vacuum left by the demise of local authorities, has brought together schools which share ideals of cooperation and accountability. The Co-operative Trust has a chain of 140 schools which are committed to working together, sharing expertise, valuing local accountability and being fully comprehensive in intake.

Gone from political thinking, however, is the idea of locally maintained schools – a tradition which had strenuously been preserved against the all-powerful state and business interests. But who now exercises legitimate power in the system? Can it really be private businesses, rich philanthropists, for-profit entrepreneurs, voluntary groups (whether religious or not), football teams, each with their own agenda and educational vision?

If there is to be secondary education for all, then cooperation rather than competition must prevail, teachers' professional expertise shared rather than hidden in 'property rights', decisions made in the interests of the local community rather than of the 'vision' or 'brand' of a distant sponsor. Can we afford to lose that? Despite the often hostile media presentation, such locally led and accountable cooperation works. According to the Ofsted Report before the closure of London Challenge in 2011,

> the programmes of support for schools are planned with experienced and credible London Challenge advisers using a shared and accurate audit of

need. Excellent system leadership and pan-London networks of schools allow effective partnerships to be established between schools, enabling needs to be tackled quickly and progress to be accelerated.

(Ofsted, 2010a)

What Ofsted highlighted was

the clear sense of moral purpose among teachers and school leaders; their sense of commitment to all London children; their sense of pride in being part of a city-wide education service, irrespective of whether they were receiving or providing support; their appreciation of effective professional development opportunities; use of data and well supported interventions for individual children.

(Ofsted, quoted by Millar, *Guardian*, 8 November 2011)

It is important to remember that, as with the performance management examined in Chapter 1 and the testing regime associated with it examined in Chapter 12, the deeper philosophical issues underpinning the creation of academies and free schools are part of a global trend and doctrine. To that we now turn, bearing in mind the key question: 'Who should control thousands of publicly funded schools without accountability to the public whose children go to those schools?'

Choice, diversity and markets

In 1992, the Conservative government produced a White Paper *Choice and Diversity: a New Framework for Schools*. It embodied both a philosophical view about the supremacy of individual choice and an empirical view about the improvement of standards through the exercise of choice in an open market of educational providers. Subsequently, the belief has developed that diversity and 'consumer choice' would 'drive up standards', new sorts of school would provide that diversity, the independent sector would be welcomed to manage state-funded schools, measures of success or failure would be published (and league tables created) to provide the evidence for rational choice. Thus the Director General of E-Act, Sir Bruce Liddington, was keen to support free schools and academies so that his chain could respond to what parents want (*TES*, 18 March 2011).

But what do we mean by choice? And can some people, by reason of their social position and location, have more choice than others? 'To be able to choose' is to be contrasted with 'to be determined' or 'to be caused' by circumstances or events against one's will. There are various ways in which a person can be said to be determined or caused. They could be physically forced, or denied the relevant information, or denied the means to carry out their wish, or not have sufficient understanding of the issues. At the same time, schools, in responding to parental choice, market themselves, some more effectively than others, even though the expertise in marketing might have little correlation with expertise in educating.

Furthermore, given this choice and the inevitable imbalance in parental first choices, the *schools* exercise choice, inevitably tempted to choose those students who are more likely to raise the school in the league tables – thereby affecting the choices which potential 'clients' make and increasing the future choice options of the school. A simple *word* 'choice' is not a simple *concept*. Once again we are easily bewitched by the use of language.

Allied to the use of choice is that of 'market'. The system of education becomes a market when the educational wares are laid out and parents are able to move from stall to stall to compare similar products in terms of price and quality. But what is a perfect market?

In a perfect market, there would be complete freedom of the producers to produce the goods which they want to sell. There would be no unfair inducements from those who control the market, giving some producers advantages over others. There would be no aim other than satisfaction of consumer taste. The customers would get what they see.

However, it is clear that the system cannot be a perfect market providing the conditions for fair choice.

First, 'school producers' do not have freedom over the goods they sell; they are subject to constant intervention from the Secretary of State. The indicators of quality are themselves constantly changed and become the moving targets. As Crouch puts it 'the use of the market *per se* negatively changes the sought after good itself' (Crouch, 1997: 8).

Second, there are substantial inducements to some producers and not to others. For example, large sums of money are given to those that become academies, thus providing state-of-the-art buildings and substantial increase in salaries to attract staff.

Third, given the two-fold aims of education to serve not just the personal good but also the good of the wider community, there is always a balance to be struck between freedom of choice and the pursuit of greater equality within society.

Finally, although the new wave of schools are publicly funded, their essential services are increasingly contracted out to private organisations which seek to maximise profits long-term and are unaccountable to parents or the community.

It is not surprising therefore that the OECD report, following 20 years of academic studies on market reforms such as the Charter Schools, voucher pro-grammes and abolition of catchment areas, found that the 'effects of market mechanisms in education are small, if they are found at all' and that in very general terms, it seems that regimes providing parents with more choice bear a risk of increasing segregation between schools in terms of ethnic, socio-economic and ability segregation (OECD, 2010).

If one puts together the complex nature of choice with that of the distorted market, then the broader educational vision of a more equal and socially cohesive society is undermined, the most disadvantaged suffer, and education fails to be a *public* service.

Privatisation

The public system may well preserve the core business of education – the buildings and the teaching, for which money will be paid from the public purse. But in two senses it becomes privatised, and subject to the wishes of organisations outside the public domain.

The first sense is where the schools, although largely financed by government, are handed over to private and for-profit organisations. In the USA, Edison Learning runs Charter Schools, and is now involved with the academy and free school developments in the UK. It was awarded a £1 million contract to turn around a failing school in Enfield (Wilby, *Guardian*, 25 May 2010). In Sweden, the private company Kunskapsskolan runs 30 state-funded schools and plans to sponsor two academies in England. Serco has, in fact, now taken over the running of three local authorities just as they have taken over aspects of social services elsewhere.

One problem with handing over public services to the private sector is that those contracts are often further subcontracted such that the parents and community have even less knowledge of who is responsible for what.

A further problem arises from the inevitable selection of those 'customers' who will provide most profit for the privatised system within the chain of schools, although remnants of the public sector which the private sector does not want will, as in a privatised health service, no doubt remain.

The second sort of privatisation is indirect – for example, the contracting out of central school services such as management, finance, information technology and IAG. Serco provides IT software for on-line solutions. E-Act has created E-Act Enterprises to sell intellectual property and services such as school improvement. The Public Private Partnerships through which many much needed schools were built put those schools in hock to private companies for as much as 30 years – private control of a public asset – for a wide range of profitable services (see H. Brighouse, 2003).

But the for-profit enterprises enter into the system in other ways, too, with a potential distortion of educational aims and values. Pearson, which claims to be 'the world's leading learning company' with interests in 70 countries including English-language centres in China, primary education in Kenya, and the UK, owns the examination board Edexcel and publishes the textbooks geared to getting good results in those examinations. The National Literacy Strategy was contracted out to Capita. Seventy-eight per cent of school inspections, once carried out by HMI, were contracted out in 2009/10 to for-profit companies, Serco, CfBT and Tribal, costing £126 million over the last three years.

Characteristic of this shifting ownership of public education, and of services to it, is the global reach of the organisations involved – far removed from the local communities to which the schools once belonged. Global Educational Reform Movement (GERM, for short – a term used by Paul Sahlberg – see Edwards, 2010), has spread like a virus. It was first detected in the USA, has spread to England (though not yet to the rest of the UK) and is moving on, as do most germs, to pastures new.

Perhaps we should remember the words of T. H. Marshall (1963), 'people acquired rights to these services . . . by virtue of their status as citizens, and not because they were able to buy them in the market' (quoted in Crouch, 1997: 5).

Evidence-based policy?

In recent years there has been an explicit embracing of evidence-based policy. In the pursuit of the quite dramatic shift from a public service to one 'exported' to a range of private organisations in which choice is supposedly maximised in a more open market, reference is made to 'successful' developments elsewhere – in particular to those in Sweden and the USA. But does the evidence support this 'policy borrowing'?

Sweden

Sweden's free schools have provided a model for their introduction in England. They were claimed as the model for a more competitive market and the enhancement of parental choice. They claim to be parent-led but often schools have been taken over by private businesses – many of them not Swedish. Seventy-five per cent are run for profit. Such profit is often gained through economies which diminish the educational value (for example, in the employment of fewer qualified teachers than in the public schools). Not all bodes well for Sweden as a result of this 'experiment'. 'Free' schools divide the community and can take pupils away from successful local schools, threatening their success and increasing social segregation.

According to Per Thulberg, Director General of Sweden's National Agency for Education:

> This competition between schools that was one of the reasons for introducing the new schools has not led to better results [and] we have had increasing segregation and decreasing results, and so we can't say that increasing competition between schools has led to better results.
>
> (Skolverket Report, 2004, www.skolverket.se)

Swedish schools slid in the global rankings of PISA to nineteenth out of 65 in 2009. PISA revealed a growing disparity between high- and low-performing students and a strengthened role in that disparity of socio-economic background.

SNS, a prominent business-funded think-tank, published a report which reversed the normal pro-market stance. Entry of private operators had increased segregation. According to Dr Vlachos, author of the report, 'The empirical evidence that competition is good is not really credible because they can't distinguish between grade inflation and real gains' (www.guardian.co.uk/world/2011/sep/10/sweden-free-schools-experiment).

Swedish free schools, though much appealed to, do not provide evidence that free schools are likely to work in England.

Charter schools

A second major influence on the promotion of free schools has been the Charter Schools movement in the USA, which are publicly funded but privately managed by a mixture of for-profit and not-for-profit companies (see Glatter, 2010). By 2009 there were 4,700 Charter Schools, enrolling 1.4 million children in four federal states – less than 3 per cent of the school population. New York City (NYC) in particular is pointed to as a model of how Charter Schools can show better results than traditional public schools with less funding.

But, a word of caution. As was pointed out above, the perfect market is one which is not distorted by inducements to some producers but not to others. NYC Charter Schools, however, were given public facilities; two-thirds being housed in public school buildings. They were boosted by federal grants (*New York Times*, 27 July 2011). And the evaluation of the Charter Schools at the Center for Research in Educational Outcomes, Stanford University, tells a different story. A five-year longitudinal study showed that 17 per cent of Charter Schools did better than their public school equivalents, 37 per cent did worse, and over half showed no significant difference (Baker and Ferris, 2011). The city's Charter Schools serve disproportionately lower percentages of the poor and English-language learners who need more resources.

The story is not so bright elsewhere. Sixty Charter Schools had to close in Ohio in the last five years due to issues such as financial mismanagement, with 31 others put on the 'watch list', following a warning from the US Education Secretary, Arni Duncan (*TES*, 5 November 2010).

Once again, there is no evidence that free schools are likely to work in England.

Academies

In view of the commitment to evidence-based policy, how does current policy reflect the conclusion of the five-year independent evaluation by PricewaterhouseCoopers that there is insufficient evidence to allow judgement to be made about the academies as a model for school improvement (PwC, 2008: 10.5). The National Audit Office, too, warned that the planned expansion of academies carried significant risks of not providing value for money (NAO, 2010).

Furthermore, the examination results do not support the claims of the superiority of the academies. In 31 per cent of the academies, no pupils gained the EBac, compared with only 17 per cent of non-academies and secondary moderns with the same proportion of pupils on free school meals and with special educational needs (*TES*, 28 January 2011). Only six academies had more than a third of students attaining the EBac and five of these were recent converts from the independent sector. This apparent reversal of competitive success was no doubt due to the fact that many academies, to demonstrate their superior performance, had focused on the vocational GCSE equivalents which were criticised by the Wolf Report (2011) as being in no way equivalent in standard to the 'pure' GCSE.

Once again, the evidence appealed to by politicians is simply not there.

Conclusion: the end of public service?

The changes in the provision of education and training must be seen as part of a more general political philosophy according to which the state's monopoly over public services should diminish and the 'consumers' or 'customers' be given greater 'choice and control'. This requires opening up the public sector to private companies, charities and mutuals, according to the Public Services White Paper, 2011, entitled *Public Services: Who Should Control?* In this way a market is created in which choices can be exercised and services bought by the 'consumers', thereby 'driving competition' and raising standards. Government would provide basic market regulations concerned with transparency on quality, costs and services. To that end there would be measured data on the basis of which rational choices could be made.

We have seen, however, the problems in the application of 'the market' to public services and the inequalities arising from maximising choices within such markets. There is no perfect market. They are subject to interference. They are distorted by preferential treatment for some. They are beholden to the interests of their sponsors. They are susceptible to market failure (as in the case of Southern Cross homes for the elderly), for a perfect market allows the weakest to collapse. The good of the community does not necessarily arise from the good of its individual members.

Furthermore, 'buyers' choices' are limited by the circumstances of the buyer – those with cars, for example, have a wider range of choices than those without, and one person's successful choice is another's lack.

Mark Britnell, former director of commissioning for the NHS and now head of health at the accountancy KPMG, advising Prime Minister Cameron on reforming the NHS, told a New York conference of executives from the private sector that future reforms would offer a big opportunity for the for-profit sector. The NHS would ultimately end up as a financier of care similar to an insurance company rather than as a provider of hospitals and staff (*Observer*, 15 May 2011). Why not also the provision of education? It is beneficiary or victim of the same social philosophy about the relation of the state to individuals – the supremacy of personal choice in a supposedly perfect market.

However, a public education service starts from different premises, namely, those in which the schools serve the community as well as the individual members, in which there are principles of fair distribution of resources that cannot be achieved through the ability to play the market, and in which decisions always arise from the needs of the learners and their communities, not from the profit or interest of the providers.

That tradition of public service, once deeply embedded in public life, is being quickly eroded. If we are to have *secondary education for all*, then it needs to be revived.

16 Providing for all

Fit for the twenty-first century?

You can still see in inner London the schools built following the 1870 Education Act. Towering (at least then) above the surrounding houses, they are still impressive – monuments to the belief that education, elementary though it was then, was important for all. The classrooms on each of the several floors radiate off from central halls where all could gather for games, assemblies or practical activities. In the 1960s and 1970s, when there was an urge for integrated studies, these became central meeting places for all sorts of curriculum experiments, many influenced by Goldsmiths College Curriculum Laboratory (see James, 1968). Classrooms were large and windows high so that pupils would not be distracted by the passing scenes outside.

We still retain the Victorian idea of formal education taking place within a single establishment which therefore should provide the resources, facilities and teaching expertise across the curriculum and across the range of learners. That was possible in elementary schools with a limited curriculum, but not in secondary schools with a much wider vision of learning.

The new academies and free schools (as indeed the Charter Schools in the USA) are no exception to this Victorian model. They are stand-alone institutions, separated from their neighbouring maintained schools, no longer subject to the same regulations and codes. Moreover, these schools have different admission arrangements (some selective, others not), different financial inducements to 'convert', different funding arrangements depending on whether they are deemed 'specialist' or not, different religious affiliations or none, different admissions arrangements. It is a hotchpotch and, with academies and free schools, there is no longer 'free education under a single secondary code for all children after the primary stage'. Each school will eventually have its own distinctive contract with the Secretary of State.

Is not *free* school yet another example of the intelligence being bewitched by the use of language? No one is simply free. One is either free *from* something or free *to do* something. Free schools are certainly free from local accountability, but now enslaved by contract to an all-powerful Secretary of State. The balance of power, established in 1944 to prevent such concentration of power, has thus been destroyed.

Moreover, they are now encouraged, as independent units, to compete in an open market, since competition for 'customers' supposedly 'drives up standards'.

But is the Victorian idea of the elementary school as an inclusive unit, independent of all the other schools, and dependent on its own resources and expertise, fit for secondary schooling in the twenty-first century?

Problems

Hark back to the two-fold aims of education for all: first, enabling each person to acquire the capacities to live a distinctively human life and, second, promoting the good of the community as a whole. Public education is not just for the personal good of each; it is for the communal good of all in which each partakes. We all have a stake in the publicly funded educational system.

There are therefore in the system, as that has developed and is developing further, two sorts of problem. The first is that no school on its own can provide the range of expertise and the resources to meet that wider vision of learning described in Chapters 7 and 8. The second is that an increasing emphasis upon differentiation and competition between schools divides society rather than creates community.

No one school can go it alone

Take the example of science. There are nearly 500 secondary schools in England which have no qualified physics teacher, thereby denying to thousands of young people the inspiration and the opportunity to advance in that most important subject. It is necessary, too, to anticipate similar problems in the teaching of modern languages. Innovative science departments covering the range of sciences and technologies need a critical mass of qualified teachers together with modern laboratories and resources. That can be achieved only if schools and colleges work together.

With the reduction in resources and influence of local authorities, so there has been a serious decline in the teaching of the arts, particularly music. Local authorities can no longer provide the peripatetic instrumental teaching. The participation in youth orchestras of young people from non-independent schools has declined. The arts are suffering from lack of teachers and resources which obviously are expensive. The omission of the arts from the Secretary of State's idea of general education, on which public assessment will be based, itself exacerbates this decline.

The need for a wider vision of learning to embrace more practical activities such as engineering, and those related more closely to the world of work, calls for closer connections with the facilities and expertise beyond the school. The Kingswood Partnership near Bristol is an excellent example of what can be achieved in engineering where several schools share the state-of-the-art engineering workshop, backed by local engineering businesses. Employer involvement in such partnerships is crucial. The Centre for Engineering and Manufacturing Excellence (CEME), Dagenham, brings together employers, colleges, schools and universities as part of the London Thames Gateway Regeneration Scheme. The world-class engineering facilities and expertise serve over 20 schools, thereby enriching courses in engineering, and providing routes through school, apprenticeships and foundation degrees.

We have seen the central importance of advice and guidance through the different pathways (and providers) into higher education, further training and employment. But this requires an independent and impartial service shared by the different schools and colleges.

Unfortunately, the emphasis on single schools going it alone, rather than being part of a wider network of schools, has encouraged schools formerly without a sixth form to develop one. But the evidence is clear from many sources (see Fletcher and Perry, 2008: 21) that the small sixth form leads to there being fewer post-16 subjects to choose from and poorer results in those subjects which are chosen. Furthermore, they use resources much less efficiently than larger sixth forms or college provision. The National Audit Office, following earlier reports as far back as 1996, reports that 'smaller sixth forms generally have worse performance than larger ones. The percentage of schools adding more value than expected decreases consistently with size of institution, below 400 students' (NAO, 2011).

The arguments for collaboration not competition, for partnerships rather than autonomous institutions are overwhelming. No one school can go it alone.

The Big Society – solidarity not division

The argument for the common school – or the common local learning partnership – is strong indeed if we are to develop the cooperative, mutually supportive society in which we can learn to be human.

The American philosopher John Dewey saw the common school as an essential part of the educational experience of all young people as they came to learn from interacting with the different traditions which made up society. The school was an essential part of learning how to live within a diverse society – how to develop the skills, attitudes and understandings required of active citizenship. Dewey was writing when people from different religions and cultures were entering the USA and when the school was seen to be the place where young people would learn not only to tolerate such diversity but also to be enriched by it.

In that vein, the Ouseley Report (2003), following riots in Oldham, warned of a socially segregated Britain and of a growing minority feeling alienated from mainstream society. Northern Ireland is often cited as a society divided on religious grounds, supported by a segregated school system, and there is a growing movement for 'integrating schools', where the different communities learn together and where each comes to appreciate the beliefs, aspirations and fears of the other. Developing mutual respect would seem to be crucial.

In the fragmented, competitive and increasingly segregated school system which is now developing, not only are many individuals being denied the opportunities and resources for their personal achievements, but also society is becoming less cohesive, less a community. It is failing to heed Ouseley's warning 'of a socially segregated Britain and of a growing minority feeling alienated from mainstream society'.

For reasons given above, a common school by itself, whatever its merits in advancing social cohesion, cannot meet the needs of all. But partnerships between schools, colleges and youth services can. What is needed is not a common school but a locally organised and locally accountable cooperative system, in which no young person is denied the teaching and the resources which too often are accessible only to the few.

Learners, not institutions, come first

The development of pre-vocational courses (referred to in Chapter 12) for many young people from the age of 14 required access to facilities and expertise which often were available only in colleges of further education. Partnerships were established between schools and colleges. Indeed, partnerships between schools and schools, and between schools and further education, were a condition for the development of the new Diplomas and the more flexible post-14 curriculum. As a consequence, over 100,000 young people each year aged between 14 and 16 have been completing a substantial part of their curriculum in these colleges. Only there will they benefit from the expertise of the different crafts and technologies.

That need for collaboration was recognised by the previous government as it sought to bring about a wider vision of learning.

> Our vision for the 14–19 phase sets out a range of opportunities that should be available to young people in every area of the country. Schools, colleges and training providers will need to collaborate, because no single institution will be able to provide them all on its own.
>
> (DfES, 2005: 78)

One main message of this book is that we are dominated by narrow aims of education and, consequently, a narrow vision of learning. Broader aims, relevant to all young people, call upon resources, opportunities and expertise which are scattered over a range of institutions within the community. How can we so organise education as to ensure that all can benefit from these? It requires collaboration, partnerships, not the competition which is presently encouraged by government policies.

The significance of collaboration is brought out well by Higham and Yeomans in their study of partnerships (Higham and Yeomans, 2010). As they say, the 14–19 phase includes a range of different types of courses – general education often referred to as 'academic', pre-vocational courses, vocational training, different pathways into higher education and apprenticeships, complex deliberations about careers, and a plethora of qualifications. Providing the right structure for such a complicated phase of education and training is far from easy, and certainly not in the power of a single school.

This is reflected in the different kinds of partnership which have grown:

- arrangements for students from several schools to access, in other schools or in neighbouring colleges, many more different courses relevant to post-14 education than their school can provide;
- shared post-16 courses so that strengths in some schools (e.g. in physics or modern languages) can be enjoyed by other schools which have other strengths;
- use of virtual learning facilities such that there can be shared teaching across schools and colleges and shared assessment of work;
- mobile transportation of teachers, practitioners and resources between schools in more rural areas, opening up opportunities otherwise denied young people.

However, despite the policy promoting partnership and despite the many good examples of it in practice, achieving it is not easy as Higham and Yeomans' research shows. Collaboration runs counter to the traditional conception of the school as a stand-alone institution, accountable to its pupils and parents. There is the need for a formal federation of institutions with appropriate constitutional arrangements for joint funding, joint teaching appointments, leadership and local accountability. (See Higham and Yeomans, 2010: 386, for a more elaborate account of the different kinds of collaboration that have developed formally and informally.)

In ensuring 'secondary education for all', we should start with the needs of the learners, not with those of the current institutions.

Who are the partners with schools?

Further education

So far, the emphasis has been on the schools. But we need to remember that over half of young people who are in full-time education in England are registered in colleges of further education. Many will be engaged in A Level studies, but more will be on vocationally oriented courses or college-based apprenticeships. In addition to these are the many part-time students who complement their work-based training with the theoretical underpinnings taught at college. To be seen, too, are those who, having finished school with no qualifications, no doubt having dropped out of school at various stages, are rescued by the colleges – encouraged to enter the world of learning once again. The crucial and varied educational activities offered by further education are rarely acknowledged. And where funding is related to meeting measurable and standardised targets, the colleges get poor rewards for rescuing those who need to be re-engaged with education.

The importance of further education after compulsory schooling has been a theme of major reports since Crowther in 1959. It is 60 years since it recommended that all young people should be in some form of full-time or part-time education up to the age of 17. That was when the leaving age was 15 (Crowther Report, 1959: para. 675). The County Colleges for the part-time students who were engaged in more vocational studies and on day-release from employment, should, it was argued, be closely linked with 'a strong Youth Service as an essential complement' to them. There was concern that their learning should not be narrowly vocational, but include 'an appreciation of the adult world in which young workers suddenly find themselves', guidance and counselling, development of physical and aesthetic skills, and a continuance of basic education (ibid.: para. 675d).

Despite this plea 60 years ago, the key importance of further education in 'education for all' seems to go unrecognised. It is funded 10 per cent less than schools for doing the same work. The Education Maintenance Allowance (EMA), which enabled young people from poor backgrounds to attend, has been cut. The scheme replacing the EMA is, according to the 157 Group of top colleges, £200 million short of the bare minimum needed to support the poorest students (*TES*, 17 December 2010).

Youth work

Youth workers have a distinctive part to play in the provision of this wider vision of learning. What is distinctive about it is the voluntary participation by teenagers who are often disengaged from education. But, more than that, because participation is voluntary, the relationship between youth and workers has to be different from that between student and teacher. The youth worker starts from the interests and concerns of the teenager, builds up trust with young people who are generally distrustful of adults, opens up new opportunities, supports them in facing difficult circumstances, provides opportunities for further learning should those be wanted. This is illustrated in the story of one girl:

> Ashby Youth Club was a big part of me whilst being aged 13–18. It kept me safe and . . . from getting myself and my friends into trouble. But it wasn't all about being kept off the streets. At the age we were we didn't care about anything and found it hard to communicate with parents and teachers. When it felt like the whole world shut you out there was always Jenny that you could just go to talk about anything in the world and she would be more understanding and give you the best advice any could give. A lot of people called her their second mum (she was to me). There was always the education side of being at a youth club, too, learning the things we really didn't learn at school and being able to do projects with other people and learning how to really work as a team.

Such an approach to learning finds little understanding from successive governments which cannot see beyond formal programmes leading to standardised measures of success. At a time when so many young people are leaving school without further education, training or jobs, the youth club is the one place in which they can find safety, adult support and opportunities for further learning. And yet, whilst money is being poured into free schools, often creating surplus places, the cuts to youth work are savage. Many youth projects across London have closed due to funding cuts. The Crib Youth Club in Hackney, for instance, a safe place for dozens of children who want to avoid trouble, has lost three-quarters of its funding and had to reduce its opening hours. Nothing now goes on in the summer. Yet 44 per cent of Hackney children live in poverty. In Haringey youth project funding has been slashed by 75 per cent, and eight out of 13 youth clubs have been shut.

Employers, independent training providers, and the third sector

Given the importance of work-based learning for many young people, not only in apprenticeships, but also as an enrichment of their general education at school, partnership with local employers and providers of real work opportunities is essential. Reference has been made to CEME in Dagenham which provides engineering opportunities for local schools. There are many examples. But the facilities for it are rarely found in schools. JHP Group Ltd is one of the largest vocational training providers in the UK with over 2,400 apprentices and over 1,000 on other training programmes. SKIDZ provides motor mechanics and vehicle maintenance workshops for schools. Established in High Wycombe, it now has projects in the Thames Valley, Milton Keynes and, thanks to a donation from Porsche, in the London Borough of Hillingdon.

The RSA's Open Minds Project, Paul Hamlyn Foundation's Learning Futures, Future Lab's Enquiring Minds, Learning to Lead, Rathbone and many other foundations and voluntary bodies provide innovative and specialist services which enhance the quality of learning in schools, particularly for those who are easily disengaged from the mainstream curriculum.

Higher education

Not too long ago, before the expansion of higher education following the Robbins Report in 1963, the relationship between universities and schools was relatively simple. Only a small proportion of school students aspired to university – no more than 7 per cent matriculated. Acceptance depended on performance in the A Level examinations, the several examining boards for which were, with one exception, based in universities. A Level was, in effect, a qualification and preparation for entry to university.

But the world has changed. Universities no longer exercise control. In this matter, as in others, they are subject to the rules and regulations of a government quango. Higher education has expanded enormously to an entry of over 40 per cent of the cohort. A Levels serve other purposes as well. Qualifications for entry now include more vocational and pre-vocational ones. There are access courses to encourage wider participation. In this more complicated world closer relationship between higher education and schools and colleges becomes ever more important. They, too, become partners in the network of educational providers – organising summer schools for aspiring undergraduates, offering specialist teaching as in the cases of University Technical Colleges (referred to in Chapter 1), opening the universities to visiting schools, helping with advice and guidance. *Aim Higher* has provided a framework in which these partnerships can be developed and there are now many examples of higher education collaborating with schools in local partnerships.

Public services

There are many ways in which the public services can be more closely linked with the schools within a partnership. One example is the development of 'restorative justice', first tested out in the Banbury area of Oxfordshire, but now spreading throughout Britain. The police work with the school in confronting the law-breakers with the victims of their crime. Often these young people have been in trouble with the police or come from families where there has been trouble. By seeking reconciliation rather than punishment the situation changes and many are kept away from court or probation or custodial sentences.

All these different partners should be seen not as extras but as integral to, and an enrichment of, what locally based partnerships of learning providers can offer.

Local partnerships or central control?

The major difficulty in obtaining the kind of collaboration necessary for all young people to receive an appropriate education is the death of the Local Education Authority, which once had the powers to organise local schooling and further education in response to local needs and wants. This has been replaced by an ever-more centralised (what Peter Newsam describes as 'totalitarian') control as each school abandons its allegiance to the local community of schools and takes out a contract directly with the Secretary of State.

Following the 1944 Education Act, the then Minister of Education had but three powers – control over the supply of and training places for teachers, the approval or rejection of local authority requests to open or to close a school, and authority to remove air raid shelters from school grounds (see T. Brighouse, 2012). Those powers have increased to over 2,000 and government interventions increased with them, with 35 Education Acts in the last 30 years – and now with power to close, create or leave open any one of the 20,000 schools he will control.

Such a centralised system must surely be a cause of concern. Presiding over 20,000 or more schools, it cannot recognise local needs and possibilities, apart from the inherent danger of so much power over the education of young people put into the hands of one person – something which the post-war settlement was anxious to avoid.

The way forward to ensure secondary education for all is to return to a system which is locally accountable, is responsive to local needs and possibilities, and is able to harness the contributions which the different partners are able to bring to the service of all.

Local learning partnerships

Local Education Authorities, as we once knew them, will not do. For one thing they were too large to ensure that local network of partners which this book has argued for. In any case they are dead, and their resurrection is highly unlikely after the slow strangulation through which they have met their end. What should we be looking for in their place?

Smaller networks of schools and colleges of further education are required which serve an area and which draw upon the resources of the community they serve – Youth Service, employers, training providers, voluntary bodies. Such a network should have an overall management and leadership with funding divided on a formula agreed within the partnership. It is the partnership which is accountable to the local community. Such a partnership would recognise the different needs of young people – those with special educational needs, those who have dropped out of education and training, those with academic aspirations – and it would ensure that there is available the support needed from trained youth workers, employers with work-based learning opportunities, higher education and the different voluntary bodies and social services within the community. The partnership would be large enough to have an independent and well-informed Information Advice and Guidance service, knowledgeable about local training and employment possibilities as well as the different pathways into higher education. Such partnerships would have the critical mass for professionally based curriculum and teacher development.

Heed, again, the wise words of the White Paper: 'the need [is] for a stronger and revived local democratic element in the governance, funding and accountability process for schooling' (DfES, 2005).

Perhaps in the immediate future this could be achieved, as T. Brighouse (2012) suggests, by looking back to 1870 and the creation of local School Boards, the beginnings of local community-related schooling – but better renamed as Local Education and Training Boards. And perhaps, too, 30 years later, we might have, as in 1902, the coordination of local resources and partners, but this time to provide a secondary education for all.

Several difficulties might be foreseen.

First, those who have power are reluctant to lose it. It is difficult to imagine the present and future Secretaries of State being content with reducing their powers to those of removing air raid shelters – or whatever is the peace-time equivalent. On the other hand, the newly acquired powers of the Secretary of State, the individual contracts made with each school, the exclusion of these schools from current legislation and thus from parliamentary protection, make it easy for a future government to close these schools down and to restore once again a maintained system.

Second, are those in power convinced that there should be *secondary education for all* such that there needs to be the kind of partnerships as set out above? The ghosts of the Black Paper writers are once more appearing.

Third, what would happen to those innovations which so often have had to take place outside 'the system'? Academy status has enabled people with a particular educational ideal to establish schools that were not possible under local authority control – for example, University Technical Colleges (UTCs). These are the brain-child of Lord Kenneth Baker, Secretary of State for Education 1986 to 1990. Fifteen are already funded; 100 are intended by 2015; there are aspirations for 200–300 eventually. These teach engineering, product design, health sciences, construction, environmental services, and food technology. Employers can name specialisms which will be of most use locally. They will involve 40–80 days' work experience a year.

Fourth, there will be a need for administrative mediation between central government and the distribution of funding to the partnerships. These could possibly be the remains of the local authorities, but educational expertise, curriculum development, and teachers' in-service training would remain in the partnerships. These should identify the needs of the learners. And these should ensure the provision of the services which the different partners together can provide.

Fifth, should there not be differential funding to a much greater extent than is now the case? The extent of disadvantage was spelt out in Chapter 5, and with the present recession the situation can only deteriorate. But as the Webb Report argued, in the context of Wales, maybe, but applicable to England, too:

> Writing of health care over 30 years ago, Tudor Hart argued that an Inverse Care Law was in operation: those most in need received less care than the less needy. There is a distinct danger that this is also the case in education. Moreover, the total expenditure on the disadvantaged groups is falling short of what is needed. Certainly, the size of the groups remains stubbornly high. Whilst these decisions are for politicians, the Inverse Care Law also raises questions about the proportionality of spend on these most needy people compared with that on such differentiated groups as university students and adult leisure learners.
>
> (Webb Review, 2007)

Finally, would this mean the end of faith schools which have allegiance to distinctive communities and traditions within society? To that vexed question we turn in the next chapter.

Conclusion

With all the changes over the last few decades (socially, economically, tech-nologically, demographically, social aspiration) we should be questioning whether 'the school' which we have inherited is the right sort of institution for educating young people for the twenty-first century. In many respects, the government believes not, and therefore we are witnessing a radical transformation of the system. Local authority control is being destroyed; private profiteers are moving in; parental choice in an educational market is being created.

All that, however, will not provide *education for all* for two reasons: 'no one school can go it alone' and the increasingly fragmented system will not nurture the social cohesion in an otherwise divided society.

The solution must lie in the creation of collaborative learning providers – local learning partnerships which embrace schools and colleges, youth service, voluntary bodies, training providers, employers and independent IAG.

17 Have faith in schools?

Policy and protest

Schools: Building on Success (DfES, 2001) promoted the policy of yet more publicly funded faith schools on the basis of their being popular, academically successful and contributing to the diversity of provision which made choice possible. Many different faith groups are now seeking state funding under the academies programme for the creation of their own distinctive faith schools. This policy, however, is not popular in some quarters and is challenged.

First, the cohesiveness of society is seemingly threatened by too much diversity – by the increasing number of ethnic and religious groups. The 'common school' would provide a 'common culture' shared by the diverse traditions, an 'overlapping consensus' of values and commitments, one of which would be respect (based on understanding) for the different religious traditions. Communities brought up entirely separately sow the seeds for distrust and discrimination.

Second, faith schools, in effect, with their own admissions policies, are accused of 'hidden selection'. Ethnic minority students are sometimes denied a place at their neighbourhood school on grounds of not belonging to the appropriate faith.

Third, in a secular society, many see it as wrong to use tax-payers' money to promote minority religious beliefs and practices. Though 30 per cent of school students are in faith schools (either voluntary aided or voluntary controlled), only 7 per cent are regular church-goers. 'No popery on the taxes' was the cry in 1902, and it is the same in 2012.

These challenges have been effective and there has been a political drive for all publicly funded faith schools to admit 20 per cent of students not of that faith.

Historical context

It is important to be reminded of how the present context came about – unique, I think, to Britain. In the first half of the nineteenth century there was no state provision of education. That was provided by endowments, by charitable trusts and, above all, by the Churches, in particular the established Church of England. That is why so many of the village schools in England, dating back to that time, are still in trust to the Church of England. It was not until 1870 that the government felt it necessary to supplement the education provided by the Churches in places where there was no provision, mainly in the big and growing cities. In 1902 Local Education Authorities were created which maintained this 'dual system' – against not a little opposition.

Basically, the dual system supported both community schools and church schools, though the latter would maintain their partial independence by having to cover part of the cost. The 1944 Education Act maintained much of this through creating three kinds of maintained schools: community, voluntary controlled and voluntary aided. On the whole the Church of England went for the voluntary controlled and the Catholic Church adopted voluntary aided. That gave the Catholic trustees greater control over governing bodies, admissions policy and staffing. A Catholic school in staff, ethos, religious teaching and pupils was the aim, but at a price, namely, the payment of 50 per cent of the cost of building of new schools and their external alteration. Furthermore, they had to comply with the basic education standards as monitored by HMI and, after 1988, with the National Curriculum.

Three significant points emerge from this that affect our understanding of current developments and aspirations.

The first concerns the role of the state in determining the aims and content of education. Not until the 1988 Education Act did government have control over curriculum (except the requirement that there should be religious education). The government was there to support provision, to ensure there was enough of it, to ensure basic standards through Her Majesty's Inspectors, but not, in a society with different views of educational aims, to determine what precisely those aims should be.

Second, however, not just anyone could set up a school and win tax-payers' support. Assurance was required that basic standards would be maintained in the general curriculum, in teaching quality, and in learning resources and facilities. Was there sufficient demand from the religious affiliations to make the proposed school viable – able to offer a general curriculum and not disadvantage the learners from progression to, say, higher education?

Third, there was a need to assess the impact on the wider provision – the creation of a new school could make other local schools non-viable if a sufficient number of students transferred to it. Such reorganisation would be expensive.

But that is history. Should the state continue to support faith schools? If so, under what conditions should that support be given?

Facing the problems

There is a new difficulty in deciding what should be included in faith schools. Would atheist schools be included? Would humanist schools? Presumably so, but one can imagine the problems that might arise in the comprehensive organisation of education if every belief system claimed entitlement to full funding.

When it comes to particular religious groups, should there be entitlement to the sub-sects within these – for example, Sunni schools alongside Shi'a and Ismaili schools, Liberal Jewish alongside Orthodox Jewish schools? Seventh Day Adventists alongside Church of England? There could be no end.

Thesis: arguments for continuation

Different reasons are given for the preservation and expansion of faith schools. Appeal is made to the 1998 Human Rights Act which states that

> in the exercise of any functions which it assumes in relation to education and to teaching, the state shall respect the rights of parents to ensure such education and teaching in conformity with their own religious and philosophical convictions.

Back to the historical account given above, there are seen to be limits to the state in any claim to set educational aims where those aims necessarily embody values that might not receive universal assent. We do live in a pluralist society and there is a necessary connection between our conception of education and our understanding of what it means to be and to grow as a person.

It follows from that that a school, serving communities within a particular tradition of what it means to be and to grow as a person, would wish to support those traditions. There should not be, so it might be argued, a conflict between the values of the school and those of the community which embodies a particular set of beliefs about how life should be lived.

Let us take the example of the education of girls. Within some religious traditions it is important for girls to be educated separately from boys. There are deeply rooted norms of appropriate conduct. That surely should be respected, and opportunities for the exercise of such understandings should be available. However, girls' schools, once very common, have for the most part been closed, thereby denying to Muslim parents something very important in the education of their girls. In consequence, many Muslim girls are kept at home, denied the opportunity of secondary schooling.

This commitment to a valued way of life, formed through particular beliefs and practices, is well expressed in the Church of England's Consultation Report of 2000.

> Pupils will experience what it is like to live in a community that celebrates the Christian faith; to work within a framework of discipline and yet to be confident of forgiveness; to begin to share the Christian hope and the Christian experience.

The religious dimension to life is, for many, inseparable from the growth of a person – an initiation into a way of life which transforms their view of the world and how to live within it. That is made more possible through faith schools which embody that way of life, and indeed is necessary if 'the great chain of learning and wisdom' is not to snap (Sacks, 1997: 173). It is no business of the state to put a stop to that within the national system. The state is made up not so much of individuals as of different communities and different traditions, and its job is to support, not negate those traditions.

Antithesis: arguments against

There is serious concern over the divisiveness of faith schools – young people from very different religious and cultural traditions educated separately, without knowledge of other traditions and without close experience of others from those traditions. As we have seen, the Ouseley Report, following the riots in Oldham, warned of a socially segregated Britain and of a growing minority feeling alienated from mainstream society. Communities learn together and each comes to appreciate the beliefs, aspirations and fears of the other. Developing mutual respect would seem to be crucial.

Dewey saw the common school as an essential part of the educational experience of all young people as they came to learn from interacting with the different traditions which made up society. The school was an essential part of learning how to live within a diverse society – how to develop the skills, attitudes and understandings required of active citizenship. Dewey was writing when people from different religions and cultures were entering the USA and when the school was seen to be the place where young people would learn not only to tolerate such diversity but also to be enriched by it.

A 'common school' need not homogenise young people – diminish their different religious understandings and allegiances. There are many examples where the timetable and the curriculum have been adapted to accommodate and indeed support such differences – so organised that there can be separate times for prayer in accordance with the religious traditions, distinctive options within the humanities for an exploration of the respective religious understandings of what it means to be human, and accommodation made for different dietary and dress requirements.

Second, appeal to human rights can arrive at different conclusions from those argued in the section above. The European Charter of Human Rights emphasises that the child is not the parents' property and that the child has the right to develop his or her own views on matters which are controversial within society. The stress is upon autonomy, not upon the transmission of beliefs.

Finally, the quotation above from the Church of England Consultation Report is of a kind which deeply concerns the humanist or the member of the secular society. Does it not smack of indoctrination, the inculcation of beliefs where those are a matter of doubt within the broader and secular society? Religious belief is no longer the 'default position' within our society, and we have no right to use taxpayers' money to teach minority and controversial views, not accepted by the majority. Unlike the conclusions of science, religious beliefs lack evidence, and to teach as true that which cannot be proven is to indoctrinate – the very antithesis of education properly conceived. Religion is a private matter.

A few words are necessary on what we mean by a secular society because of the radical changes that have taken place in the last few decades. Fifty or more years ago a basic religious background to society was hardly questioned – the Established Church, the religious consecration of the monarch, the oath on the Bible in court, the closure of shops in respect for Sunday as a day of worship and on such days as Good Friday. One could go on. Even for unbelievers, there was a religious backcloth to the culture which we had inherited and through which we made sense of life.

However, as Charles Taylor explains in *A Secular Age* (2007), all that has changed. Religion is no longer connected with society's 'self-concept' and with its political organisation – even in the United States where religious belief is very much part of society. There is a complete separation of state and religion. Religious belief would therefore not be taught in school. In such a secular society, belief in God is but one option amongst many. It is no longer the 'default position'. Instead, there is presumption of unbelief, and it is the religious believer who has to argue the case, not the other way around. Hence, the need for a secular common school – with, if necessary, special arrangements for those who want 'religious options' by way of teaching or specific practices. Such would not be part of the mainstream way of life of the school.

Synthesis

First, clearly the most important issue is that of indoctrination. Is the secularist right in seeing that the induction into a religious tradition is necessarily to indoctrinate, whereas the pursuit of autonomy through the formation and exercise of reason escapes such a charge?

Let us work through examples. To teach basic mathematics as unquestionably right would not seem to be indoctrination because of the nature of the beliefs, even though we might be asking for unquestioned belief where there is little understanding. Indoctrination would seem, therefore, to be concerned with the nature of the belief rather than with the mode of reaching it. But what, then, about moral beliefs? They are very different from mathematical beliefs. There are disagreements in society about fundamental moral questions – abortion, bank bonuses, eating meat, capital punishment, nuclear warfare. These differences are not just on the particulars but on the principles by which particular moral dis-agreement might be resolved. Would, therefore, the initiation into a moral form of discourse be regarded as indoctrination? Furthermore, the 'default position' of a secular society is itself open to challenge – by no means self-evident to those who remember the past. The prevailing idea of the liberal autonomous individual is itself a 'background' to the questions we are raising, and might itself be questioned and open to critical scrutiny. Is not its unquestioned assumption, manifest in countless ways, another form of indoctrination?

All young people need to be initiated into a particular form of life which embodies the kind of values, evolved over generations, which make sense of the human condition and which enable them to understand the physical, social and moral worlds they have inherited. The great religious traditions offer that, alongside the humanist and secular. The important thing is to enable their adherents to recognise the depth of wisdom in their respective traditions and then to see the overlapping consensus between them. But, first, 'initiation' is essential if there is to be the wisdom and depth of understanding which each tradition is able to offer.

Furthermore, such initiation requires the introduction to the social practice of that tradition. We are constantly deceived by the false idea that first we think and then we act. Rather, it is the case that we learn practically and then we come to reflect upon the understandings embodied within the activity or practice. You do not learn how to become a good citizen by reading books on good citizenship, but by engaging in citizenship-type activities. Similarly, religious truths are embedded in religious practices. You come to understand the sacred through participation in activities which express the sacredness of life. And that is why faith schools seek a distinctive schooling if they are to embrace a way or 'a form of life', which has evolved over the millennia and which reflects a distinctive way of seeing the moral and social worlds we have inherited.

Faith schools – but under what conditions?

There need, however, to be conditions attached to gain public support.

First, such schools need to meet agreed educational standards in terms of quality of teachers, resources, breadth of curriculum, progression to further training and to higher education, and quality of learning. Inspection from the Inspectorate is vital.

Second, such schools need to be viable in terms of numbers, in order to ensure the range of subjects and the width of experience, and in terms of resources (e.g. in science). And questions could quite legitimately be raised about the viability of the school system if a new faith school were created, thereby making other schools non-viable. There is a need to think of the system as a whole.

Third, such faith schools need to be open to others who are not of that faith, where special circumstances apply, for example, where there is no other local school.

Fourth, the faith school, to get public support, must have an explicit, distinctive and defensible vision of education for the young people attending. That defence must include openness to discussion of controversial issues. The dogmatic assertion of creationism, as against evolutionary explanation of the physical world, would not be acceptable.

Fifth, admissions arrangements need to be carefully drawn up. There is a deep suspicion (with some justification) that proclaimed adherence to a faith may, in many cases, be a ploy to gain admission to a 'good' school, thereby depriving people in the neighbourhood from attending it. Under the cloak of faith, there must be no surreptitious selection on grounds other than that of 'faith'.

But, finally, and most importantly, such faith schools would need to be part of the local partnerships, sharing, drawing upon and contributing to the resources of other schools and the wider community. They would not 'go it alone'. The possible isolation of different ethnic and religious communities as a result of segregated faith schools would need to be addressed through the close links established with other schools in the local collaborative partnerships this book is advocating. The 'integrating schools' in Northern Ireland are addressing the deep divisions, bolstered by distinctive religious beliefs, by bringing the two communities together and by making the very divisions the object of curriculum exploration. Thereby, it is hoped, distinctive traditions might be preserved, albeit with increased under-standing of and respect for the differences. That could well be achieved by making mutual and respectful understanding of different traditions, fostered in separate schools, the focus of shared experience and curriculum within the partnership.

For Dewey, experiential access to diversity was a source of growth for, not a barrier to, the preservation of significant traditions, religious or otherwise. Social cohesion requires not sameness, but respect for difference, and we need to find ways in which the different traditions might be maintained, but intelligently so and in such a manner that the 'overlapping consensus' between them might be recognised. That is one important job for the local partnership.

Conclusion

Faith schools of various kinds are but one part of the mosaic of schools which has emerged. But they are an important part, and the principles to which they are now asked to comply may not necessarily tally with those that are central to the school's ethos. But society is a collection of communities, not an aggregate of individuals. And, until recently, this has been acknowledged through the maintenance or building of schools for these separate faith communities, which remain within the national system.

However, the arguments for their continued existence must recognise that individual schools cannot very often provide all the expertise necessary for education for all. Faith schools, as much as all the other kinds, must be members of their local learning partnership.

Part IV

Conclusion

18 'Secondary education for all'

Must it be but a dream?

Hope and disillusion

We have seen both the hope for and the aspiration to achieve *secondary education for all*. In England and Wales it was firmly embodied in the 1944 Education Act. We saw, too, how it was the dream of the American High School.

Its attainment in England and Wales was sought, over time, through different routes – on the one hand, three types of school for three types of learner, and, on the other, comprehensive schools for all. Such comprehensive schools would overcome the inequities and the loss of opportunities, which segregation at age 11, on the basis of questionable tests, had created. There would be greater social mobility, the generation of a greater sense of community, the opening to the cultural riches previously limited to a few, equal respect for all irrespective of social background or ability.

However, we have seen, too, disillusion set in. For some, 'more means worse', because, so it is claimed, it leads to a dilution of the culture into which those to be educated need to be initiated. Critics point, too, to the many failures – those, especially, who become disengaged from serious learning. Performance against defined standards may well have risen but still standards of literacy and numeracy remain low, and employers complain about poor standards generally.

In response, new solutions have been advanced: the creation of more vocational opportunities for the 'less academic'; a greater focus on targets and on the explicit standards which they represent; greater accountability of schools and teachers through a burgeoning testing industry and through the publication of results in publicly available league tables; encouragement of parental choice as a way of encouraging schools to perform better; the undermining of local responsibility and accountability as schools seek to be more autonomous in performing their duties; the contracting of schools under the title of academy or free school to the person of the Secretary of State; the growth of sponsors (some for-profit) to bring 'business efficiency' to the running of schools and colleges.

Permeating it all has been a massive shift in the language of education as teachers are required to *deliver the curriculum* so that externally imposed *targets* might be reached, *performance indicators* established, *audits* carried out, *efficiency gains* pursued, the satisfaction of *customers* sought as they exercise their choices in an educational *market*. Such language, drawn from 'performance management' would have been risible, if not incomprehensible, only a few decades ago.

But the result? Higher scores in tests, certainly, but less knowledge, less understanding, less enthusiasm for learning – indeed, less education. And that applies not just to Newsom's 'half our future', but also, as so many testify, to the other successful half. As the book has demonstrated, education has been impoverished by the high-stakes (and highly profitable) testing industry.

Was *secondary education for all*, then, but a dream?

Think first: what does it mean to educate?

Standards necessarily embody judgements about what is worth learning, and therefore, ultimately, about the aims of education. Narrow those aims and inevitably many are excluded. Impoverish those aims further through a high-stakes testing regime, yet more are judged to be failures. Take no account of social disadvantage, then education cannot compensate for society.

Therefore, this book has argued throughout that it is essential constantly to ask, *What counts as an educated 19 year old in this day and age?*

In seeking an answer, we need to think hard about those distinctively human qualities that we need to teach and nurture. Remember the words of the high school principal:

> So I am suspicious of education.
>
> My request is: Help your students become human, . . . Reading, writing, arithmetic are important only if they serve to make our children more human.

That broader view of education must embrace the ways in which we have come to understand the physical, social and moral worlds in which we live, but also that practical know-how through which we are engaged with that world. It must include the moral seriousness through which we accept responsibility not just for our own destinies but also for those of other persons and of the wider community. It would seek, too, to ensure that all, whatever their abilities, have a sense of fulfilment and self-worth. There is much more to becoming human than academic success.

Furthermore, as the book has persistently argued, education is for the good not just of the individual learner but for the good of the wider community. We are all stakeholders in our schools, colleges and universities. Education is essential for the good of all. Individual choice has to be balanced against community benefits – subject therefore to local accountability.

But our intelligences have been bewitched by the Orwellian 'newspeak' of performance management as referred to above. Such language has no place for the essentially moral language through which we seek to understand what makes us human and how, through learning, we can become more so – the very stuff of the arts and the humanities through which understanding is developed through the exploration of ideas, not through the pursuit of targets. Return to a different set of metaphors, a different language, and you get a different understanding of education and its aims. In that language (one that does justice to the complexity of human nature, of knowledge in its different forms, of the young person's struggle to make sense of his or her experience) the false dualism, which shapes the organisation of learning, between academic and vocational, between theoretical and practical, becomes exposed. Is not education an introduction to the 'conversations between the generations of mankind' through which we have come to understand the physical, social and moral worlds we inhabit? Is not education the empowerment of all young people to manage their lives more intelligently, to find fulfilment and a sense of dignity in those lives, and to be able and disposed to make a valuable contribution to the wider community?

To educate is to embrace a wider vision of learning and teaching

Therefore, the book has argued for a 'wider vision of learning' – one that respects the practical as well as the so-called academic, the importance of the arts and humanities too often neglected in the academic/vocational divide, involvement with the community and its needs, respect for the voice of the learners as they are helped to articulate their needs and aspirations. Central to that wider vision is an independent and well-informed IAG service which helps all young people to develop realistic aspirations for the future in the light of their abilities, the different pathways through education and training and the employment possibilities.

Secondary education is possible for everyone, but it requires a more generous understanding of education, of teaching, of its provision. Teachers are central, not as 'deliverers' of knowledge and skills, but as custodians of traditions of learning, of culture, of criticism and of creativity. To be such custodians, their professional autonomy must not be (as it has been) undermined by government control, performance management and a narrow testing regime. And it must be enhanced through continuing professional development responding to the teachers' understanding of their needs – the opportunity constantly to renew intellectual and creative interests as well as the skills of pedagogy.

But who should control?

We are presently witnessing the erosion of the delicate balance of power established by the 1944 Education Act. That balance ensured that no one should be too powerful, that there should be local responsibility and accountability for the provision of *education for all*, that the different community bodies (the Churches in particular) should have their traditions respected, and that the expertise and professionalism of the teachers should play a key role.

That balance has been overturned. Local authorities' responsibility for education is now negligible – gone is the principle of local accountability. Academies and free schools are not covered by the legislation for the erstwhile maintained system. These schools are contracted to an ever more powerful Secretary of State – the very thing that the Butler Act, noting what had happened in Germany and Italy, sought to avoid. In place of local authorities has grown a plethora of sponsors seeking to run our schools, many for profit as they seek, as in the USA, some of the huge amounts of money to be made in the 'education industry'. We are seeing the destruction of a tradition of public service – and all without a squeak from political opposition.

Way forward

Therefore, secondary education for all requires the following:

Aims

Start with (and continue to ask): *'What counts as an educated person in this day and age?'* This might seem an obvious question. Yet it is rarely asked in a systematic way. There may be little consensus in answers given. But the constant asking of this question reminds us of what is needed for the personal well-being of each and of the public good of all.

Relevance

Answers must be relevant to all young people, not just those who are academically able. All are capable of developing the capacity to think, to be practical, to be morally serious and responsible, to contribute to the wider community, to have a sense of pride and dignity, to feel fulfilled – in the words of the high school principal, 'to learn to be human'.

Stop blaming the schools for the ills of society

The political mantra of 'no excuses' for 'educational failure' must be seen for the empty, though dangerous, rhetoric that it is. It confuses 'explaining' with 'excusing'. Social conditions (dire poverty, family breakdown, generational unemployment, and so on) provide the unavoidable backcloth to many teachers' attempts to bring a better life to young people. Education can 'compensate for society', but only partly, with immense struggle and with the direction of resources to those most in need.

Wider vision of worthwhile learning

From asking about the development of 'the whole person' and about their contribution to an ever-better society, a wider vision of worthwhile learning arises. This should be practical and vocational as well as so-called academic. It would draw on the 'different voices' within the sciences, arts and humanities. It would build on the experiences and informal learning acquired in home and community. It would provide the motivation for life-long learning. It would meet very different personal, social and economic needs.

Testing has failed its own test

Such learning must not be killed by a testing regime that tests only what is measurable, narrows learning to passing the tests, marks out so many from an early age as failures, and leads to disengagement.

Respect the teachers

Recognition must be given to the central role that teachers play in any educational and training system. No policy, howsoever well thought out, has merit unless thoughtfully implemented by those who teach. They alone have the pedagogical expertise to communicate the knowledge, values and skills, which we have inherited, to the developing minds, interests and aspirations of the learners. But that expertise needs to be nurtured through rigorous initial training and then through continuing professional development. That professional development should respond to the perceived needs of teachers. After all, there is no curriculum development without teacher development – despite what the 'deliverologists' think.

Progression

Learning builds on what has been learnt before and provides a springboard for what is yet to be learnt. Guidance is required, routes need to be lit up, distant goals envisaged. Progression routes, therefore, through different paths and qualifications into further and higher education and into employment, are essential. Hence, the importance of independent IAG.

Local partnerships: collaboration, not competition

We should make sure that the provision of educational opportunities begins with the needs of the learners, not with the interests of the providers. No school can go it alone. Local collaborative partnerships need to be created and funded. These bring together schools and colleges, employers and independent training providers, higher education and youth workers, third sector organisations and members of the local community. All bring to the partnership their respective and much needed expertise, opportunities and resources for realising that wider vision of worthwhile learning.

Public service, not private gain

The education of all in a society, which is increasingly characterised by social segregation and massive financial differentiation, must be seen as a public service for the benefit of all, not a private service for the benefit of some. With reference to Rawls' idea of social justice, what sort of arrangements would you create if, 'from behind the veil of ignorance', you did not know what position you were to have in society – that of the many young people (poor, vulnerable and disadvantaged) or that of the much fewer very rich and privileged? It would not be one where education for all is subject to choice on an open market, nor one where schools and educational services are opportunities for private profit. There must be a return to the tradition of public service and its values.

Government: know your limitations

There are limits to how central interventions can change a complex system which requires the daily difficult and professional work of teachers and detailed knowledge of the learners, their circumstances and their communities. Government has acquired too many powers, and these are exercised almost whimsically. Furthermore, governments and their ministers change, often at frequent intervals. Policies come and go. Too much power gained by one minister may be used for the opposite purposes by the next.

Therefore, *secondary education for all* was and still is a dream. But it could come true.

References

Abbs, P., 1994, *The Educational Imperative*, London: The Falmer Press.

ACME, 2011a, *Mathematical Needs: The Mathematical Needs of the Learner*, London: Royal Society.

ACME, 2011b, *Mathematical Needs: Mathematics in the Workplace and in Higher Education*, London: Royal Society.

American National Research Council, 2011, *Incentives and Test-based Accountability in Education*, National Academy Press.

Andrews, D., 2008, *Careers and Guidance Education*, Nuffield Issues Paper, no. 5.

AoC (Association of Colleges), 2004, *Survey on Transition to Adulthood*, London: AoC.

Assessment Research Group, 1999, *Assessment for Learning: Beyond the Black Box*, University of Cambridge School of Education.

Auld Report, 1976, *William Tyndale Junior and Infants Schools Public Enquiry*, London: ILEA.

Baker, B. and Ferris, R., 2011, *Adding Up the Spending: Fiscal Disparities and Philanthropy among NYC Charter Schools*, Boulder, CO: National Education Policy Centre, University of Colorado.

Ball, S., 2012, 'Performativity, commodification and commitment: an I-spy guide to the neo-liberal university', *British Journal of Educational Studies*, 60(1): 17–28.

Bantock, G.H., 1971, 'Towards a theory of popular culture', *Times Educational Supplement*, March, reprinted in Hooper, R. (ed.), 1972, *The Curriculum: Context, Design and Development*, Open University Press.

Barnardo's (Glover, J. and Clewett, N.), 2011, *No Fixed Abode: The Housing Struggle for Young People Leaving Custody in England*, Ilford: Barnardo's.

Beard, C. and Wilson, J.P., 2002, *Experiential Learning*, London: Kogan Page.

Beloe Report, 1960, *Secondary Schools Examinations Other than GCE*, London: HMSO.

Benn, M., 2012, *School Wars: The Battle for Britain's Education*, London: Verso.

Benton, P. (ed.), 1990, *The Oxford Internship Scheme*, London: Calouste Gulbenkian Foundation.

Berliner, D. and Nichols, S., 2007, *Collateral Damage: How High Status Testing Corrupts American Schools*, Cambridge, MA: Harvard University Press.

Berliner, W., 2011, 'Bullied, belittled, . . . and that's just the staff', *Guardian*, 4 October 2011.

Bernstein, B., 1970, 'Education cannot compensate for society', *New Society*, 15(387): 344–347.

Bloom, A., 1987, *The Closing of the American Mind*, New York: Simon and Schuster.

Blower, C., 2010, 'Preface: standing by public education', *Education Review*, 23(2).

Brighouse, H., 2003, 'Against privatizing schools in the UK', *London Review of Education*, 1(1): 35–45.

Brighouse, T., 2012, 'Decline and Fall: are state schools and universities on the point of collapse?' First annual lecture of the Oxford Education Society.

Britton, J., 1970, *Language and Learning*, London: Penguin.

Brockmann, M., Clarke, L. and Winch, C., 2011, *Knowledge, Skills and Competence in the European Labour Market*, London: Routledge.

Browne Report, 2010, *Securing a Sustainable Future for Higher Education in the UK*, London: Stationery Office.

Bruner, J., 1960, *The Process of Education*, Cambridge, MA: Harvard University Press.

Bruner, J., 1966, 'Man: a course of study', in *Towards a Theory of Instruction*, Cambridge, MA: Harvard University Press.

Bryce Report, 1895, *Royal Commission on Secondary Education*, London: HMSO.

Bullock Report, 1975, *Language for Life*, London: HMSO.

Cambridge Assessment, 2011, *A Better Approach to Higher Education/Awarding Body Interaction for Post-16 Qualifications*.

Careers Profession Task Force, 2012, *Towards a Strong Careers Profession*.

CBI, 2010, *Report into the Role of Business in Education*, London: CBI.

CBI, 2012, *Time for the UK to 'Power Up' and Begin Rebalancing the Economy*, London: CBI.

Chubb, J.E. and Moe, T.M., 1990, *Politics, Markets and America's Schools*, Washington, DC: Brookings Institution Press.

Church of England, 2000, Dearing Report, *Church Schools as an Instrument of Revival for the Church of England*, London.

Coleman, J. *et al.*, 1967, *Equality of Educational Opportunity*, Washington, DC: US Government Printing Office.

Coleridge, S.T., 1830, *On the Constitution of the State and Church*, republished by Dent, 1972.

Council for Science and Technology, 1998, *School Science: Fit for the Future?* London: CSE.

Cox, B. and Dyson, A.E., 1969, 'Black Paper, No. 1', *Critical Quarterly* (Summer).

Crawford, M., 2009, *The Case for Working with Your Hands*, London: Penguin.

Crick, B. and Porter, A., 1978, *Political Education and Political Literacy*, Harlow: Longmans.

Crick Report, 1998, *Education for Citizenship and the Teaching of Democracy in Schools*, London: QCA.

Croll, P., Attwood, G. and Fuller, C., 2010, *Children's Lives, Children's Futures*, London: Continuum.

Crouch, C., 1997, *Commercialisation and Citizenship*, London: Fabian Society.

Crowther Report, 1959, *15 to 18*, Report of the Central Advisory Council for Education, London: HMSO.

Cuban, L., 2005, *The Blackboard and the Bottom Line: Why Schools Can't Be Businesses*, Cambridge, MA: Harvard University Press.

Dale, R. *et al.*, 1990, *The TVEI Story*, Milton Keynes: Open University Press.

Davies, N., 2000, *The School Report: Why Britain's Schools Are Failing*, London: Vintage.

DCSF, 2004, *Education and Skills*, London: Stationery Office.

DCSF, 2008, *21st Century Schools: Your Child, Your Schools, Our Future: Building a 21st Century Schools System*, London: DCSF.

Demos, 2011, *The Forgotten Half*, London: Demos.

DES, 1977, *Education in Schools*, London: HMSO.

Dewey, J., 1897, 'My pedagogic creed', *School Journal*, 14(3).

Dewey, J., 1902, *The Child and the Curriculum*, reprinted in Garforth, F.W., 1966, *John Dewey: Selected Writings*, London: Heinemann.

Dewey, J., 1910, *The School and Society*, reprinted in Garforth, F.W., 1966, *John Dewey: Selected Writings*, London: Heinemann.

Dewey, J., 1916, *Democracy and Education*, New York: Free Press.

Dewey, J., 1938a, 'Experience and Education', in Boydston, J.A., 1991, *The Collected Works of John Dewey 1882–1953, Later Works*, Carbondale, IL: Southern Illinois University Press.

Dewey, J., 1938b, *Logic: the Theory of Inquiry*, New York: Holt.

DfE, 2010, *The Importance of Teaching*, Schools White Paper, London: DfE.

DfES, 2001, *Schools: Building on Success*, White Paper: London: DfES.

DfES, 2003, *The National Strategies: Invitation to Negotiate*, London: DfES.

DfES, 2005, *14–19: Education and Skills*, London: DfES.

Donnelly, J., 2005, 'Reforming science in the school curriculum: a critical analysis', *Oxford Review of Education*, 31(2): 293–309.

Donnison, D., 1974, 'Policies for priority areas', *Journal of Social Policy*, 3(2): 127–135.

Dorling, D., 2010, *Injustice: Why Social Justice Persists*, London: The Policy Press.

Drake, P., 2011, Presentation to the Joint Mathematical Council, 22 Feb.

Dyson, J., 2010, *Ingenious Britain: Making the UK the Leading High tech. Exporter in Europe*, Report of the James Dyson Foundation.

Education and Employment Task Force, 2011, *Collaborate to Compete: Seizing the Opportunity of On-line Learning for UK Higher Education.*

Edwards, D., 2010, 'How international solidarity networks can beat the GERM', *Education Review*, 23(1).

Eisner, E., 1976, 'Educational connoisseurship and criticism', *Journal of Aesthetic Education*, 10(3–4): 135–150.

Eisner, E., 1986, 'The role of the arts in cognition and curriculum', *Journal of Art and Design Education*, 5(1–2): 57–67.

Equality and Human Rights Commission, 2010, *How Fair is Britain?*

Evans, J., 2010, *Not Present and Not Correct: Understanding and Preventing School Exclusions*, London: Barnados.

Findlay, G., 2010, 'Building successful partnerships in hospitality education', *The Hospitality Review,* July.

Fletcher, M. and Perry, A., 2008, *Accident or Design: Is Our System of Post-16 Provision Fit for Purpose?* Reading: CfBT Education Trust.

Franklin, B.M. and McCulloch, G. (eds), 2007, *The Death of the Comprehensive High School?*, New York: Palgrave Macmillan.

Gillborn, D. and Youdell, D., 1999, *Rationing Education*, Milton Keynes: Open University Press.

Glatter, R., 2010, 'Changing organisational structures: will we never learn? *Education Review*, 23(1): 21 (referring to and quoting from Hill, 2010).

Hadow Report, 1926, *The Education of the Adolescent*, London: Board of Education.

Halsey, A.H., 1992, *Decline of Donnish Dominion*, Oxford: Oxford University Press.

Higham, J. and Yeomans, D., 2010, 'Working together? Partnership approaches to 14–19 education in England', *British Educational Research Journal*, 36(3): 379–401.

Hill, R., 2010, *Chain Reactions: A Think-piece on the Development of Schools in the English School System*, Nottingham: National College for School Leadership.

Hirst, P., 1974a, 'Liberal education and the nature of knowledge', in *Knowledge and the Curriculum*, London: RKP.

Hirst, P., 1974b, 'What is teaching?', in *Knowledge and the Curriculum*, London: RKP.

HoC, 2002, Science and Technology Committee, Third Report: *Science Education from 14–19*, London: The Stationery Office.

HoC, 2003, Education and Skills Select Committee, *Secondary Education: Pupil Achievement*, London: The Stationery Office.

HoC, 2008, Education Select Committee, *Testing and Assessment*, London: The Stationery Office.

HoC, 2010, Education Select Committee on Youth Service, London: The Stationery Office.

HoC, 2011a, Education Select Committee on EBac, London: The Stationery Office.

HoC, 2011b, Education Select Committee, *Services for Young People*, Third Report of the Session 2010–2012, London: The Stationery Office.

Hoggart, R., 1957, *The Uses of Literacy*, London: Chatto and Windus.

HoL, 2008, House of Lords Select Committee on Economic Affairs, *Apprenticeships: A Key Route to Skills*.

Holt, M., 1978, *The Common Curriculum*, London: RKP.

IUSS, 2008, Innovation, Universities, Science and Skills Select Committee, 7th Report, *Pre-legislative Scrutiny of the Draft Apprenticeship Bill*, London: Houses of Parliament.

Jackson, P., 1968, *Life in Classrooms*, New York: Rinehart and Winston.

James, C., 1968, *Young Lives at Stake*, London: Collins.

James, M. *et al.*, 2006, *Learning How to Learn: Tools for Schools*, London: Routledge.

James, M., 2012, 'An alternative to an objectives model: the process model for the design and development of curriculum', in Elliott, J. and Norris, N. (eds), *Curriculum, Pedagogy and Educational Research*, London: Routledge.

Jenks, C. *et al.*, 1972, *Inequality: A Re-assessment of the Effects of Family and Schooling in America*, New York: Basic Books.

Jessup, G., 1991, *Outcomes: NVQs and the Emerging Model of Education and Training*, London: Falmer Press.

Jewish Museum Prague, 1993, *I Have Not Seen a Butterfly Around Here*, ISBN 80-85608-18-9.

Kilpatrick, W.H., 1918, 'The Project Method', *Teachers College Record*, 15.

Kilpatrick, W.H., 1923, 'Introduction to Collings', *An Experiment with a Project Curriculum*, New York: Macmillan.

Kohlberg, L., 1982, 'Recent work in moral education', in Ward, L.O. (ed.), *The Ethical Dimension of the School Curriculum*, Swansea: Pineridge Press.

Lawton, D., 1975, *Class, Culture and the Curriculum*, London: RKP.

Lawton, D., 1989, *Education, Culture and the National Curriculum*, London: Hodder and Stoughton.

Learning Futures, 2010, *The Engaging School: Principles and Practices*, London: Paul Hamlyn Foundation.

Leitch Review, 2006, *Prosperity For All in the Global Economy: World Class Skills*, London: H.M. Treasury.

Looney, A., 2010, 'Between brutality and fairness', *Le Cheile*, No. 4: 93–104.

Lumby, J., 2011, 'Enjoyment and learning: policy and secondary school learners' experience in England', in *British Educational Research Journal*, 37(2): 247–264.

Macmurray, J., 1957, *Self as Agent*, London: Faber and Faber.

Mager, R.F., 1962, *Preparing Objectives or Programmed Instruction*, San Francisco: Fearon.

Mansell, W., 2007, *Education by Numbers: The Tyranny of Testing*, London: Politico.

Mansell, W. and James, M., 2009, *Assessment in Schools: Fit for Purpose?* London: ESRC/TLRP.

Marmot, M., 2011, *Fair Society, Healthy Lives* (The Marmot Review), London: UCL Institute for Health Equity.

Marshall, T.D., 1963, *Sociology at the Crossroads and Other Essays*, London: RKP.

Mattock, R., 2009, *Conservation Management Plan, Summerfields School Oxford*, University of Bath.

Midwinter, E., 1975, *Education and the Community*, London: Allen and Unwin.

Millar, R. and Osborne, J. (eds), 1998, *Beyond 2000: Science Education for the Future*, London: KCL.

Moran, G., 2008, *Speaking of Teaching: Lessons from History*, New York: Lexington Books.

Morrell, D., 1966, *Education and Change*, Joseph Payne Memorial Lecture, London: College of Preceptors.

Morris, M., 2004, *The Case for Careers Education and Guidance for 14–19 Year Olds*, Slough: NFER.

Moser Report, 1999, *A Fresh Start: Improving Literacy and Numeracy*, Sudbury: DfEE.

NAO, 2010, *Value for Money: The Academies Programme*, London: National Audit Office.

NAO, 2011, *Getting Value for Money from the Education of 16–18 Year Olds*, London: National Audit Office.

Newsam, P., 2011, 'Towards a totalitarian education system in England', Oxford Education Society website.

Newsom Report, 1964, *Half Our Future*, London: HMSO.

NISAI, 2010, *Case Studies and Feedback: Andrew*, www.nisai.com.

Noddings, N., 2005, *Philosophy of Education*, 2nd Edition, Boulder, CO: Westview Press.

Norwood Report, 1943, *Curriculum and Examinations in Secondary Schools*, London: HMSO.

Nuffield Review, 2009, *Education for All: The Future of Education and Training for 14–19 Year Olds in England and Wales*, London: Routledge.

Oakeshott, M., 1962, 'Voice of poetry in the conversation of mankind', *Rationalism in Politics*, London: Methuen.

Oakeshott, M., 1975, 'A Place of Learning', reprinted in Fuller, T. (ed.), 1989, *Michael Oakeshott and Education*, New Haven, CT: Yale University Press.

OECD, 2009, *PISA: Assessment Framework – Key Competencies in Reading, Mathematics and Science*, Paris: OECD.

OECD, 2010, *Markets in Education: An Analytical Review of Empirical Research on Market Mechanisms in Education*, Paris: OECD.

Ofqual, 2011, *GCSE and A Level Regrades*, London: Ofqual.

Ofsted, 2005, *The Secondary National Strategy: An Evaluation of the Fifth Year*, London: Ofsted.

Ofsted, 2008, *Learning Outside the Classroom*, London: Ofsted.

Ofsted, 2010a, *London Challenge*, London: Ofsted.

Ofsted, 2010b, *Moving through the System: Information, Advice and Guidance*, London: Ofsted.

O'Hear, A., 1987, 'The importance of traditional learning', *British Journal of Educational Studies*, 35(2): 102–114.

O'Hear, A., 1991, *Education and Democracy: The Posturing of the Left*, London: Claridge Press.

Ouseley Report, 2003, *Community Pride, Not Prejudice*, Bradford: LEA.

Payne, J. and Keep, E., 2011, 'One step forward, two steps back: skills policy in England under the coalition government', *SKOPE Research Paper 102*, University of Oxford: SKOPE.

Pedley, R., 1963, *The Comprehensive School*, Harmondsworth: Penguin Books, Ltd.

Peters, R., 1965, *Ethics and Education*, London: Geo. Allen and Unwin.

Phenix, P., 1964, *Realms of Meaning*, New York: McGraw-Hill.

Plaskow, M. (ed.), 1985, *Life and Death of the Schools Council*, London: Taylor and Francis.

Plato, *The Republic*, Part I, Book I.

Popham, W.J., 1969, 'Objectives and Instruction', in Popham *et al.* (eds), *Instructional Objectives*, Washington, DC: Rand McNally.

Popper, K., 1972, *Objective Knowledge*, Oxford: Oxford University Press.

Power, S. *et al.*, 2008, *Out-of-School Learning: Creation, Variation in Provision and Participation in Secondary Schools*, Cardiff University: Research Papers in Education.

Pring, R. and Hudson, C., 2003, *Report on the Banbury Schools and Police Project*, University of Oxford: Department of Education.

PwC, 2005, *The Market for Qualifications in the UK: Final Report*, London: Pricewaterhouse-Coopers.

PwC, 2008, *Academies Evaluation: Fifth Annual Report*, London: PricewaterhouseCoopers.

QCDA, 2010, *Evaluating Mathematics Pathway Project*, End of Year Report, London: QCDA.

Raffo, C. *et al.*, 2003, 'Disaffected young people and the work related curriculum at Key Stage 4', *Journal of Education and Work*, 16(1): 69–86.

Ravitch, D., 2008, in 'NYC Public School Parents', 17 February 2008.

Ravitch, D., 2010, *The Death and Life of the Great American School System*, New York: Basic Books.

Reeves, M., 2011, *The Life and Thought of Marjorie Reeves (1905–2003)*, edition of unpublished memoirs, Lampeter: Mellon Press.

Robbins Report, 1963, *Higher Education*, London: Stationery Office, cmnd.2165.

Robinson, K., 1999, *All Our Futures*, National Advisory Council on Creativity, Culture and Education.

Royal Society, 2011, *Brain Waves Module 2: Neuroscience: Implications for Education*, London: Royal Society.

Rubinstein, D. and Simon, B., 1969, *The Evolution of the Comprehensive School*, London: RKP.

Rudduck, J. and McIntyre, D., 2007, *Improving Learning through Consulting Pupils*, London: Routledge.

Rury, J.L., 2007, 'The Comprehensive High School, enrolment expansion, and inequality: the United States in the post-war era', in Franklin, B.M. and McCulloch, G. (eds), *The Death of the Comprehensive High School?*, New York: Palgrave Macmillan.

Rutter, M., *et al.*, 1979, *Fifteen Thousand Hours: Secondary Schools and their Effects on Children*, Shepton Mallet: Open Books.

Sacks, J., 1997, *The Politics of Hope*, London: Jonathan Cape.

Sacks, J., 2002, *The Dignity of Difference*, London: Continuum.

Sandel, M., 2009, Reith Lecture, *A New Citizenship*, London: BBC.

Schools Council Working Paper, 1965, *Raising the School Leaving Age*, London: Ministry of Education.

Schuller, T. and Watson, D., 2009, *Learning through Life*, Leicester: NIACE.

Schwab, J.J., 1964, 'Structure of the disciplines; meanings and significance', in Ford, G. and Pugno, L., *The Structure of Knowledge and the Curriculum*, Chicago, IL: Rand McNally.

Searle, C., 1975, *Classrooms of Resistance*, London: Writers and Readers.

Sennett, R., 2008, *The Craftsman*, London: Penguin.

Shaw, B., 1983, *Comprehensive Schooling: The Impossible Dream?* Oxford: Basil Blackwell.

Simon, B., 1985, *Does Education Matter?* London: Lawrence and Wishart.

Simon, B., 1991, *Education and the Social Order*, London: Lawrence and Wishart.

Skinner, B.F., 1968, *The Technology of Teaching*, New York: Appleton Century Croft.

Smith Report, 2004, *Making Mathematics Count*, London: The Stationery Office.

Stenhouse, L., 1967, *Culture and Education*, London: Nelson.

Stenhouse, L., 1975, *Introduction to Curriculum Development and Research*, London: Heinemann.

Strom, M.S., 1981, 'Facing history and ourselves: integrating a holocaust unit into the curriculum', *Moral Education Forum* (Summer).

Sutton Trust, 2010, *The Educational Background of Government Ministers*, London: Sutton Trust.

Sutton Trust, 2011, 'Note for the House of Commons Education Select Committee on the new Admissions Code', London: Sutton Trust.

Tawney, R.H., 1938, *Equality*, London: Geo. Allen and Unwin.

Tawney, R.H., 1943, 'The problem of the public schools', in Hinden, R. (ed.), 1966, *The Radical Tradition*, Harmondsworth: Penguin Books.

Taylor, C., 2007, *A Secular Age*, Cambridge, MA: Harvard University Press.

Thompson, E.P., 1957, *The Making of the English Working Class*, London: Gollanz.

TIMSS, 2007, *Trends in International Mathematics and Science Study*, Washington, DC: U.S. Department of Education.

Tyler, R., 1949, *Basic Principles of Curriculum and Instruction*, Chicago, IL: Chicago University Press.

Vernon, P., 1957, *Secondary School Selection*, London: Methuen.

Waldfogel, J. and Washbrook, E., 2010, *Low Income and Early Cognitive Development in the UK*, London: Sutton Trust.

Watson, A. and De Geest, 2008, *Changes in Mathematics Teaching Project*, http//cmtp.co.uk.

Webb Review, 2007, *Promise and Performance: The Report of the Independent Review of the Mission and Purpose of Further Education in Wales in the Context of the Learning Country*, Cardiff: WAG.

Wilde, S. and Wright, S., 2007, 'On the same wavelength but tuned to the different frequencies', *London Education Review*, 5(3): 299–312.

Willetts, D., 2010, First keynote speech as Minister for Universities and Sciences, 20 May, University of Birmingham.

Williams, R., 1961, *The Long Revolution*, Harmondsworth: Penguin.

Williams, R., 2010, Evidence to the Wolf Committee.

Willis, P., 1977, *Learning to Labour: How Working Class Kids Get Working Class Jobs*, Farnborough: Saxon House.

Winch, C., 2010, *Dimensions of Experience*, London: Continuum.

Wittgenstein, L., 1958, *Philosophical Investigations*, Oxford: Basil Blackwell.

Wolf Report, 2011, Review of Vocational Education, London: DoE.

Young, M. (ed.), 1972, *Knowledge and Control*, London: Methuen.

Name Index

Subject Index

academic *see* learning
academic/vocational dualism 3, 51–2
academies *see* schools
accountability 2, 3, 4, 21, 131–4, 154
  see also assessment for accountability
ACME (Advisory Council of
    Mathematics Educators) 102–3,
    107–8, 143, 147
admissions 156, 166, 177, 182
adolescents 7, 17, 86, 91, 96
Aim Higher 172
apprenticeship 14, 15, 29, 51, 85,
    137–9, 144–6
ARIS (Achievement Reporting and
    Innovation Systems) 89
ARK 158–9
arts 36, 46, 51, 76–7, 110–11, 118,
    127, 167, 188
Arts Council 7, 77
ASDAN 135–6
assessment 3, 22–4, 56, 71, 80
  for accountability 79
  for learning 79, 80
  national 125
Assessment of Performance Unit (APU)
    132
Association of Teachers and Lecturers
    (ATL) 25
'Atlantic bridge' 2
Audit Commission 143
audits 2, 31, 125, 187
autonomy 50, 55, 90

Babcocks Lifeskills Careers 140
Bally-Hoo 76–7, 86
Barnardo's 64, 69
behaviour
  difficulties/ADHD 62, 88
  modification 54, 55, 79
Beloe Report, 1960 10

Big Society 153–4, 168–9
Birmingham
  Royal Ballet School 76
  University of 75
Black Papers 14, 174
British Medical Association 121
Browne Report 137
Bryce Report, 1895 13
Bullock Report 86, 112, 119
business/edubusiness 17, 21, 31, 42,
    101, 156, 158

Campbell's Law 124, 127, 129
Capita 128
careers advice *see* IAG
Careersoft 140
Catholic Church 178
CBI 33, 143, 189–90
Central Advisory Council for Education
    (England) 155
Centre for Engineering and
    Manufacturing Excellence (CEME)
    167, 172
Centre for Policy Studies 157
CfBT 84, 162
Chief Inspector for Schools 24, 62, 64,
    128
child-centred 20, 105
China 18, 109
choice 3, 7, 12, 21, 23, 37, 64, 137,
    160–2, 187, 192
Church of England Consultation Report
    178–9
citizen/citizenship 11, 38, 100, 104,
    112, 154, 163
clerisy 13, 37, 44
Cognita 158
collaboration, cooperation 1, 4, 7, 9, 16
  see also partnerships
common good 38